THE
PEACE CORPS
EXPERIENCE

"It is required of a man that he should share the passion and
action of his time at peril of being judged not to have lived."
—JUSTICE OLIVER WENDELL HOLMES

President Kennedy on the White House lawn saying farewell to volunteers bound for Indonesia, May 18, 1963.

THE
PEACE CORPS
EXPERIENCE

Edited by *ROY HOOPES*

With a Preface by
Hubert H. Humphrey
Vice President of the United States

 *Clarkson N. Potter, Inc./Publisher* NEW YORK

Distributed by Crown Publishers, Inc.

To the Peace Corps Volunteers
and Staff Photographers Who
Made This Book Possible

Library of Congress Catalog Card Number 67-27354

Manufactured in the United States of America
First Edition

Acknowledgments

This book would not have been possible without the cooperation of Jack H. Vaughn, Director of the Peace Corps, his staff, and the thousands of volunteers whose efforts and dedication forged the Peace Corps. However, certain members of the staff were especially helpful in putting this volume together and I wish to express my appreciation. They were: Stewart Awbrey, Pat Brown, Carol Condon, Suzanne Evans, Lorraine Farinha, Robert Hatch, Lacy Hinkle, John LaHoud, Jack Keyser, Tom Page, Barbara Prikkel, Carl Purcell, Coates Redmond, and Paul Reed.

CONTRIBUTORS / Volunteers

Most of the reports by volunteers in this book originally appeared in the Peace Corps magazine, *The Volunteer,* and are reprinted with its permission, as is the essay on "Transculturation" by Maurice Sill, which appears in Chapter 9. A few reports, however, appeared in other Peace Corps documents and literature, and are reprinted with permission of the Peace Corps. The volunteers who contributed to this volume are:

Chapter 1
Vicki Soucek
and Nancy Keith

Chapter 3
Moritz Thomsen

Chapter 4
Gwynne Douglas
Samuel Abbott
Bennett Oberstein
Raymond Brodeur

Chapter 5
Louis Rapoport
Tom Clark
Truman E. Howell, Jr.
William Krohley
Ed Cheira
Joan Marasciulo

Chapter 6
Moritz Thomsen
Ronald Venezia
Philip A. Schaefer

Chapter 7
Patty Schwartz
Gerald Patrick
Carole Watkins

Chapter 8
Roger and Ellen Watson
Brooke Baker
Magdelena Tapia

Chapter 9
Charles Katz
Gary Engelberg
Judith Nordblom
William Martin
Nancy Tucker

Chapter 10
David Schickele

Purcell   *Conklin*   *Scherman*

CONTRIBUTORS / Photographers

The great majority of photographs in this book were taken by the three Peace Corps photographers: Carl Purcell, current Director of Photography for the Peace Corps; and past photography directors, Paul Conklin and Rowland Scherman.

In addition, a few photographs in the Introduction were taken by volunteers or members of the overseas staff. The photographers and their photographs are:

John Hand: Hillside Dwellings in Nigerian Village
Jim Rugh: Farmer Planting Peanuts in Senegal
Dr. William Anderson: Togo Blacksmith
Dr. William Anderson: Little Boy Carrying Boxes
Martha Cooper: Indian Women Coming Home
   from Market
Nick Mills: Children Looking Under Door
Jim Rugh: Children Playing Cards
Charles Marden Fitch: Cholo Indian
Dr. William Anderson: Togo Farmer

Table of Contents

Vice President Humphrey shakes the hand of PCV Joy Hudson in the Dominican Republic. Behind the Vice President are PCVs Wayne Watts and Mike Sweeney.

Preface

We hear a lot nowadays about people having to do their "thing." Doing their "thing" is very personal to them, and very compelling. This, of course, is nothing new. There have been times in all our lives when we just *had* to do or say or support a certain thing. For example, I have had a few "things" in my public life—causes or ideas that meant a great deal to me. One of them was my advocacy of the Peace Corps, and my legislation that brought it into being.

I believe this country—the American people—also have a "thing." And Peace Corps Volunteers are doing it. Our "thing" is the knowledge, deep within our marrow, that to live in prosperity while others live in deprivation is wrong—and that we have a responsibility to help the less fortunate lift themselves. Our "thing" is the belief that justice and human dignity should be the blessings of every man—and not just those of a chosen few. Our "thing" is helping our fellowmen "in the huts and villages of half the globe," as John Kennedy pledged us, "not because the Communists may be doing it, not because we seek their votes, but because it is right."

I can remember when the Peace Corps was just an idea that a lot of people were talking about—an idea for some kind of national service. Out of that general talk, from the public platform, came a lot of speeches, especially in the Senate and the House of Representatives. But it also produced a proposal that was not accepted at first. In fact, it was rejected. There were the cynics, as there always are, who thought that it was a pie-in-the-sky foolish idea. There were others who thought it was just another way for young men to escape their responsibilities to the military service.

However, the idea was a powerful one, and would not be stifled. In fact, it was discussed in the 1960 primaries that Senator John F. Kennedy and I engaged in, and of course it became an important issue in the 1960 presidential campaign. And when John Kennedy became President of the United States, I remember his calling me to the White House one day and saying: "Hubert, I want to take that proposal of yours that we talked about a great deal in the primaries, and I want to send it up to Congress. We want to make it the law of the land."

The proposal had been introduced in 1959. It was debated in 1960. It was reintroduced as an Administration proposal in 1961. And the President of the United States gave me the high honor of introducing that bill as an Administration bill. The Chairman of the Foreign Relations Committee, Senator William Fulbright, gave me the high honor of holding the hearings. And the majority leader, Senator Mike Mansfield, gave me the high honor of managing the bill on the floor of the Senate. Those were very happy days.

But I want you to know that it did not come easily. Practically everybody praises the Peace Corps now. But anyone who has ever taken the trouble to look at the votes on the amendments to the Peace Corps proposal at the time we were debating it in the Congress, or read all the speeches, knows that it wasn't easy. But it did come about because there were people who cared, people who had ideas and commitments and feelings.

The truth is that this country and the American people have very strong feelings about a number of things. I think they have a very strong feeling about the role of the United States in a troubled world. And I believe that the American people have a strong feeling about the Peace Corps and the Peace Corps Volunteers. The greatest testimonial to our moral fiber and moral stature and moral commitment is that at a time when we are rich and affluent and powerful, we are also deeply concerned about the weak and the sick and the illiterate and the poor and the unfortunate and the despairing, both at home and abroad.

I think it is fair to say that America could literally withdraw from any responsibility in the world today and have a ten-year lost weekend—live it up just having the time of our lives. There are those, even in this generation, who fail to remember and have not learned the lessons of the 1920's and the 1930's when "living it up" was exactly what we did. We closed our mind, closed our heart, closed our purse, closed our thinking to the rest of the world. And we soon closed up our banks, and lost our farms and businesses, lost our self-respect. That happened once, in my lifetime. And I see the seeds of it beginning to grow again in this part of my lifetime.

The excuse for it is: "Well, we are involved in struggle and war. And therefore I am disenchanted. I don't like it; it is a dirty business."

That is a sheer rationalization with very poor evidence. What is really going on is that some people just do not want to be bothered with the problems of other people. They prefer to take it easy.

However, there are those who are really interested in peace, and who really are the peacemakers, not the peace-talkers or the peace-walkers. The peacemakers are the ones who take time to help people live a good life. The peacemakers are the Peace Corps Volunteers abroad and the Community Action group at home. They are the people who have the courage to go into the ghetto of the urban slum and help people find a new life. They are the people who have the courage to go to faraway places with a Foreign Aid program or a Peace Corps program or a volunteer program of some voluntary agency, and help build, help in the process of nation-building.

Personally, I think the Peace Corps is the finest living expression of the purpose and the meaning of America that has ever been put in the field and put to the test. It *really* exemplifies the qualities of first-class citizenship and the meaning of America. I believe in public service, and so do the Volunteers or they wouldn't be here. The rewards of public service are the rewards of knowing that you have been of some help to someone other than yourself. The reward of public service is the feeling that you have been able to help others help themselves—lift themselves to a more meaningful life. And the Peace Corps has preserved a posture in our overseas programs that has enriched its meaning and, in fact, improved its efficiency and its applications to the tasks assigned to it. Peace Corps Volunteers are not engaged in the politics of a country, nor should they be. They are helping people—without any regard to their race, their creed, their color, their religion, or their political preference. The Peace Corps is a "pro-people" organization, an organization of volunteers dedicated to helping individuals as well as communities, and that is why it has had such a remarkable reception all over the world.

The meaning of the Peace Corps is most evident in the experiences of the Volunteers, and there is no better way to understand this meaning than showing them in action overseas and having the Volunteers tell their own stories, which they do in this stirring and perceptive book. In letters home, official reports, and advice to those who will follow, Volunteers tell in the most sensitive terms how they faced the challenges of their assignments—and profited by it. The photographs and stories are compelling in their simplicity, adding up to an extraordinarily rich and moving testament to the essential spirit of the Volunteers: They are idealists.

I know many people say: "What we need is more practical men in this world." Well, there is no conflict between having ideals and being practical. As a matter of fact, the realization of ideals and idealism comes through practical application of one's endeavors and talents and capacities. But Peace Corps Volunteers have to be idealists. They have to really believe they make a difference, that one person can make a difference in what happens in this world. And it is this belief that one person does make a real difference in the outcome of a contest or the development of a community or in the progress of a nation or in the cause of peace—this belief that one person makes a difference—that gives them the strength and courage to carry on. This belief that one person makes a difference is the hope of the world.

One of the most encouraging things about the Peace Corps is what it has done for America at home. In the speech I delivered in the Senate when we presented the bill for authorizing the Peace Corps, I said the Peace Corps will do more for America in America or as much for America in America as it will do for others in other parts of the world—and it has. It has brought out the best in our young people. It stands as a symbol and a reminder to all Americans of what we are and what America stands for. And it brings back to this nation a host of mature leadership. This generation of Americans has had a unique experience, and they are returning home and asking hard, penetrating questions.

The returning Volunteers are injecting imagination and new energy into public services. They are becoming involved in some of our toughest, most difficult social problems, trying to find modern solutions. Fortunately, they are not afraid to roll up their sleeves and do a little hard work. They are giving our country a lift by their spirit and their determination, and they are giving our country quite a bargain, too.

Young men and women who have learned something about the world in which they live, and who have gone out to help the world out of conviction, have come back much more mature, ripened and improved in their sensitivity and judgment as a result of their experience.

Those of us who have been a part of the Peace Corps are proud to see this idea, which was our export, come back as our best import, to see that which we practiced abroad come home and do as much for our own country as we were able to do for others in other parts of the world. For the Peace Corps will blend again with the people from whom it sprang—or should I say from which it never quite left?—imparting new vigor, new promise, and new conviction for Americans that this nation's "thing," or commitment, was right in the first place, and that it is still worth doing anytime, anywhere.

HUBERT H. HUMPHREY
Vice President of the United States

Introduction

A Variety of Nonreligious Experience

Since August, 1961, when the first Peace Corps volunteers sent overseas landed at a dusty airstrip in Accra, more than 25,000 young—and many not so young—Americans have gone abroad in a modern version of William James's Army of Peace. "To coal and iron mines," James wrote in 1910 in his *Moral Equivalent of War*, "to freight trains, to fishing fleets in December, to dishwashing, clotheswashing and windowwashing, to road-building and tunnel-making to foundries and stoke-holes, and to frames of skyscrapers, would our gilded youths be drafted off, according to their choice, to get the childishness knocked out of them, and to come back into society with healthier sympathies and soberer ideas. They would have paid their blood-tax, done their own part in the immemorial human warfare against nature; they would tread the earth more proudly. . . ."

Today, having endured everything James conceived, with the possible exception of the frames of skyscrapers, and quite a few situations that even James could not have imagined, thousands of our no longer "gilded" youth tread the earth more proudly. They have endured a variety of nonreligious experiences, and whether an individual Peace Corps volunteer's mission was a success or a failure, and regardless of whether the Peace Corps itself is the most impressive achievement of the Kennedy Administration, as many say it is, or a colossal boondoggle, as a few die-hard cynics persist in describing it, a volunteer's two years in the Peace Corps will no doubt stand out in his or her life as something never to be forgotten. The volunteers have seen strange sights, lived in unusual dwellings, eaten food they never dreamed existed, learned languages no American had ever spoken before, played games you would not believe,

Herons in Niger.

Elephants in Uganda and . . .

. . . a gorilla skull in Gabon.

danced dances that defy description, walked through incredible slums, come upon vistas most Americans never see except in travel films or the pages of the *National Geographic*—exotic cities, dark jungles, beautiful harbors, and desolate plains. But most important, they have lived with the people of more than fifty nations on every continent on the planet.

Trying to describe the "typical" Peace Corps volunteer is as difficult as trying to describe their collective experience abroad. "Frankly," former Peace Corps Director Sargent Shriver once said, "there is no typical volunteer, unless you believe in the hazy concept of a 'typical' American.

"Peace Corps volunteers look like any Americans you might pass in the supermarkets or like a neighbor who lives down the street. They average twenty-four years of age for men, twenty-five for women—although almost eighty of them are over sixty. The things that make them different from the average don't show—their good will, their sense of adventure, their willingness to sacri-

fice for others and to work hard under difficult conditions.

"They go abroad with no special privileges, no hardship pay. They are subject to the laws of the country in which they work. They do not have the commissary privileges enjoyed by most Americans abroad. They speak the local language. They live on the economic level of local citizens who do the same kind of work.

"They are the best and best-liked unofficial ambassadors this nation ever sent overseas."

In the early days of the Peace Corps it was thought that Shriver's "ambassadors" would be skilled technicians or people with two or three years of experience in an activity which would be of use in the developing nations. But it quickly became apparent that experienced technicians would not be available in large enough quantities to satisfy the demand. "For every blue collar sought," says one Peace Corps recruiting brochure of these early days, "twenty Shetland sweaters appeared." Deluged with what it calls "A.B. generalists,"

The anthills in the desert of North Somalia sometimes rise to a height of 30 feet.

the Peace Corps selected them in—and out (one was chosen for every five that applied)—trained them in a skill and a language, and turned them loose in the great big, awesome developing world—with remarkable results. "We are discovering," says Peace Corps Director Jack Vaughn, "that the special hero of the Peace Corps is the Forgotten Man of the '60's: the generalist—the liberal arts graduate with a decent education and lots of ambition. At best, he resembles the Renaissance man —round in spirit and judgment rather than versed in science. . . . Fortunately, we are able to train such people, and naturally, where highly technical skills have been requested, we have followed suit in training. But the highest skill for the Peace Corps volunteer usually is his attitude."

The attitude of the volunteers has surprised the cynics who said that young Americans were too soft to live out on the frontiers of ignorance, poverty, and disease. As one management expert who makes long-range studies

of the volunteer's effectiveness put it: 'Who else but the educated young generalist from the established middle class can take two years off, learn a new trade, work like hell, maybe live in a dump, and not get paid much? He is the missing link in all our economic development efforts overseas. What more can you say."

The volunteers may go abroad as the missing link in an economic development program—"middle level manpower" is the term most often used in government and academic circles—but they also go as students. Collectively, the Peace Corps experience has been the greatest eye-opening, mind-stretching education any generation of Americans has ever had. But individually, the Peace Corps experience has often meant two years in an isolated village high in the mountains, or lost in a teeming city slum to which thousands of people have migrated to escape the hopeless life of the village. Loneliness is the only return on his contribution, and this contribution, as Sargent Shriver once said, "measured in the

Hillside dwellings in a Nigerian village.

Photo by PCV John Hand

A rubber farm near Kuala Lumpur, Malaysia.

"This is the hardest thing I've ever done. Absolutely nothing is familiar and I often feel totally alone—the physical difficulties actually help, as they take my mind off myself and the feeling of suddenly being cut off from the rest of the world. You cannot imagine the gulf between East and West, and it makes me laugh now to think that I expected to bridge it with a smile and a handshake."

—Peace Corps volunteer Patricia MacDermott, Philippines

Planting peanuts in Senegal.

Photo by Jim Rugh

Irrigated rice paddies in Malaysia.

Hillside near Mamou, Guinea.

A boy on a cart—in Konya, Turkey.

whole spectrum of the world's difficulties, will probably cast only a sliver of light—and that sliver may go unseen."

But the volunteer's contribution cannot be measured solely in terms of children taught, bridges built, roads laid, communities developed, people inoculated, or crops harvested. "In twenty-eight languages," says Jack Vaughn, "the word for 'stranger' and 'enemy' is the same. By communications on a person-to-person level, the peoples of the world may some day eliminate the word and its negative meaning from their vocabularies. Communications, after all, can breed understanding. And understanding can breed peace. I like to think that is what the Peace Corps is all about."

That is at least one of the things the Peace Corps experience is all about. But there is more, as I hope to show on these pages—with the help of the volunteers themselves describing some of their own experiences and the superb collection of photographs taken by the Peace Corps staff photographers. "The art of photography," says Edward Steichen, "is a dynamic process of giving form to ideas and of explaining man to man."

The village smith—Togo style.

Photo by Peace Corps physician **Dr. William Anderson**

And I am convinced, after having written thousands of words about the Peace Corps, that the essence of the Peace Corps experience cannot be explained in words alone—even the words of those who shared these experiences. To see the faces the volunteers have seen, to appreciate how they have lived, to understand the beauty, the squalor, and the hunger for food and knowledge the Peace Corps volunteers have encountered, photographs are essential. But even the camera has its limitation in showing the impact the Peace Corps volunteer has had on the world (and vice versa), for as one volunteer has written: "How do you photograph the mind of a child?" And how do you photograph the mind of a returning volunteer?

If we *could* photograph their minds, some of the things we would see would be the scenes depicted in this book. The volunteers have seen a world most Americans do not know—but most of all they have seen faces —and on these faces they have seen indifference, despair, curiosity, resignation, hostility, apathy, ignorance, suffering, intelligence. But the thing they look for most is the smile of friendship. For once they have achieved friendship, their job is more than half done—and until they achieve it, the job cannot be done at all.

Just as there is no such thing as the "typical" volunteer, there is no "typical" Peace Corps experience. As these pages reveal, every volunteer has a different experience—even two volunteers serving together on the same "team" in an isolated African village. Two such volunteers are Nancy Keith and Vicki Soucek, two young ladies who lived in the heartland of Niger, Africa, two young Americans who asked not what the human race could do for them, but what they could do for the human race.

A St. Louis (Senegal) merchant.

Little girl and beer boxes in a Togo village.

Photo by Dr. William Anderson

Anything Singer makes, the girls of Gabon can carry.

In the Peace Corps Countries . . .
People Use Their Heads

Indian women coming home from market.

Photo by PCV Martha Cooper

Ecuadorian waterfront.

(*Opposite page*) Street scene—Rabat.

A Chilean village.

14

"There is nothing to make one indignant in the mere fact that life is hard, that men should toil and suffer pain. The planetary conditions once for all are such, and we can stand it. But that so many men, by mere accidents of birth and opportunity, should have a life of nothing else but toil and pain and hardness and inferiority imposed upon them . . . this is capable of arousing indignation in reflective minds."
—William James, in the *Moral Equivalent of War*

(*Opposite page*) Movie theatre in Tunis.

Village in Somalia.

"There may be a road connecting it [the village] with the next village; but it is in no way connected with the rest of the country in the way, for example, in which Keokuk, Iowa, is connected with Chicago and from there to Boston. This village simply does not have that kind of national consciousness.

"You will find people living here who do not know the names of the leaders of their country, who have never heard of the United Nations, who have heard of the United States in only a vague, distant way and who could not find it on a map because most of them have never seen a map. They are aware of the next village, and perhaps the village beyond that, and perhaps of the major city in their province. Beyond that, their knowledge of the world ends.

"In this village, people work on land they do not own and make a subsistence living at the pleasure of the man who does own the land. Classically, in this village there are a priest, a teacher, and perhaps one or two government officials—depending on the size of the village. . . .

"Into this situation, where there is no one indigenous to the town who has anything to say about how his economic, political, or social system is run, we move, as part of a host country effort, a Peace Corps volunteer or two."

—Frank Mankiewicz, former Peace Corps Director for Latin America

Volunteer George Seay, of Buffalo, New York, with his "Exercise Club" in Conceição de Castelo, Brazil.

"Peace Corps volunteers look like any Americans you might pass in the supermarkets. . . ."
—Sargent Shriver

Volunteers Eve and Chris Lotze, 1964 graduates of LSU, in the Medina in Sousse, Tunisia.

". . . In his loneliness by a foreign roadside, this man or that ceases to be a Government Issue, a mass commodity produced by a mass response out of a mass need and hope. He once again becomes man's issue, and woman's too."

—John Mason Brown

A girl, taking lunch to her father, passes an unidentified volunteer in Senegal.

Everywhere, There Are the Children

View from the bottom floor—in Bogotá, Colombia.

Photo by PCV Nick Mills

Mother and child in a cart—Lomé, Togo.

Photo by Dr. William Anderson

"I call you"—young boys in Keur M'Bire, Senegal.   *Photo by Jim Rugh*

(*Below*) In Chijnaya, Peru, students rest in a school built with the help of Peace Corps volunteer Ralph Bolton, called by Cornell University anthropologists "a model volunteer" (see page 293).

The Greatest Challenge of All . . . Getting to Know the People

(*Left*) An old woman of Kikuyu. Earrings show that, as a girl, she was properly circumcised, a custom rarely practiced in modern Kenya.

A Cholo Indian, Colombia. *Photo by Charles Marden Fitch*

A young girl in the Souloulou area of Niger.

Buddhist monks in Thai howdah.   *Photo by Charlotte Hutchinson*

Revelers at the annual fiesta in Urubamba, Peru.

Young girl in the atoll of Woleai, Micronesia.

Togo farmer with hoe—in Sokode.

Photo by Dr. William Anderson

Uruguayan police.

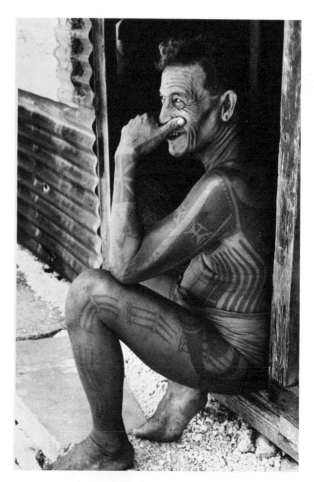

Ulithe islander.

"We have learned in Ghana, in the Dominican Republic, and a dozen Vietnams that progress for mankind can never really be measured in causes and coups, but in precious inches of human understanding and enlightenment, scantly noticed, grudgingly surrendered from indifference and despair, toiled after, lost, missed, and sought after again.

"These are the unseen battles and the silent victories of Peace. They are won by quiet heroes whose politics are people, whose nationality is mankind. These are the men and women who serve the cause of Peace by grappling at the very level where results count; where people live and must survive.

"These are the Peace Corps volunteers."

—Jack Vaughn, Director of the Peace Corps

In twenty-eight languages, says Peace Corps Director Jack Vaughn (pictured *right* at a ceremony in Micronesia) the word for "stranger" and "enemy" are the same—a linguistic peculiarity that the Peace Corps would like to change.

Chapter 1

Two Young Ladies in Niger

Illéla Niger, is a small village of 7,000 people. It is the center to an agricultural area containing approximately 94,000 Nigeriens and the *chef de canton* lives there. It is 120 kilometers north of Birni N'Konni and 15 kilometers west of the main road. The public buildings in Illéla consists of a school (for 200 students), the government office, a dispensary, an unopened post office, an inn for government travelers, the abbatoir, and a *Maison des Jeunes.* There are no factories or mills, no electricity, no running water; and no European products are available in Illéla, except for tomato paste and cocoa.

Although most of Illéla's citizens are members of the Hausa tribe, there are also a few Djermas, and Tuaregs. The village is divided into several *quartiers,* and the people of the different *quartiers,* or the different tribes, rarely associate with one another. Hence, town projects involving the cooperation of everyone are difficult to organize.

There are a few government employees in Illéla, but most of the town's income is from farming. Peanuts and beans are grown for export, millet and sorghum for home consumption. Although the women help some in the fields, most of the work is done by the men. The women usually raise gourds, pimento, squash, and spices in the yards of their compound. Most families raise chickens, goats, a cow, pigeons, and guinea hens in their yards, mostly for home consumption.

During the farming season, which runs from June to early November, many families move to bush homes near the fields. In the off season some men migrate to other towns to work, or work in Illéla at various odd jobs, such as masonry. They also repair their homes, granaries, and fences which have been damaged by the rains. Cash is very short in Illéla; often the women have to look after themselves, and they usually don't have enough food, and there is litle money for soap, sugar, or milk.

There is one dispensary in Illéla. It serves not only the village but all the 94,000 people in the surrounding area. It is staffed by two male nurses and two female assistants. In addition to the dispensary, there are a four-room hospital for out-of-town patients, and a residence for the head nurse. The dispensary has three rooms: one where patients are diagnosed and medicine is dispensed, one for bandaging and giving shots, and a small pharmacy.

The dispensary has no vehicle of its own. If an evacuation is necessary, the dispensary may request the use of a government vehicle, but often a vehicle is not available or there is no gas. Evacuations are usually made to the hospital at Tahoua. If a patient needs an operation, he may be sent to the Protestant hospital at

Vicki Soucek (*left*) and Nancy Keith. "We love the people and we love our work," says Nancy. "But I doubt whether we would ever do it again."

Galmi where there is a surgeon. If the roads to Tahoua are washed out, the patient may be evacuated to Konni.

Children from the school in Illéla are brought to the dispensary two days a week to receive treatments for minor ailments. The ten schools in the surrounding bush area are furnished medicine by the dispensary through the teachers. A large supply of aspirin, niva-quine, meningitis prophylactic, mercurochrome, and compresses is given at the beginning of the year, and the teachers replenish their supplies during the year. In 1965, the head nurse made one trip to the ten bush schools by horseback. He would like to do this every two months, but the lack of a vehicle makes this very difficult. If a student becomes seriously ill, he is sent to the dispensary on horseback. When an epidemic is reported, an *infirmier* goes to the town by horseback or by car.

Although Illéla's market is very small, market day draws many people from the bush towns up to 20 kilometers away. These people sometimes stop by the dispensary for medicine, but they usually don't come until complications have set in, and they return home before the illness has been cured. There are almost always from two to ten people staying in the hospital, usually adults who have a serious problem such as crippling complications from a guinea worm, a knife wound in the stomach, a woman who ran a stick into her eye, or a child who had been hit by a car.

The majority of the people from the bush who come for medicine, however, come with the idea that after they have received one shot or one dose of medicine they have received "the cure" and can go home. If the medicine works, they get well. If it doesn't work, then it was "Allah's will."

Many people are suspicious of the dispensary and simply refuse to go. They think that the medicines in syrup are only water; they are afraid the nurse will cut a gangrenous sore. Since the concept of time is so vague, many people arrive at the dispensary during rest hours. They are told to return during regular hours to receive the medicine but seldom do return. The unfamiliar procedure in the dispensary intimidates some people, who refuse to return. As a result, they prefer native medicines supplemented by amulets and prayers.

In the fall of 1965, two young American girls fresh out of college were sent to work in Illéla's dispensary as Peace Corps public health volunteers. They are Vicki Soucek and Nancy Keith, and they are typical of the "A.B. generalists" who have become the backbone of the Peace Corps.

Vicki Soucek was twenty-three when she joined the Peace Corps. She is from Winchester, Massachusetts, and was graduated from Tufts University in 1965, with a major in English. She also attended Marymount College and the University of London. Nancy Keith was twenty-two. She is from North Brookfield, New York,

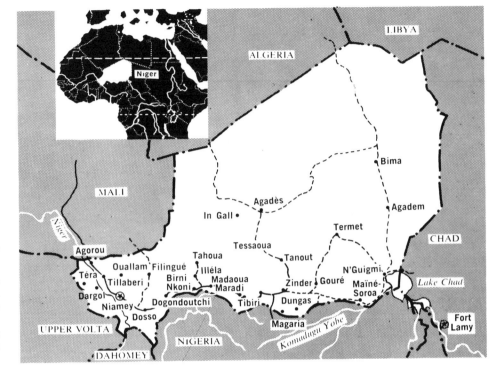

Niger is larger than the combined area of Texas and California, but most of its 3 million people are concentrated along the southern border from Niamey to Lake Chad. Its output averages $75 per person annually, mostly in peanuts and cotton (the chief export crops), live-stock, gum arabic, tin, tungsten, and hides. Niger's literacy rate is estimated at 5 percent. The average life-span of its people: thirty-eight years.

(*Below*) The main street of Illéla. Camels and donkeys are the normal means of transportation in Niger. These camels are bringing in millet (grain) from the outlying areas. Because of its climate, Niger will probably always have economic problems.

and majored in French at the State University of New York at Albany, where she was graduated in 1965.

Before being sent to Niger, both girls were given training with other Niger-bound volunteers at the University of Southern Illinois at Carbondale, Illinois. The group was scheduled to teach adult literacy, and to work in public health and agriculture. The curriculum consisted of courses in world affairs, communism, and the history and customs of the area: 360 hours of French and one of the various African dialects prevalent in Niger (Nancy and Vicki studied Hausa); physical education; personal medical training; and technical studies, which for the girls meant public health. The health program was developed by Dr. David Nicholas, Peace Corps staff physician in Niger, who says, "If you can teach public health to a Nigerien mother, you can certainly teach it to an A.B. generalist"—or, as the Peace Corps puts it: "If you can't teach it to a liberal arts graduate in three months, you probably can't teach it to a Nigerien housewife."

After three months at Carbondale, and a short week's home leave, the girls flew to Niamey, the capital of Niger, then went by bus to Illéla. The trend today in the Peace Corps is toward volunteers working in pairs or groups rather than alone, so Vicki and Nancy were assigned to work as a team teaching public health to the mothers and housewives of Illéla.

After six months on the job, they wrote an extensive report on the problem of getting started with their work in the village. Printed below are excerpts from that report, which constitutes one of the best descriptions of the Peace Corps experience I have read. The photographs were taken by Peace Corps Director of Photography Carl Purcell, who visited Illéla in the summer of 1966:

On October 15, we were "dropped off" in Illéla to begin our Peace Corps tour overseas. We greeted the commandant and explained briefly our role in public health. We wanted to help the town improve its health, especially to teach the women child care. We would have to become more fluent in Hausa, learn about the town and available resources before we could begin a specific project.

Our relationship with the dispensary proceeded very slowly at first, for the head nurse was ill in Tahoua for a month. Mornings we sat as observers at the dispensary learning Hausa, about various prevalent diseases, and having people become used to us. Afternoons we explored the town, trying to ease the strangeness. Because there had never been a European living in Illéla, we found that we had to proceed very slowly. In some ways this was harder because we didn't have a specific job, and people found it difficult to figure out what we were doing in Illéla, despite our repeated statement that we had come to help in the dispensary. Our limited ability to speak Hausa was a great drawback during the first two months.

After two weeks we felt we needed more help with Hausa quickly, and we asked the commandant to suggest a good teacher. For the next two weeks we spent from 8:00 to 9:30 in the dispensary, and then walked around town with our teacher. We were introduced to different compounds, and we learned Hausa and worked on our survey at the same time.

Our house had not been repaired, so we lived in an "inn" for travelers near the government office. It was isolated from town, which slowed us down for we had no neighbors with whom to chat. The simple greetings or a household visit in town were all on a superficial level. Women appeared very hesitant and reticent when we entered a compound, and often conversation seemed very forced.

People began to think of our teacher more as a translator; they also couldn't understand why we were paying someone to teach us Hausa. So we began walking around town on our own and had our Hausa classes at the house, for we felt we were better able to reach the townspeople by ourselves. People seemed more relaxed. After four weeks of Hausa lessons, we dropped our

(Opposite) A dehydrated Nigerien baby, flies clustering around her eyes and mouth, clutches at her mother's dry breast. Until the mother's milk comes in, the baby is given unboiled cow's or goat's milk, or more often "samka," skimmed sour milk. The girls feel that the use of unboiled milk has been the cause of digestive tract and diarrhea problems in very young babies brought to them. If the mothers had been ill, often the milk would not come in. Two babies were brought to Nancy and Vicki about two weeks after birth, in a state of extreme starvation and acute diarrhea. The mothers were very young and shy about their babies. They did not enjoy the attention, and usually refused to answer questions, giving the responsibility and work over to the baby's grandmother. They both refused to admit that they didn't have enough milk, and insisted that the babies didn't have diarrhea.

Endemic syphilis is also a major source of illness. Schistomiasis, guinea worm, and other parasites are common. Although there do not seem to be any mosquitoes in Illéla during the dry season, people often have recurrent attacks of malaria. Since all fevers are designated as malaria ("agana"), it is difficult to know precisely. The girls say they have seen many children with enlarged spleens and liver troubles resulting from little or no treatment when they had malaria as infants.

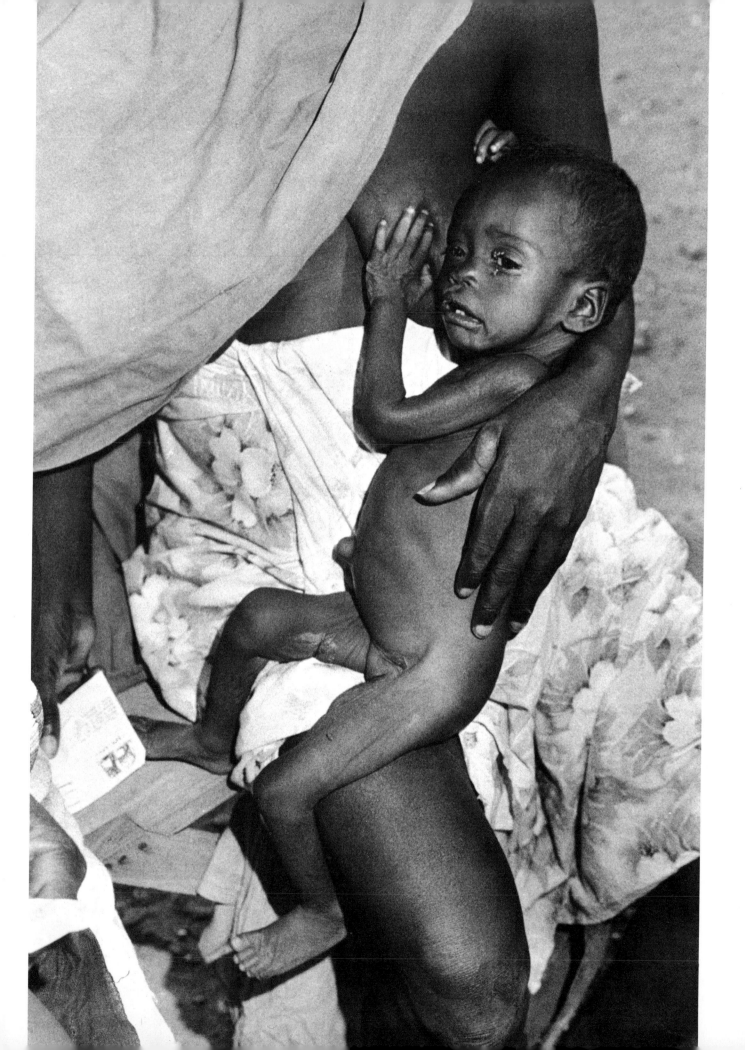

teacher and decided it was more beneficial to learn Hausa on our own, often questioning a young schoolboy in the vicinity if the Hausa became too difficult.

On our second day in Illéla, the Minister of Education had delivered a political speech, including us as helpers in the progress of Niger. He told the crowd of schoolchildren, *anciens militaires,* and the men not to fear us, because we had come to improve health conditions. We gave a short speech in French, and then the Minister explained that we were not interested in exploiting them because, as Americans, our fathers were millionaires and we didn't need their money. There were no women present at this meeting, and the impression transmitted to them was that we were here to give out money and medicines. The concept of public health, of improving health without donating either money or medicine, was incomprehensible. Consequently, we have had to make a tremendous effort to define our role as public health workers in terms which the people will understand.

We had decided at the onset not to dispense any medicines, even for headaches or simple cuts, for this would detract from the dispensary, which had adequate but limited materials. One of our goals is to encourage the early and frequent use of the existing facilities of the dispensary rather than destroy its function by doling out limited supplies ourselves. Many people have lost faith in the dispensary because the medicines do not always cure. This is not because the medicine is worthless, but because people wait too long before receiving treatment, return to an unsanitary compound, or don't go often enough.

We decided that our goals for the first two or three months would be to inspire trust, learn Hausa, work on our survey of the town's problems and resources, encourage using the dispensary, and do public health work using only available materials.

The introduction of foreign elements such as powdered milk, bottles or diapers, foreign dietary habits such as scrambled eggs, rice, salad, meat might provide short-term results if the people have the money to buy these products. But when these things would no longer be available, people would quickly revert to their old habits, and the work would be wasted. We were determined to learn about their foods, the nutritional quality and methods of preparation, their customs and work through the existing system to produce results. Sometimes the introduction of a change is worse, if the new method is not done correctly: the addition of a place to wash with a drain into the street, instead of a dry well, creates more of a sanitation problem than the old system which uses water more sparingly. The introduction of diapers, if women are unable to wash them often with soap and hot water, would be a less sanitary method than letting the child straddle the mother's legs in order to go to the bathroom in the sand.

We have also found that it is essential to work on changing one small idea at a time to make sure it is successful before confusing the issue with many new concepts. If we are teaching a mother to boil milk, we sometimes forego commenting on the animals near the house or the necessity to boil all drinking water. As we return for each home visit, if our advice seems to be working, we offer a new idea, and we always try to stress washing often with soap and going to the dispensary the moment one is ill.

One day, as we were walking around town working on our survey, a mason approached and asked us to help his three-month-old child. The mother had died when the child was one month old. Although it was being cared for by the grandmother, it was very tiny.

Whereas before our suggestions had been met with fear or distrust, our conversations had convinced this man that we wanted to help him. We decided to concentrate on this small object in order to learn how to proceed with other women, how to gain the parents' confidence, what to suggest for the child, and to learn the pertinent Hausa phrases.

The first night we just chatted, asking how old the child was, what she was fed, whether she had diarrhea. After checking with Doctors Nicholas, Jelliffe (author of the paper "Public Health in a Rural Village"), and Spock, we decided on a formula of cow's milk, for they had a cow in the yard; we returned the next morning

(*Opposite*) A Hausa mother and child.

(*Below*) One of the first things the girls decided to do was to make a "survey" of the health conditions in the compounds. They found that animals are usually tethered to posts in a corner of the compound. Almost every family has a cow, horse, several goats, chickens, and guinea hens. Goats are often turned loose at feeding time to save carrying water and food to them. The goats wander around, shoving their noses into food vessels, stumbling into living quarters, around the cooking area or area where millet is pounded, until someone shoos them away. The goats are given water which has been used to rinse the millet, thus freeing the women from carrying even more water. Chickens are allowed to run free, nesting under beds in the house at all times and scratching for food where they can find it—in the cooking area, the pounding area, or among the animals.

The cooking area is often allowed to build up to two- or three-foot heaps of ashes. In homes where the animal tethering area is not swept regularly, the combination of manure-laden sand and heaps of light ashes can quickly contaminate foods and the air, whenever there is a slight wind.

Homes in Illéla generally have a large hole in the yard, left over from digging for clay to build the house and fence of the compound. The women usually walk to the edge of this hole, if it isn't too far away from the cooking area, to throw away garbage. Often when the animal-tethering area is swept, those wastes will be thrown into the hole and sometimes burned. The idea is to get the wastes out of the way while gradually filling the hole. There is no attempt made to cover the trash.

There are many homes which are regularly swept and where the animals are kept confined. In some compounds the animals are actually fenced off from the rest of the compound and are located far from the living quarters and cooking areas. The problems seem to be most accentuated in those compounds which are crowded because of a large number of wives, children, and dependent relatives. The crowding forces the small living space left between buildings to function also as the cooking area and animal-tethering area.

at milking time. We were lucky to spot a spoon, bowl, and soap in the house so we told the grandmother to wash everything. The grandmother wasn't very confident, but we had her do each step, although she kept trying to have us do it because she didn't know how. We returned that evening to watch her, occasionally adding a comment praising her so that she would continue when we weren't there.

The father had bought two cans of powdered milk from Tahoua, for he was told by the nurses that powdered milk was better for the child. We had to show them how to use it because the father insisted, thus further complicating the situation. Since they had been using the powdered milk in a very diluted formula, the child was receiving practically only water. After a week we convinced the father that there was nothing wrong with powdered milk, but that it was expensive, not readily available, and more complicated to use. The cow's milk was always there, much less expensive, and easier for the grandmother to work with.

One day we returned to find that the child had been given nothing for almost two days because the cow had not come in from the bush. We borrowed some milk from a neighbor's goat, and went through the process again, explaining to the grandmother that she should feed the child either powdered milk, cow's milk, or goat's milk, whichever was available, as long as she was fed. The inability to substitute one thing for another is a common problem.

Now, after six months, the child is fat and healthy. We have also taught the grandmother to make millet cereal; we give her a papaya occasionally to mash and feed the baby for vitamins A and C. We tell her to use a scrubber rather than sand, to buy soap and sugar when she can, and jokingly order her to sweep the yard. The atmosphere has relaxed so that this is possible; when we first came, these suggestions would have just made matters worse.

We have found that working closely with a few cases, with neighbors watching, has brought other people running to us asking for help. They are willing to accept our method because they know that it has helped someone else. Merely teaching a new method does not ensure that it is being carried out; public health has to inspire the will to change, and at the same time provide the method of improvement and the reasons.

After two months in Illéla, we told the commandant we would like to speak to the *chefs* again in simple Hausa to show them we were learning through our home visits. We wouldn't be able to continue the home visits for two years because we wouldn't reach many people this way. We wanted to tell them that we would start to weigh babies soon, and later, when we became more fluent in Hausa, that we would begin classes in health.

The commandant elaborated on our speech and clarified some points. Afterwards we also found out that he had made a public apology to the townspeople for our Hausa teacher's behavior. Men are not allowed into another man's compound, especially the cloistered homes, without the specific permission of the man of the household. Although we were permitted to enter because we are females, our teacher should have remained outside the compound. Our Hausa teacher never explained this, always entered with us, and people were too polite to say anything when we paid a visit. The commandant said that we weren't to blame, for we were ignorant of the custom. He also explained that we wanted to get to know the women and children in order to help them, and urged the men to welcome us into their homes.

After this, the town literally opened up to us. Everyone wanted us to visit his home, and we didn't have enough hours in each day. We were very lucky that this breach of etiquette did not create a permanent rift between us and the town. People have been very understanding when we make mistakes, and we have tried to learn the customs and act accordingly.

In November, we decided that our Hausa and knowledge of the town had increased to the point that we could do more than just make home visits. In December, the Peace Corps provided us with a bright, shiny scale which gave us a *modus operandi*, for people had trouble comprehending how our visiting in the compounds was related to health work. With our new scale proudly established on a rickety old table *en plein air* under the *nime* trees in the dispensary lawn, we opened for business the following Tuesday. We chose Tuesday, market day, in order to reach, in some small way, the people from neighboring bush villages who come to the market and occasionally the dispensary.

The first day, attendance was over a hundred. We weighed all the babies and examined them carefully. Our mouth-to-mouth publicity for three previous days had helped considerably. We emphasized that the mothers continue to bring the babies every week to see

(*Opposite*) The visits to Illéla homes also helped the girls improve their Hausa, although at first they said, "The simple greetings or a household visit was all on a superficial level. Women appeared very hesitant and reticent when we entered a compound and often conversation seemed forced."

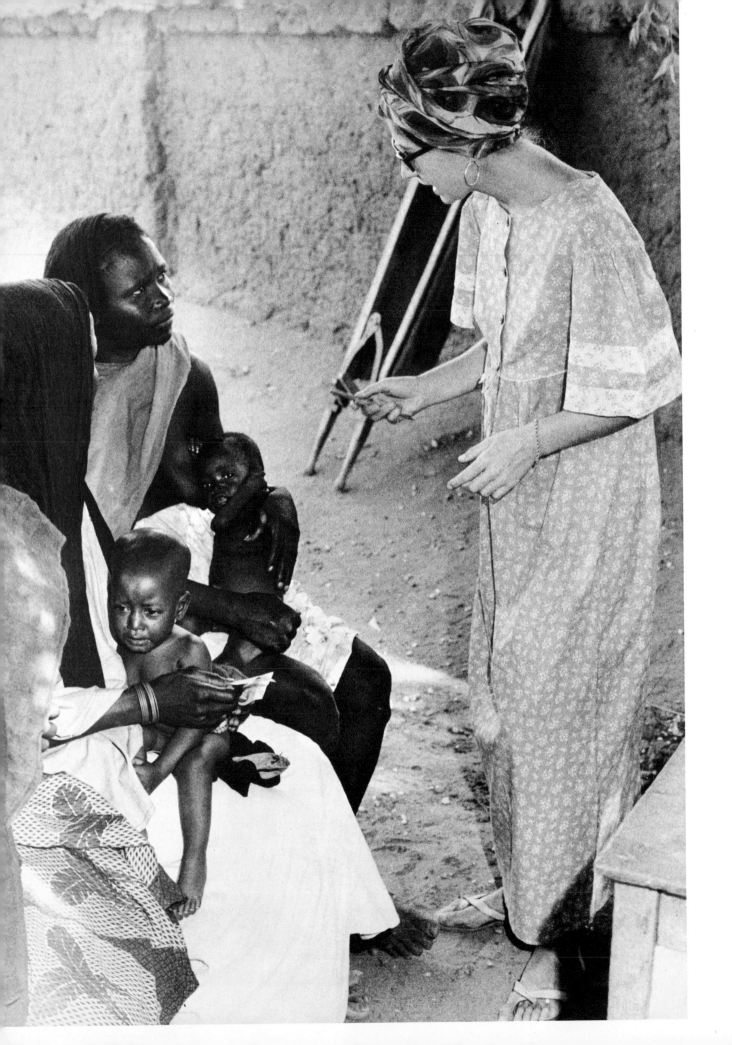

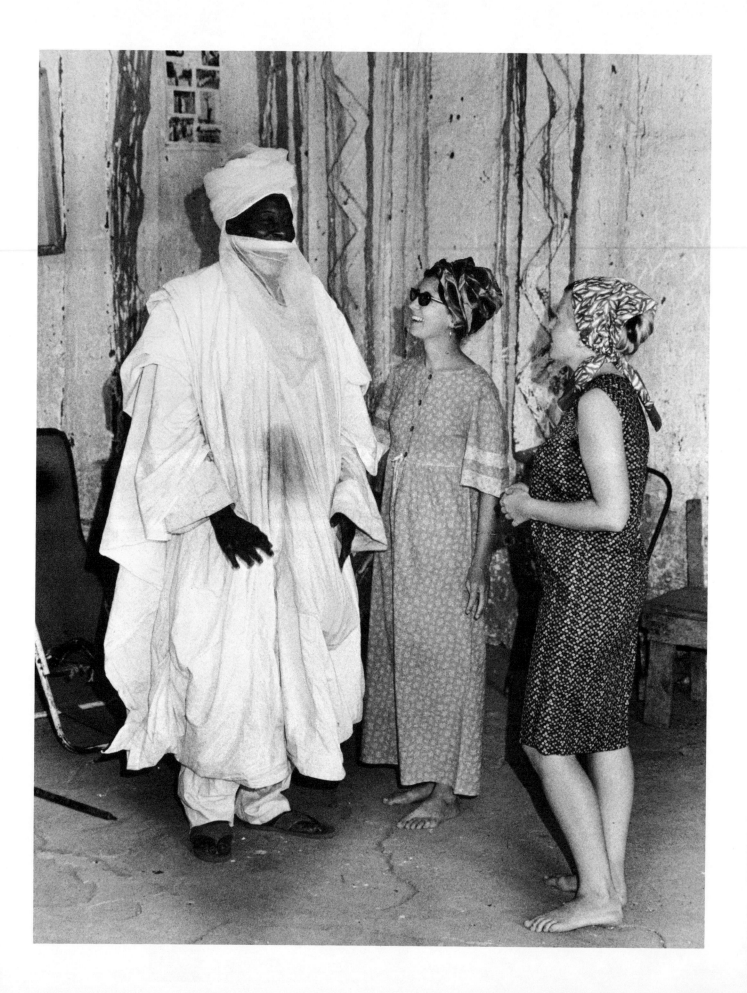

(*Opposite*) Gradually, the people of Illéla became more receptive, especially after one of the government officials explained to the people that the girls had come to improve their health conditions, and did not want to exploit them. They were Americans who didn't need money because their fathers were millionaires. One man who became their friend is Sarki, a tribal chief. Once they brought him a gift of melons from the local market. Sarki, a gracious host, expressed great appreciation, although later the girls learned that their melons were used mainly as goat fodder.

if they had gained weight and so we could make sure they were healthy. We singled out as many of the cases needing special help as we could manage, and spent the rest of the week visiting their homes to prepare milk and water. The mothers loved having us hold and weigh the babies.

The second week, attendance was still about a hundred. The sarki's and functionaires' children returned, but a large percentage of the infants were newcomers brought to the dispensary for treatment. Obviously a bookkeeping system was needed, so we decided to give out small, numbered pieces of paper containing the child's name, date of weighing, and illness, if any. In our black book, we had the corresponding numbers, child's name, mother's name, age, *quartier* (or town), and a large blank space for the successive weights to be recorded. The age turned out to be a rough approximation, for we were told that the baby was born "when it started raining" or "when we harvested the millet." At

(*Below*) After some resistance, Vicki and the child's mother finally persuade a young child to drink some powdered milk. Because of dehydration, the child's system could not tolerate whole milk, and the powdered milk, made with boiled water, was the perfect solution. The child probably would have died without the powdered milk

The majority of illnesses of babies under six months are related to insufficient food intake. If the mother's breast milk is insufficient, the unboiled milk given to the child is often the cause of diarrhea. After six months, the illnesses seem to be fevers, colds, rashes, eye and ear infections, and malnutrition. Unsanitary conditions, infrequent and delayed use of the dispensary, and the lack of a good diet promote the vicious circle of illness and weight loss.

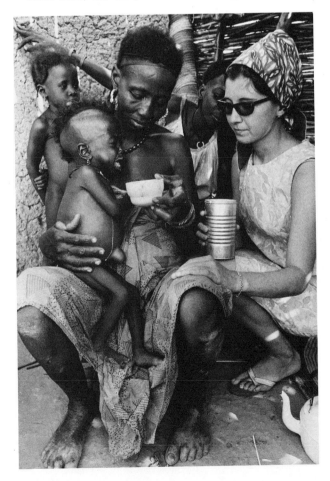 

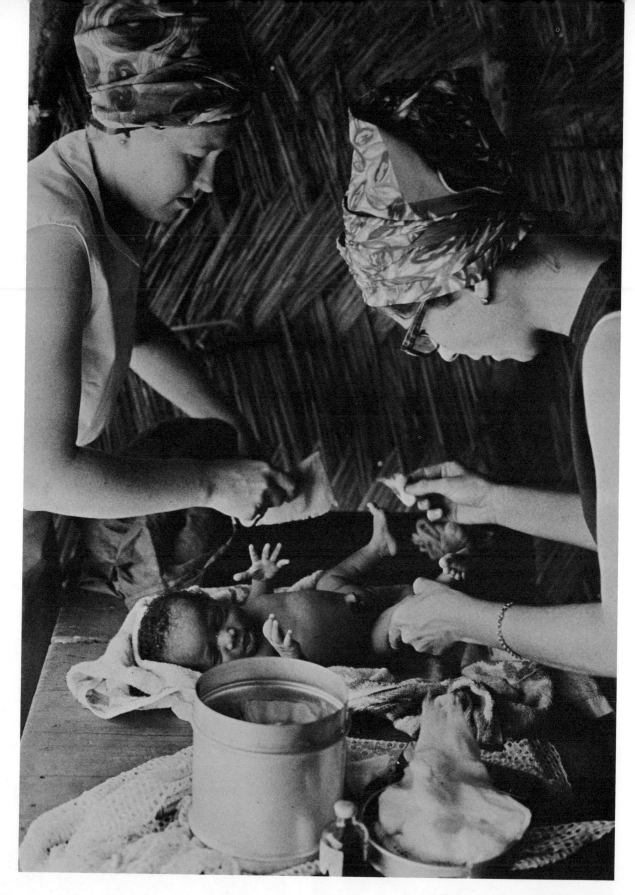

(*Above*) Nancy and Vicki treat a baby's skin rash at the dispensary. After they were accepted by the town, people flocked to the clinic and "everybody wanted us to visit his home and we didn't have enough hours in the day," the girls said in their report.

first, before we had learned many of the terms, we miscalculated a month or two, but our improvisation works fairly well, except that the little slips of paper are often lost and are not very durable.

One of the greatest problems with weighing is the irregular attendance. Although we have over three hundred children in our books, many come only once or twice when sick. The average attendance is approximately forty to fifty. The children from bush villages often have the more serious cases of malnutrition and complications from a disease. Rarely do the same people from *en brousse* return the next week or remain in Illéla until the child has improved. Although many of the families in Illéla have at least some goats and perhaps a cow, the busy villagers frequently have none. It is almost impossible to help them, for they have only a subsistence existence.

Even among the women in town, we have found it impossible to keep them returning weekly if the child is healthy. Thus, our well-baby clinic deals generally with only the ill children. Our demonstrations thus far, with the exception of daily baby washing, are geared to the curative aspect. If a child is ill, women are more apt to listen; if he is healthy, we have little success.

After establishing Tuesday as baby-weighing day, for healthy babies as well as sick babies, the next thing was to prepare the women for classes. The first two Tuesdays we weighed babies in the yard outside of the dispensary, because we had no room of our own. In January we asked the commandant to build a straw lean-to where we could hold classes and weigh babies. The shelter helped people begin to understand the purpose of our work. Since we had already made many home visits, working with individual cases that needed special help, we decided to pick a larger number from the babies that came on Tuesday to return on Wednesday. We wanted to use the established weighing day as a means of checking all babies and catching those who needed extra help. We wanted to find a way to help many of these cases at one time so that more time could eventually be devoted to classes for well babies, to keep them healthy.

Our first weighing day in the shelter was used not only for sending those who needed medicine in to the dispensary and telling all mothers to wash their babies, but also to pick out those who needed the dehydration formula or supplementary milk. Their mothers were told to return the next day with a clean bowl, cover, and spoon. If they were going to learn to boil milk, they were to bring the bowl full of whatever milk was available, goat's or cow's milk. We also painted the old table bright blue to lighten spirits.

Wednesday, as each mother arrived, we talked to her about the reasons for the dehydration formula or supplementary milk. We explained what we were going to

(*Above*) Vicki gives a demonstration in basic hygiene. "Rural people here do not connect disease and dirt," wrote Vicki and Nancy in their report. "Dishwashing, personal hygiene, and compound cleanliness [therefore] suggest our major theme: Dirt causes sickness." They tell the mothers that it doesn't matter whether or not they can see the dirt; "if you don't wash everything with soap, you will become sick."

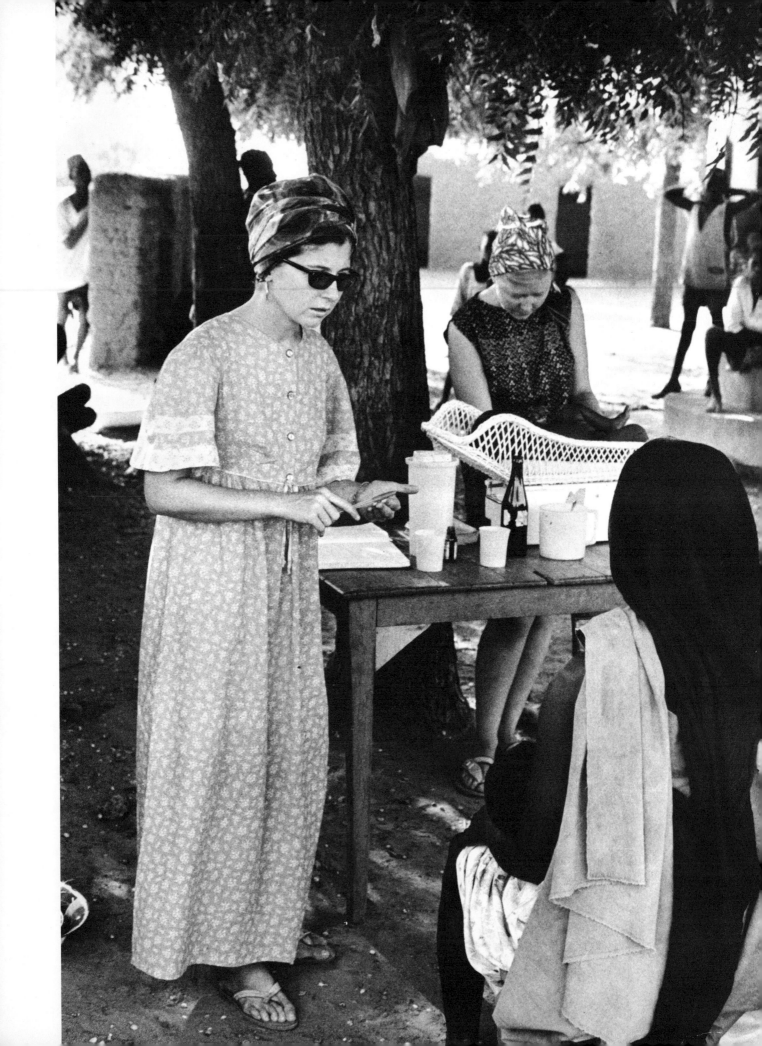

(*Opposite*) In December the girls decided to establish a weighing day, and set up their scales on a rickety table, *en plein air*, under the *nime* tree on the dispensary lawn. On the first day, attendance was over 100, and the women loved having the girls hold and weigh their babies.

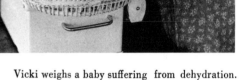

Vicki weighs a baby suffering from dehydration.

do, and then went carefully through the procedure, having the mother do most of the preparation on the open fire in the dispensary yard.

This first week we decided to have the same mothers come back for two more days to report on their progress, to check the baby's reaction, and to adjust formulas. Thursday was spent strengthening formulas to full strength appropriate to the baby, and switching some of the diarrhea cases, now cured, to milk formulas.

We used the afternoons and weekends to visit these cases in their homes. This first time we had asked the women to bring whatever milk they had. We simply used what was available and added the proper proportions of water and sugar. The following Wednesday we asked all of these mothers to bring what they were feeding the baby so that it could be measured to determine how nearly it was fulfilling the child's nutritional and caloric requirements figured from their weights and ages.

We had thought about starting a women's class for some time but there were many problems to consider. We wanted to make sure that each previous project was established before starting a new one. It would be difficult to establish a specific time for a class, for the women had no conception of time. Time is considered in terms of "when I get back from the well" or "when I have finished pounding millet." These times vary within each household, depending upon when the men climb into the granary to get out the day's supply of millet.

Women seem to have very little free time, except during the hottest hours of the afternoon when it would be difficult to persuade them to come to a class. On weighing day, women constantly threaten to leave before we've seen their baby if they have to wait for fifteen minutes, because they have to get back to their work. At least one-third of the children and babies brought to the dispensary for treatment are brought on the backs of small children because the women either have no time or are cloistered.

In April we decided to start an experimental *quartier* class with the guards' and functionaires' wives. We picked them for the pilot class because they are a closely knit group, socially and economically. They are faithful to our established program of baby-weighing and come often to the dispensary. They are somewhat more

used to new ideas, and have the means to get new materials. Many of the homes in town don't have the money to buy soap or sugar, so often our simplest suggestions are ineffective. These women have some free time in the afternoon, and are anxious to learn about improving the health of their families. Because they are a close-knit group, they are easier to watch for changes or reactions. Also, we feel that it is more important to be successful with a limited number of people than to try to reach everyone, and know that our suggestions are not being carried out.

When we began the class, the women decided we should meet at the chief of the guard's house, where they often meet to chat. Thus, the women themselves chose a common meeting place, which is an important consideration for any type of gathering.

The young girls of Illéla have no organization of any sort. They help with the housework until they find a husband, and spend their free time playing with the children close to home or walking around town with one or two friends. Before starting any type of class for women or girls, we tried to think of the advantages and disadvantages, and how we could be most effective. After discussing the possibility of a class with women and girls in different parts of town, we decided to begin a small girls' class. The girls have more free time than the women; they seem more anxious to learn because they don't have firmly set habits; they will be preparing themselves for the time when they will have their own families. We didn't want this class to be an end in itself, but saw the possibility of extending our influence further into the community by having these girls help us with demonstrations at the dispensary, their homes, neighbors' homes, and cloistered homes. We would like to incorporate the 4-H system of having the girls work up their own projects and demonstrations.

The first day of class, April 15, we handed out index cards which had bouquets of flowers crayoned on the back. We wrote each girl's name, her father's name, and her *quartier* on it. Then we explained that for each class we would write down what they learned and whether they had given the demonstration. We then demonstrated how to wash a baby with a live model, stressing the importance of washing thoroughly with soap every day. Then the entire group of six girls went with us to the home of one of the girls, where she did the same demonstration for all the women in the compound. The girls were very excited about being able to teach something, to show off their cards, and to have their pictures taken while washing the babies.

The second week we showed some posters on conjunctivitis and baby washing. We had told a mother of

(*Below*) The next move was to organize a well-baby clinic. "People think of our job as curative," the girls wrote. "They think we have medicine for sick babies. They also believe that as soon as the illness is better they can stop following our advice. People want to be given medicine, not a new way of doing everyday chores. This is partly because they don't perceive the connection between the way you perform a daily task and the result of health or illness. Thus, our lessons on baby-washing are labeled "*maganin ciwon ido*," medicine for conjunctivitis. Boiling baby's milk and cereal are called *maganin kiba*, medicine to get fat. As soon as the anxiety for the baby's illness disappears, so does the newly formed habit of washing children daily with soap or cooking supplementary foods.

"This connection of our work with curative techniques also follows through to our baby-weighing and diet day. If a child has a fever or cold or is underfed, the women come to the dispensary and remember to have the baby weighed. After a few weeks, though, the babies we have helped no longer come regularly. Thus, every week we have a small group of regulars and a much larger new group of sick babies. We are constantly reminding women we have already visited to bring the babies each week but they rarely do unless the infant becomes ill again.

"Many adults even come to us for medicine, before going to the dispensary, despite our constant reminders that we have no medicine. Part of this seems to be a need to be led or to depend on someone else to show the way."

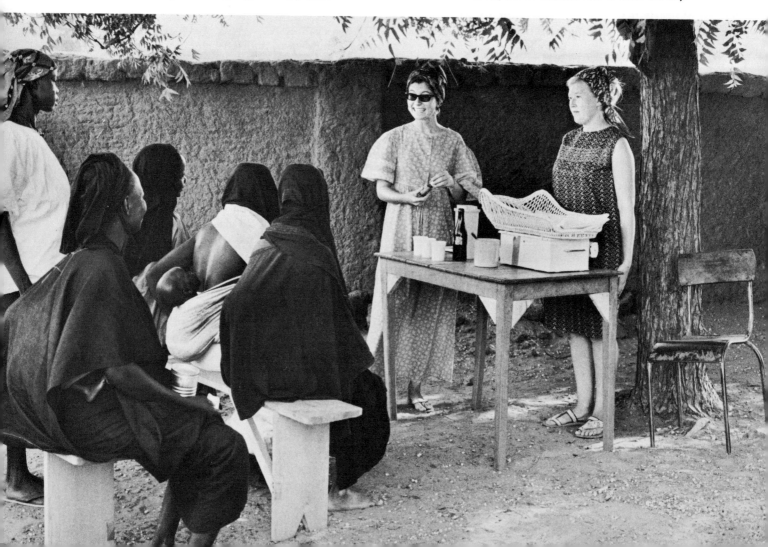

an underfed child to come at the class time so that we could teach her to prepare baby cereal while the class watched. After the cereal was prepared, the entire class went to another of the girls' homes. Two of the girls demonstrated washing three babies with the appropriate lecture. During the intervals before the babies were brought for the bath, one very self-confident girl took charge of the posters on conjunctivitis and conducted a lively discussion. A woman from another compound came in with her baby and a small bowl of milk, saying that she wanted to learn how to cook the cereal. Another girl took charge of helping the woman. We observed all the demonstrations, and we added comments occasionally and asked questions to stimulate thought about what they had learned.

The girls learn the material very rapidly and are not as hesitant to change their methods. They are very demonstrative and enjoy telling others what they have learned, especially with the help of posters and live materials. Once they have heard the lesson, they elaborate with their own words. Each week we chose one girl to help us on "weighing day" and one for "diet day." Occasionally one or two of the girls accompany us on home visits.

Because the attention span of the girls is short, we try to limit each class to a simple demonstration, and then visit alternate homes where the demonstration is repeated. The subjects for the class are variations on the themes of the relation between dirt and disease, personal and compound cleanliness, and proper nutrition.

We have found that live demonstrations are much more effective than posters at first, especially among the women and girls; if they do the actual demonstration themselves, using their own utensils, they remember

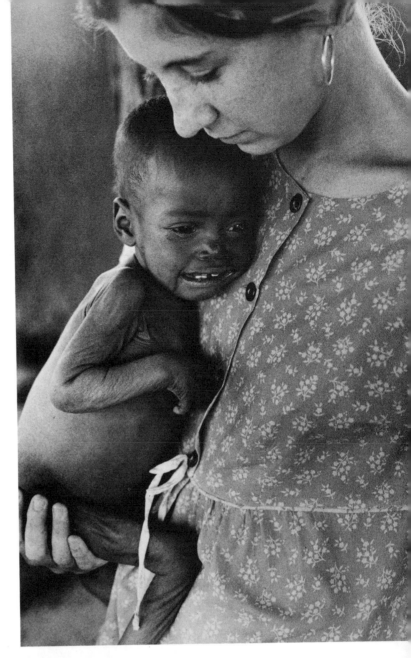

A trip to the well. There are twenty-one wells in Illéla, most of them cement and about 16 to 24 feet deep. In the newer, more sparsely populated *quartiers*, the wells are evenly distributed. But the oldest, most densely populated area of town is located on the hill overlooking the marsh; and because the hill consists of sand which is constantly shifting, it is impossible to dig wells in this *quartier*. Consequently, women have to walk a long distance to carry water. If the marsh water doesn't look dirty, the women sometimes prefer to use this more conveniently located water for drinking and household purposes. The marsh water is undoubtedly heavily infested with schistosomes and guinea worms. The schoolboys who have both of these diseases, swim and play in this water. The people from the new *quartier* often walk through the marsh in order to get to the main section of Illéla.

During the rainy season the majority of the town's population move to thatched huts in the bush for the farming season. Here the water supply is often stagnant water holes and shallow hand-dug wells.

Treatment of the marsh with chemicals to combat schistosomiasis and guinea worm would be an effective way to combat these diseases. However, since the people are exposed to these diseases when they go to their farms and use water sources which can't be controlled, this would probably be a waste of time. Vicki and Nancy are trying to discourage the use of marsh water for drinking and washing. The problem is not so much a lack of water, but of unequal distribution of good wells in relation to the location and numbers of the population. The girls, of course, boil all the water they use and try to encourage the townspeople to do the same.

more easily. But only with constant repetition and varition on a theme are our suggestions remembered.

We have found that going to the homes of people whom we are trying to help is absolutely essential. With the diarrhea and malnutrition cases, the attitudes and habits of the mother in her home are responsible to a large extent for the condition of the child. We are convinced that these attitudes and habits are little changed by one or two lectures or demonstrations at the dispensary. A mother may carefully follow directions, and prepare the milk herself at the dispensary. When she returns home, she may lose confidence. Many come back to tells us that the child refused the milk or that the baby goats have to have the evening milk. Several personal visits to the home may get the mother on the right path. A pep talk to the whole family about the logic of feeding a hungry baby, along with the appropriate joking and usual Hausa visiting conversation, will often do much to win their confidence in us and restore their own confidence in doing the task. Usually we visit a case three to seven times within the week. The first few visits are the longest. After the mother becomes confident, a brief chat to see how all is coming is all that's necessary. These brief visits are essential; otherwise, the mother will likely discontinue what has been taught. We have found that women are afraid to force-feed a child even if he is starving. People are afraid to take the initiative to go to the dispensary. It is essential that the man of the house meet us, understand the problems and what we want done to alleviate them.

Our relationship with the people of Illéla began with friendships, in conversations on their own mats in their own homes. We are continuing this approach and hope it will succeed.

(*Above*) A tree grows in Illéla. Trees, which are scarce in the barren Sudan, must be protected from the goats by thorn fences. The heat and scarcity of open water are the most difficult things about life in Illéla. "It may sound crazy," says Vicki, "but, you know, night after night I dream about the ocean and the beach."

Visitors in Illéla are rare, so when volunteer Paul Lubeck, who drives a Peace Corps truck from the capital, Niamey, out into the bush drops in for a visit, he is well received.

(*Opposite page*) Vicki stands in front of their Illéla house, which is made of mud and straw.

Vicki and Nancy walk hand in hand with a young friend down Illéla's main street. "Our relationship began with friendship . . ." the girls wrote. "We are continuing this approach, and we hope it will succeed."

Chapter 2

Sarge's "Lemon" Ripens to Maturity

The story of the Peace Corps's creation has been told so often that it already has become part of the legend of John F. Kennedy. As it has been pointed out many times, the idea of sending young men and women abroad to help others less fortunate than themselves is not new. Since the early days of Christianity, many churches have sent missionaries abroad, not only to help the natives save their souls, but to improve their living conditions, the ability of cleanliness to inspire godliness being one of the ancient Christian faiths. William James proposed an Army of Peace made up of young people dedicated to war against nature; in 1901 the American government sent the "Thomasites" to teach in the Philippines; during the Depression, Franklin Roosevelt's New Deal Administration developed a number of Peace Corps-like organizations to help absorb the energies of restless, unemployed youth; after World War II, a number of private organizations, such as the International Voluntary Services, were organized both in the United States and abroad, for the purpose of recruiting and sending young people overseas to serve at the grassroots of the developing nations.

Just prior to 1960, the idea of young men and women serving abroad in the cause of peace had also been creating a considerable stir on the nation's campuses. Congressman Henry Reuss (D-Wis.) and members of the Young Democratic Clubs organized by the Democratic National Committee had been especially active in encouraging the idea among college students, and in early 1960 Reuss and Senator Richard Neuberger (D-Ore.) submitted legislation in the Congress calling for a study of the Peace Corps idea. Democratic Senator Hubert Humphrey of Minnesota went even further: on June 15, 1960, he introduced a bill in the Senate proposing that a Peace Corps be established, not studied. "There is sufficient evidence now in hand," he said, on introducing his bill, "to justify moving directly to the formation of such a corps now,

HERE AT 2:00 a.m ON OCTOBER 14, 1960, JOHN FITZGERALD KENNEDY FIRST DEFINED THE PEACE CORPS. HE STOOD AT THE PLACE MARKED BY THE MEDALLION AND WAS CHEERED BY A LARGE AND ENTHUSIASTIC STUDENT AUDIENCE FOR THE HOPE AND PROMISE HIS IDEA GAVE THE WORLD.

Kennedy asked the Michigan students: "How many of you are willing to spend ten years in Africa or Latin America or Asia working for the United States and working for freedom? How many of you [who] are going to be doctors are willing to spend your days in Ghana? Technicians or engineers, how many of you are willing to work in the foreign service, and spend your lives traveling around the world? On your willingness to do that, not merely to serve one or two years in the service, but on your willingness to contribute part of your life to this country, I think, will depend the answer whether we as a free society can compete."

rather than waiting for a study to be made."

Senator Kennedy's Presidential campaign staff had also been studying the Peace Corps idea—and the Senator had been known to discuss variations of it with a number of people during the first part of 1960. In September, Kennedy, by this time the Democratic nominee for President, asked both Congressman Reuss and Professor Samuel Hayes of the University of Michigan to submit "position papers" on an international youth service program to his campaign staff. Both responded. Early in October, the Young Democrats released a "Message of John F. Kennedy to the Nation's New Voters," which was printed in several newspapers. In it Kennedy said that if elected he would explore the possibility of an organization which would enable our young people to give from three to five years in the cause of peace. On October 14, Kennedy first proposed the idea in person—in a campaign appearance early in the morning of October 14th on the steps of the Student Union at the University of Michigan in Ann Arbor. The idea immediately caught fire, and letters supporting and applauding the proposal poured in to Kennedy's campaign headquarters and the Democratic National Committee. Aware that he had a very live issue by the tail, on November 2, 1960, in the Cow Palace at San Francisco, Senator Kennedy made a formal campaign promise that an international Peace Corps would be a definite part of his program to get America moving again.

After the election, the Peace Corps idea continued to generate enthusiasm, and one of the many studies of the New Frontier which President-Elect Kennedy ordered between his election and inauguration was one on an international youth service by Dr. Max Millikan, director of the Center for International Studies at MIT. In January, 1961, this study and several others were completed, and they all endorsed, in one form or another, an international youth service corps. Most of them, however, did not recommend a completely independent agency similar to the one President Kennedy created by Executive Order (10924) on March 1, 1964. To run the new agency, President Kennedy picked Sargent Shriver, his brother-in-law. Shriver says he suggested that the President appoint someone to whom he owed a political debt, but the President replied, half-jokingly: "If it flops it will be easier to fire a relative than a political friend."

The Peace Corps still had to be confirmed by legislation before it became official, and one of Shriver's first goals was to present Congress with a *fait accompli*. He wanted volunteers in the field by the time Con-

Peace Corps forerunner. The International Voluntary Service has been in operation since 1953. Its volunteers serve today in many countries where the Peace Corps, for various reasons, does not send volunteers, such as Vietnam, where IVS has been operating since 1957. (*Above*) An IVS volunteer (*right*) works on a 1954 well-digging project in Iraq.

gress got around to considering the Peace Corps seriously, which he knew would probably not be until later in the year. Also, the 1961 class of college students was about to graduate, which meant campuses would be free in the summer to take on training programs, and there would be a fresh batch of potential volunteers who were still fired up with enthusiasm for the Peace Corps which the Presidential campaign had sparked. "A year's delay," Shriver wrote five years later, "might well have proved fatal to a baby whose birth was being celebrated with hoots of derision."

The hoots of derision were coming from many quarters—the Daughters of the American Revolution, syndicated columnists, prominent Republicans, old State Department and AID hands, and powerful newspapers, such as the *Wall Street Journal,* which wrote: "This is so disproportionate as to be nonsensical. What person except the very young themselves, can really believe that an Africa aflame with violence will have its fires quenched because some Harvard boy or Vassar girl lives in a mud hut and speaks Swahili?" Shriver's answer, which he repeated on Capitol Hill, at Washington dinner

Several members of Congress had shown an early interest in the Peace Corps idea—among them Representative Henry Reuss (D-Wis.); Senator Richard Neuberger (D-Ore.), and then Senator Hubert Humphrey of Minnesota, shown (*above*) addressing an early Peace Corps staff meeting.

Two weeks after mentioning the Peace Corps idea at Ann Arbor, Kennedy discussed it in a formal campaign address at the Cow Palace in San Francisco.
Credit: Wide World

parties and his around-the-world travels, was simply that the volunteers were not going abroad to quench fires, but teach school, work in a village community development program or public health projects or help improve farming techniques.

But the criticism did not last—in fact, Shriver hardly gave it a chance to be heard, so quickly did he get the Peace Corps off and running. The first thing he did was assemble a bright, energetic, and alert group of young men which he drove, as one of them put it, as though they were in the last stages of a political campaign. "Shriver's boys," as they were often called, came from all walks of life—journalism, the groves of academe, business, politics, government, the professions, and the still groping field of international volunteerism—and many of them went on to bigger things after distinguishing themselves at the Peace Corps. They included a young Senate staffer of Lyndon Johnson's named Bill Moyers; William Haddad, a prize-winning journalist; Ed Bayley, former assistant to Governor Gaylord Nelson of Wisconsin; Lawrence Dennis from Penn State; Dr. Nicholas Hobbs, a psychologist who had taught at several leading universities; Franklin Williams, an NAACP lawyer; Harris Wofford, a

former University of Notre Dame law professor who had worked in the Kennedy Presidential campaign (as many of the early Peace Corps staffers had); Warren Wiggins, an ICA official; Jack Vaughn, who had

also been with ICA; William Delano, who was a young New York lawyer and an early enthusiast in the volunteer movement; and many others.

Having made the decision to get volunteers in the field by the end of

President Kennedy appointed his brother-in-law, Sargent Shriver, director of the new agency, remarking that if it failed it would be easier to fire a relative. Later, he also joked about handing Shriver a lemon from which he made lemonade. (*Above*) He hands his brother-in-law the pen with which he signed the Peace Corps Act.

Many of Shriver's Early Staffers Went On to Bigger Things....

Bill Moyers, to top White House Assistant under Lyndon Johnson, and publisher of *Newsday* . . .

. . . Harris Wofford to the presidency of the New York State College on Long Island . . .

. . . Franklin Williams to become Ambassador to UNESCO. later Ghana . . .

the summer, there were many critical decisions to be made immediately and a multitude of problems to be solved. "It was fundamentally new," Shriver wrote in a *Saturday Review* article summing up his five years in the Peace Corps, "that government should be doing such a thing and on the scale that we were going to attempt it. With the help we were able to attract to the cause, men with experience in other international programs, we started charting an unknown terrain. The solutions we found to our problems, many of them, now seem obvious. They weren't at all obvious when we started.

"For instance," Shriver continues,

citing one of the most vexing problems he faced in the early days, "I used to wake up in the middle of the night with the question tearing at me: How are we ever going to protect the health of Peace Corps Volunteers? This question seemed to have no ready answer. And yet, could we go to the parents of this nation and say to them, yes, we want your sons and daughters, and admit at the same time that for two years they would be overseas—many of them in primitive and remote towns and villages—with no medical assistance?

"In retrospect, it seems only a lucky chance that someone mentioned to me that the Coast Guard

. . . Bill Haddad to form his own political public relations firm and run for Congress in New York City (he lost) . . .

. . . Richard Ottinger, to run for Congress in New York (he won) . . .

. . . Warren Wiggins, to Peace Corps Deputy Director and to form his own firm, Transcentury Corporation . . .

. . . Ed Bayley to the vice-presidency of the Educational Television Network . . .

. . . Frank Mankiewicz to press secretary for Senator Robert Kennedy of New York . . .

. . . Doug Kiker, to become a Washington correspondent for NBC and Washington columnist for the *Atlantic* . . .

has no medical service of its own. The Public Health Service takes care of the health of Coast Guardsmen.

"I put in a call to Dr. Luther Terry, who as Surgeon-General of the United States was head of the Public Health Service. To my huge relief, Dr. Terry said, 'Yes, we would like to take on the Peace Corps.' To develop a Peace Corps health program, he sent Leo Gehrig to help us.

"Dr. Gehrig became the Peace Corps's first medical director. His knowledge, vision, and dedication to the idea of the Peace Corps enabled him to create a unique medical service keyed to Peace Corps ideals. The result? Peace Corps volunteers have

been healthier than a corresponding sample of stay-at-homes!"

It was also decided early that: Women would be eligible to serve in the Peace Corps; married couples would serve if they did not have dependents and if *both* the man and the woman were active volunteers; there would be no age limit; the Peace Corps would not make a young man exempt from the draft (although in practice, very few volunteers have been drafted either during or after their service); volunteers could not become involved in the politics of the country in which they were service; to avoid any implication that volunteers were being sent abroad to proselytize, it was decided not to en-

. . . Bill Delano to become Secretary General of the International Secretariat for Volunteer Service . . .

. . . Glenn Ferguson to become head of VISTA, Ambassador to Kenya . . .

. . . Nat Davis, to become United States Minister to Bulgaria . . .

. . . Jack Vaughn, to become Ambassador to Panama, Assistant Secretary of State for Inter-American Affairs, and Peace Corps Director . . .

One of Shriver's first acts was a nine-country tour to "spread the word" and find out if volunteers were wanted abroad. They were—in greater numbers than the Peace Corps could supply. Of Shriver, one early staffer was quoted as saying: "The boss of this operation is an idiot. The Corps has succeeded in spite of his crazy methods." Another: "The man's a genius. His crazy methods work." And all agreed he drove his staff hard. "When you join the Shriver team," said one who couldn't stand the pace, "you put yourself in line for an ulcer, a heart attack, or a nervous breakdown. I held on until I was forced to quit by all three." Shriver and members of the team arrive in Indonesia on the nine-country tour.

The first Peace Corps exams were held on May 27, 1961. David Schikele (*in the foreground*), who contributed the essay in Chapter 10, is among the applicants who took the first test in New York City.

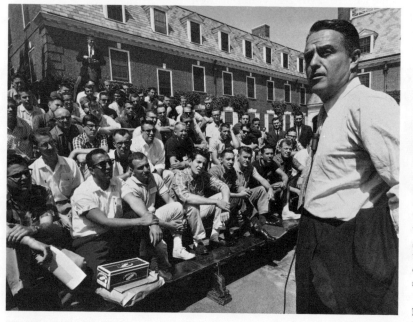

Shriver speaks to the first contingent of volunteers to go into training—at Rutgers, in 1961. "Here at last," he recalled later, "were our first volunteers! For five months we had been talking about them, arguing over them, worrying about them, and defending them, hypothetically, in the press, and here they were at last in the flesh. Now we would finally see what they were like. I had a final moment of trepidation on my way to Rutgers where I was scheduled to greet them in the name of the Peace Corps—could the critics be right, after all? When I finally stood in front of them to make a few remarks, I noticed that they were at least a fine-looking group. When I had finished, I asked them if they had any questions—if they did, I would try to answer them. Instantly, their faces, passively listening until then, were transformed. They plunged into the question session with a kind of keyed-up enthusiasm and rock-hard intelligence."

ter into working partnerships with religious organizations, although partnerships with such nonreligious organizations as CARE, Heifer, Inc., and various universities were encouraged, at least at first; volunteers would serve without pay (although there would be living allowances granted and a terminal leave payment of $75 for every month spent overseas); the volunteers would not be given the usual diplomatic and economic privileges shared by most Americans serving in an official capacity overseas, they would live exactly like their counterparts in the host country; a college degree was not necessary; volunteers had to be American citizens and at least eighteen (although in actual practice few volunteers under twenty have been selected). And, of course, it was decided early that volunteers would be

President Kennedy addresses the first volunteers to go overseas. They were teaching in the secondary schools of Ghana before Congress made the Peace Corps official. Some reporters are in the first row.

On September 22, 1961, Congress passed the Peace Corps Act. Its objectives were stated in a Declaration of Purpose—but there were many who were skeptical, including former President Dwight D. Eisenhower, who called it a "juvenile experiment." Others referred to it as a "Children's Crusade" and "Kennedy's Kiddie Korps." (Above) President Kennedy signs the Peace Corps Act as Sargent Shriver, on the far left, then-Senator Hubert Humphrey, behind and to the left of the President, and others look on.

Early Days: Problems, Decisions, Goofs, Tragedy, Kudos . . .
. . . and a Whirlwind Boss

One of Shriver's earliest worries was a volunteer health program. He solved this by calling on Dr. Leo Gerhig of the Public Health Service, who created a health program which has been remarkably effective. (*Left*) Jim Chapman, who served in West Pakistan, draws his water which he will boil before drinking—the number one rule of health for all volunteers.

It was also agreed that there would be no age limit. Two of the most publicized senior volunteers were Mr. and Mrs. Chester Wiggins, the parents of Warren Wiggins, until recently the Peace Corps's Deputy Director. The Wigginses taught school in Peru.

Mauldin in the Chicago Sun Times

"*Eenie, Meenie, Minie, Moe . . .*"

It was also decided that Peace Corps service would not exempt a volunteer from the draft, although, in practice, relatively few ex-volunteers have been called.

Married couples (such as Jim and Anne Mariner, of Kansas City, who taught in Ghana) were permitted to join the Corps, providing both husband and wife were active volunteers.

Nor did an applicant have to have a college degree. Volunteer Gerhart Wehrbein of Burchard, Nebraska, served as a mechanic in Sidi Bou Rouis, Tunisia.

Abroad, Peace Corps volunteers were to live in quarters similar to those lived in by their host country counterparts. Ron Kuhl, who taught school in Tambunan, in Borneo, is seen leaving his house, typical of the kind of houses Borneo teachers have.

And no politics! Volunteer Maureen Orth (*above*) appears to be plotting the overthrow of the government, but actually she is enjoying a farewell party given her by the people of the *barrios* in Colombia, where she lived for two years.

Nor were volunteers to have the special privileges most American government officials living abroad have. They would eat the same food everyone else did and shop in the same markets. They would receive no pay, just a small living allowance which would vary from country to country. At the end of their duty, they would be given a terminal payment of $75 for every month spent in service.

(*Below*) Volunteer teachers Mary Lou Callahan (*right*) and Gwen Dillard shop in the marketplace in Dabola, Guinea.

In the early days the Peace Corps training camp at Puerto Rico, where this young lady walks a rope bridge, was overpublicized as the Peace Corps's emphasis on physical fitness. Today, the emphasis in training is more on helping the volunteer get ready for his specific assignment—although physical fitness is not ignored, as the group (*below*) getting ready for Brazil found out.

From the beginning, the Peace Corps has placed heavy emphasis on language training. This group (*left*) is studying Spanish before going to Colombia.

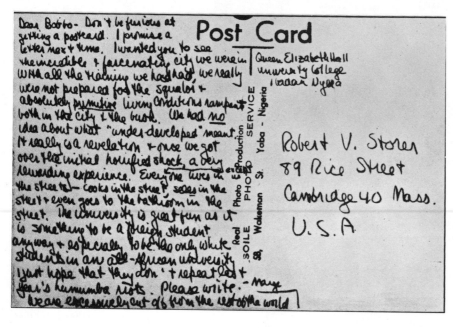

Typical of some of the early growing pains was Margery Michelmore's famous postcard which she lost in Nigeria. It was picked up and read by a Nigerian student, and caused a minor crisis. Margery (*right*) was recalled from Nigeria, harassed by the press, but continued for awhile to participate in the Peace Corps training program, cautioning others not to repeat her mistake.

Credit: UPI

And tragedy was unavoidable. "Should it come to it," David Crozier (*on foot, facing camera*) wrote his mother from Colombia in the spring of 1962, "I would rather give my life trying to help someone than give my life looking down a gun barrel at them." Two weeks later, young Crozier was killed in a plane crash. The Peace Corps named a training camp in Puerto Rico after him. To date, nearly forty volunteers have died overseas.

At first it was thought that finding the right man to fill the demanding Overseas Representative posts would be difficult, and the Peace Corps launched an intensive talent search. It wanted men who had the same motivation as the volunteers, had already pursued a successful career in the United States, the capacity to direct the mission, deal with the United States Ambassador in the host country, and the host government, be willing to forego all privileges, and to know or have the ability to learn quickly the language of the host country.

In the first two years, the Peace Corps interviewed more than 1,200 men; one in six was hired. Their average age was thirty-seven. Typical was David Elliott, first Peace Corps Representative in Nigeria, later Director of the entire Indian program. Before joining the Peace Corps staff, Elliott was the president of Solana Steel Corporation in Vallejo, California, which he founded in 1958.

There was also the much-publicized "cultural shock"—which volunteer English teacher Rosalind Pearson, twenty-two, from Detroit, must have experienced in Kabul, the capital of Afghanistan. Although volunteers do feel a psychological letdown at about the end of the first nine months, the overseas dropout rate has been less than 5 percent.

'ANOTHER CUNNING CIA AGENT HAS JUST SLIPPED INTO OUR TERRITORY. COMRADE!'

Then there were the Communists. At first they tried to convince the world that the volunteers were spies. The volunteers countered the accusation by going about their business and trying to show the absurdity of such charges. Volunteer Peter Morrissey, a champion swimmer while at the University of California, was confronted with the problem when he arrived in Sumatra, 1,700 miles from Djakarta. The local paper ran an editorial announcing that "our CIA agent has arrived—our spy is here." Children would come up to Morrissey and shout: "Spy!"

Morrissey answered by laughing and saying: "Spy? What is there to spy on?" Pretty soon all the kids were laughing with him.

To keep in touch with the volunteers, Shriver (right) spent a great deal of his five years in the Peace Corps in airports, such as this one in Zahedan, Iran, where he was forced down by a sandstorm. He is talking with newspaperman Walter Redder, who was writing a series of articles on the Peace Corps. On the far left is Robert Steiner, then in charge of the Peace Corps mission in Afghanistan, now a staffer in Washington. In five years, Shriver visited thirty-seven countries and approximately 5,000 volunteers.

In Sarawak, Shriver visited volunteer teacher June Jensby. Shriver later wrote of an incident involving June which occurred when Shriver and some volunteers, including June, were inspecting a work site in a village near Kota Belud on Borneo. Swarms of children were perched on ladders leading to the stilt-supported straw huts typical of the area. "June walked over to some of the children," says Shriver, "and spoke to them in Pasar Malay, the language we had taught her in Hawaii training. (As far as I can find out, Pasar Malay had never been taught in the United States before.)

"When the children answered, her face lit up like a full moon. She looked, in fact, as if she were immensely relieved to discover that Pasar Malay was a real language after all, and not just a lot of nonsense that we had forced her to memorize. . . ."

In some cases, Shriver gave the volunteers a bigger lift than he might have expected. Volunteer John Coyne, a teacher in Ethiopia, tells of Shriver's surprise visit to his Addis Ababa classroom in November, 1962. "In his usual manner," Coyne wrote home, "he came hurrying through the door with hand outstretched and said: 'I'm Sargent Shriver.' I flippantly replied, 'No kidding?' It was my best one-upmanship. I was pleased by Shriver's visit—it was the first time my students had been quiet since September." (*Right*) Shriver visits a similar class presided over by volunteer Robert Olson of Baudette, Minnesota, in Salihili, Turkey.

At home, Shriver also helped keep volunteer morale up by visiting training sites whenever he could and with numerous parties for volunteers at his home in Rockville, Maryland. (*Above*) He is trying to strike out a volunteer bound for Indonesia.

He also kept in touch with scores of prominent Americans who volunteered to help promote and recruit for the Peace Corps. Harry Belafonte, pictured with Shriver (*above*), was an early member of the Peace Corps's National Advisory Council.

sent only to countries that specifically requested them.

In May of 1961, with the Peace Corps only two months old, Shriver and a handful of his aides set off on a nine-country visit to Asia and Africa. "I wanted to tell the government leaders of these countries that we were in business," says Shriver, "get their reactions to the Peace Corps idea, and find out what sort of volunteers they would want—*if any*. The trip revealed I needn't have worried on the last point, even though all the 'experts' before the trip advised us that youthful Americans—'kids' as they called them—should be kept at home, not let loose to complicate work of experienced diplomats, economic development workers, bankers, businessmen, missionaries, et al. I was told everywhere that skilled volunteers were wanted in the worst way. Requests for volunteers immediately exceeded the capacity of the Peace Corps to supply them."

There was, at first, no little concern as to whether there would be enough qualified volunteers to

Behind Shriver stood President Kennedy and Vice-President Johnson, both of whom gave the Peace Corps their full support in its early, formative days. (*Above*) The new President presides over a May, 1961, White House meeting of the Peace Corps's National Advisory Council, made up of distinguished Americans from all walks of life. . . .

achieve even the limited goals of the Peace Corps—500 to 1,000 volunteers overseas by the end of 1961. In the spring, 400,000 questionnaires were sent out to post offices, colleges and universities, and the more than 25,000 people who had requested information. The turnout at the first Peace Corps exam was disappointing, which created a detectable gloom in the hall of the new agency. However, the caliber of those who did turn out was higher than expected, which meant Peace Corps officials could revise their estimate that only 10 percent of those qualifying would be selectable. In July, the picture brightened considerably when 2,700 applicants showed up for the second exam, and the chief selection officer said "we are over the hump for this year."

With Shriver and his staff often working a sixteen-hour day, seven-day week, it began to look as if they would achieve their goal: By the summer of 1960 Peace Corps volunteers were in training at Rutgers University, the University of California at Berkeley, and Western Texas College, and several projects had been announced, including a road-building program for Tangan-

. . . Lyndon Johnson presiding over a 1963 meeting of the National Advisory Council. Shriver is seated, on left; Bill Moyers, extreme right.

yika, teaching programs for Ghana and the Philippines, and community development projects for Colombia and St. Lucia. The first volunteers actually to set foot on foreign soil landed in August, 1961, at Accra, the capital of Ghana, where they would soon be teaching in the secondary schools. "This should have been an anxious moment for me," Shriver later wrote, "but frankly I had been too impressed by the caliber of volunteers in training to believe they would let us down. They didn't. . . . The fifty-one Americans who emerged from the plane were not loud and flippant, chewing gum

Most government leaders were never too busy to meet with the volunteers. For instance, Supreme Court Justice William O. Douglas invited a group of volunteers in training at George Washington University to hike with him along the famed C. and O. Canal.

And whenever possible, departing volunteers, such as these athletic instructors bound for Indonesia (above), were given a farewell by the President on the White House lawn. Kennedy also talked occasionally with Peace Corps mission directors before they went overseas, as he does (right) with William G. Saltonstall, principal of Phillips Exeter Academy for seventeen years before he became a Peace Corps representative in Nigeria.

and taking pictures of everything and everybody as some might have expected. They behaved in a quiet, unassuming manner, and the only loud thing they did was to sing a song in Twi, the commonest of Ghana's languages."

One of the more modest volunteers recalls one Ghananian remarking, after hearing a radio broadcast of the song: "Why, it sounded almost like Twi." But Shriver reported that their arrival made a real impact. "Everywhere the volunteers traveled," he wrote, "people recognized them as the Americans who sang our song. These were the Americans who had taken the trouble to learn our language before arriving." Although it is debatable just how well those first volunteers sent abroad spoke the language of the host country, it has not been for their or the Peace Corps's lack of trying. From the beginning the Peace Corps has placed a strong emphasis on language training, and more than sixty languages have been taught in the Peace Corps training camps, many of them for the first time in America.

With requests for volunteers coming in faster than the Peace Corps could fulfill them, and a tireless staff developing the logistics to support the soon-to-be-exported volunteers, Shriver was free to turn his considerable energies to selling the idea to Congress. At first there was a vocal and articulate resistance—especially among Republicans who were skeptical of any new scheme that would cost the taxpayer money, and particularly one as seemingly impractical and unrealistic as the Peace Corps. While Shriver worked tirelessly in the corridors and dining rooms on Capitol Hill, the Peace Corps publicity staff sparked a continual stream of favorable newspaper and magazine stories about the Peace Corps, and as Eric Sevareid commented in a none-too-friendly column, "there is nothing so irresistible as pure intentions backed by pure publicity." But it served its

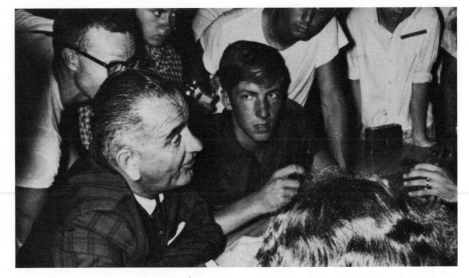

On a July, 1962, visit to Camp Radley in Puerto Rico, Vice-President Johnson had a heart-to-heart talk with volunteers in training.

purpose. The irresistible gung-ho publicity, combined with Shriver's lobbying, put down the opposition on Capitol Hill. On September 22, 1961, the Peace Corps Act was signed, endorsed by the second highest majority of any nondefense legislation submitted by President Ken-

Later that year, Johnson went back to Puerto Rico as the United States Delegate to the Conference on Middle Level Manpower, which created the "International Peace Corps." In his opening remarks, Johnson told the delegates that "we feel the need to share with others whatever skills modern science and technology have brought us, and we hope that others will share their skills with us. We have long since passed the historic point where nations can live in isolation."

(Below) Vice-President Johnson shakes hands with Giuseppe Luis, Under Secretary of the Italian Foreign Ministry. Between them is Mrs. Golda Meir, Foreign Minister of Israel; on the right, S. K. Dey, India's Minister for Community Development.

Also attending the Puerto Rico Conference were Shriver (*right*), Richard N. Goodwin (*center*) a White House aide who would be the first Secretary General of the International Peace Corps Secretariat; and William Delano (*left*), a Peace Corps staffer who would follow Goodwin as the second Secretary General of what later came to be known as ISVS—The International Secretariat for Volunteer Service.

nedy.

The Peace Corps was now an official government operation, not just a vision shared by dozens of dreamers who had been advocating such an organization since late in the 1950's. And the speed and efficiency with which it was launched was no small achievement by Washington standards. As President Kennedy once said to the Peace Corps staff, "I do not think it is altogether fair to say that I handed Sarge a lemon from which he made lemonade, but I do think that he and the other members of your staff were handed one of the most sensitive and difficult assignments which any administrative group has been given almost in this century."

This was high praise, and it is fair to say that the staff and the early volunteers were worthy of it—which was fortunate because the difficulties were just beginning. Having created an organization from which its skeptical critics expected very little and its enthusiastic supporters perhaps too much, Shriver and his staff were now faced with the challenge of developing a realistic program that would silence its enemies and not disappoint its friends.

The problems were quick to emerge. Some created small sensations, like Margery Michelmore's famous postcard. Others were less publicized but more serious—the deficiencies in the training program, which the early volunteers began reporting back almost as soon as they had settled in their jobs overseas; the problem of finding the right men to serve as Peace Corps staff representatives abroad; the psychological letdown which hit the volunteers after their first eight or nine months overseas; and the most

The idea was spreading rapidly: (*Above*) President Kennedy attends ceremonies launching the German Volunteer Service in June, 1963. Seated next to Kennedy is the then German President, Dr. Heinrick Lubke, and the then Prime Minister Konrad Adenauer. Standing (*right*) is the then Foreign Minister Walter Scheel.

Two German volunteers in Tanzania stop for **a talk.**

68

challenging development of all—the fact that the overwhelming majority of applicants were the A.B. generalists—young men and women with liberal arts degrees, lots of energy, plenty of idealism, and no particular skill. The Peace Corps was asked to leave some countries, and in others the programs were disappointing if not downright failures. And the kind of snafus familiar to anyone who served in the United States Armed Forces during World War II naturally occurred: Volunteers were placed in the wrong jobs, sent to the wrong countries, received the wrong textbooks for use in their classes, could not get the proper equipment to carry out a project they had promised, and so on.

But for the most part, the early crises and problems were the kind that were expected—the superficial ones were ignored and the more serious ones were met head on and solved with vigor, to use a word popular in the early days of the New Frontier. The training program was completely reorganized, a special recruiting program was set up to staff the overseas Representative posts, project programming was completely revamped and built around the liberal arts graduate, and the volunteers learned to live with their "cultural shock" (only to be confronted by a new psychological obstacle course, the "crisis of reentry," but this one was primarily their concern, not the Peace Corps's).

The assassination of President Kennedy came as a stunning shock to people all over the world. Many coins were struck in his honor, including this Dutch coin which was sold for the benefit of the Netherlands Peace Corps.

Despite the difficulties, the Peace Corps survived its early growing pains. By the summer of 1964, only three years after the first volunteers went into training, there were more than 10,000 volunteers in training or overseas; 1,828 had completed service; and Peace Corps programs were operating in 44 countries in Latin America, Africa, and Asia. And the goals of the Peace Corps were be-

coming crystallized—and simplified. "There is nothing complicated about what the Peace Corps is trying to accomplish," Shriver said. "The volunteer is a catalyst for self-help projects that will produce something of value that was not there before he arrived. It is that simple."

Still, there were those who argued that although the Peace Corps might be rewarding for the Americans who participated, and perhaps even beneficial in those hamlets, villages, and slums where the volunteers had served, its impact on worldwide poverty would be insignificant. There was, perhaps, some merit in this argument. But just as the Peace Corps volunteer is a catalyst at the human level, the Peace Corps itself proved to be a catalyst at the government level. In 1962, delegates from 42 nations met in Puerto Rico in a conference on middle-level manpower which had been called by President Kennedy. The conference was the result of Sargent Shriver's conviction that the moment was right to encourage the spread of the volunteer movement around the world. The experience of the Peace Corps had demonstrated that there existed throughout the world a great "hidden force" of middle-level manpower needing only direction and encouragement to turn it into a major weapon in man's age-old fight against ignorance, poverty, and disease. All the delegates to the conference, including the United States delegate, Vice-President Lyndon Johnson, agreed that middle-level manpower was essential

The new President was quick to let it be known that he would continue to support the Peace Corps—and Shriver. In May, 1964, he and Shriver met with a group of volunteers on the White House lawn. "Thomas Hardy once said that war makes rattling good history but peace is poor reading," the President said. "You people, I think, have changed that. In three years, the aspirations and accomplishments of the Peace Corps have made the pursuit of peace 'rattling good history.'"

to the economic growth of a nation, and they were of the unanimous opinion that volunteer programs such as the Peace Corps were "making a significant contribution, both a direct and indirect, to the manpower requirements of the developing nations," as the Conference's summary report put it.

As a result, the Conference created an International Peace Corps Secretariat (later renamed the International Secretariat for Volunteer Service) to encourage and promote not only organizations like the Peace Corps that export volunteers, but organizations in the developing nations themselves designed to recruit volunteers for domestic use.

Today ISVS has 43 member-nations. Australia, Austria, Belgium, Canada, Denmark, France, Germany, Israel, Japan, Liechtenstein, the Netherlands, New Zealand, Norway, the Philippines, Sweden, Switzerland, the United Kingdom, and the United States have export programs involving more than 19,000 volunteers in 94 countries in Latin America, Africa, and Asia. At the same time,

18 developing nations have launched programs which have placed 14,000 volunteers in domestic service. National Service Volunteer programs, which provide basic education and skill training for youth while they serve in their country's development program, have also been launched in many countries, especially in Africa.

At the end of 1963, volunteers began returning home, and we were soon hearing a lot about the "reentry crisis." There is, perhaps, a reverse cultural shock when the volunteer returns, but most volunteers say it is no more than you would expect and that they usually get over it in a hurry as they work their way back into the mainstream of American life. And most agree that the Peace Corps did as much for them as they did for it. Robert Laird, for instance, says of his Peace Corps experience: "Once you've tried something very hard, you have more confidence." He also thinks it helped him land a job as a reporter on the *World Telegram and Sun*, which led to his present job as deputy press secretary for Mayor John Lindsay of New York. (*Left*) Young Laird briefs Lindsay before the Mayor meets the press.

The Peace Corps was having an impact in some ways not always obvious—and in others that were easily understood. For instance, the volunteers in the Philippines were given the Ramón Magsaysay Award, the first time non-Asians had ever received the honor; Peruvian President Fernando Belaunde Terry awarded the Peace Corps the "Silver Medal

By early 1965, there were 3,000 returned volunteers, and with that many of any group wandering around, a conference is inevitable. At the request of President Johnson, a three-day conference for returned volunteers was held in March, 1965. Many government leaders addressed the conference, including Secretary of the Defense Robert McNamara, Secretary of State Dean Rusk, and Vice-President Humphrey (*above*), who told the volunteers that America expected much of them—that "you don't really have to save the world, just start saving the home town."

McNamara's message to the returned volunteers: "We have three and three-quarters million people in the Defense Department but I doubt very much that we have influenced the peace of the world as much as the small handful of you. . . ."

70

of Arequipa" (from the second largest city in Peru) for the work they did in the city's urban slums; Thailand's Chulalongkorn University awarded Sargent Shriver an honorary degree as a tribute to the Peace Corps volunteers; and verbal bouquets too numerous to reprint have been tossed at the Peace Corps, such as this one by a Somaliland official. "When they [the Somali people] saw the volunteers living in accommodations that were suitable but not luxurious, willing to share the type of life our people live . . . this was a revolutionary thing."

By living with the people and sharing their day-to-day problems, the volunteers have probably come closer to the people of other countries around the world than any Americans ever have—and in doing so, have brought others closer to us. This fact has never been revealed with more compassion than in late November and early December, 1963, immediately after President Kenne-

dy's assassination. In Iran, on November 22, 1963, a Peace Corps volunteer was approached by an Iranian co-worker who announced, with tears in his eyes: "Our President is dead." In Nepal, villagers

In the spring of 1965, a revolt took place in the Dominican Republic which resulted in the United States Marines being sent to the Caribbean to put down the uprising. Ironically, the Assistant Secretary of State for Inter-American Affairs at the time of the uprising was Jack Vaughn, an ex-professional boxer, ex-Marine, and ex-Peace Corps staffer. He says he was proud to have had a hand in stopping the bloody massacre . . .

walked five days to bring some isolated volunteers the tragic news. And below, volunteer Nancy Norton tells how she first heard the news in the village of Huarocondo, Peru. At 7:30 A.M. on the morning of the 23rd, her Peruvian friend Vilma knocked on the door, shouting: "Tu Presidente esta muerto!"

"I couldn't believe it," she wrote her parents in Illinois. "I yelled for my roommate. We both stood in the doorway too shocked to say much. Vilma left. We looked at each other and agreed we felt like crying. We decided then it was only rumor, and wouldn't believe it until we read a newspaper.

"We hurried to meet the morning train from Cuzco. On our way, three children asked if it was true. We couldn't answer. We passed the school. Half a dozen of the teachers came to the road in tears. They expressed sympathy. We arrived at the train. The usual crowd of Indians who sell food was very quiet as we came up. The town mayor came over, crying. We began to believe. It was true. He is dead.

"That was a strange ten-minute

. . . but prouder still of having sent the first contingent of Peace Corps volunteers to the Dominican Republic, which included Rob Gutowski (left) who helped forty boys organize a jewelry co-op in Santo Domingo. Vaughn says that one Dominican Republic official told him later that if they had been given the 450 additional Peace Corps volunteers they had requested, the revolt might not have occurred.

wait for the train. It came in, the newsboy leaped off and was mobbed. The big black headlines proclaimed the news. MUERTE DE JOHN KENNEDY —EN LUTO AL ORBE. Death of John Kennedy—The World Mourns.

"Then we cried—11,000 feet in the Andes, surrounded by Indians, no radio, no way of getting Lima newspapers, no way of getting more information until Monday night. The President had been dead eighteen hours, and we hadn't known. We looked around at the crowd. One of our favorite school kids had big tears rolling down his cheeks. He said, *'Senoritas, por favor, no lloran'* (Please don't cry).

"We walked slowly up the hill to our house. We decided we must, in a rural Latin community, show our sorrow as they would expect. The constant stream of townspeople who stopped us in the Plaza or came to see us, therefore, saw us dressed in black. They approved. It's funny how the President's death has affected the town. All are subdued. The bells have tolled. Tomorrow a special mass will be held. Our little school friends—really our closest companions—are fourth- and fifth-grade boys. They came to keep us company. They just sit, looking stricken.

"The paper said the whole world is in mourning. I don't know about the whole world, only about Huarocondo. Huarocondo is mourning. Everyone knows the President of the United States. They would be stricken if we weren't here. But they know we are here because of John Kennedy. They know we are sad because he is dead. They love us, so they are sad, too. Were I not here, I would never have believed that the world really cared."

Having established such a relationship, it is little wonder that the Communists have never been able to discredit the volunteers. In the early days, the Communists did their best to convince the people in the Peace Corps countries that the volunteers were spies. But they finally gave up their spy charges, and two Czechoslovakian political scientists, Jiri Hybner and Valdimir Novak, conceded the effectiveness of the Peace Corps when they wrote in the journal *Mecinarodni Politica:* 'The Peace Corps is an extraordinarily important tool for anticommunism. It achieves its goals not with subversive activities, but, on the contrary, with most effective help in those sections of national economics, culture, education, and welfare and in other branches of life where the developing countries feel the acute need for help."

Perhaps the most dramatic acceptance of the Peace Corps volunteers by the people of a developing country occurred in the spring of 1965, during the armed revolt in the Dominican Republic. On the Saturday morning when the revolt began, there were 108 volunteers in the Dominican Republic, 34 of them in Santo Domingo. The volunteers had been told that if there was an uprising, they were to remain with their friends in the *barrios,* but as the fighting swept across the city, the volunteers were soon caught up in events. This was how that period looked to one of the volunteers:

"As the initial fighting broke out, some of our Dominican friends actively participated, while others preferred to wait in their homes patiently, caught in the uprising with which they sympathized, but in which they preferred a vocal rather than physical involvement. This vocal participation was, nevertheless, no less important or real than that of those actually fighting. It was with this group that we remained during the early days of the fighting. As the conflict was centered around the Duarte Bridge, a few kilometers south of most of the *barrios,* we were able to hear the rifle fire as a steady

However, the revolt did occur and it was perhaps the Peace Corps's finest hour. As one volunteer wrote about the experience: "Most important was that the volunteers remained a neutral group in a fractionated country. Even as fighting continued, volunteers working the slums of Santo Domingo controlled by rebel commandos were warmly welcomed back into their communities. At the same time, other volunteers continued their work through loyalist government agencies in rural areas. On either side the words 'Cuerpo de Paz' were the safest conduct pass available. The economic, political, and military problems of the revolution are beyond the realm of the Peace Corps, but the human quotient is our province."

(*Right*) Peace Corps nurse Arleen Serino treats a woman who lost a leg in one of the battles. Today, volunteers are continunig to serve in the Dominican Republic.

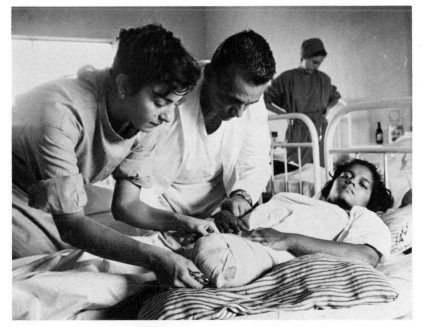

In February, 1964, President Johnson had appointed Shriver to head a task force dedicated to eliminating poverty in the United States. In the fall of that year, Shriver was officially sworn in as the Director of the Office of Economic Opportunity, although Johnson asked him to continue directing the Peace Corps. The dual responsibilities led to a difficult period in the Peace Corps's history, and by late 1965 and early 1966 Shriver and Johnson came under heavy criticism for expecting one man to hold down two important, demanding, full-time jobs. (*Right*) A somewhat tired-looking Shriver presides over an OEO staff meeting.

background to the sight of dive-bombing P-51's attacking the bridge.

"It was only a few days until the fighting reached into the *barrios*. Armed bands of civilians—mostly comprised of seventeen- to twenty-three-year-old kids—roamed the area freely where they confronted and fought the National Police. By Wednesday, April 28th, the entire northern area was under the control of the Constitutionalist forces. Up until this point, I had shared the confusion with all of my neighbors. Nobody really knew exactly what was happening—there was just a confusion of guns, shooting, planes, radio fanatics from both sides, and death. I had little sense of real personal danger as I felt completely safe surrounded by people I had grown to trust completely. But the problem was that nobody was able to predict with accuracy what might

On March 1, 1966, the Peace Corps observed its fifth birthday, and Sargent Shriver resigned, faithful to his "five-year-flush" policy which limits the amount of time an employee can work for the Peace Corps. At the ceremony were Vice-President Humphrey, Under Secretary of State George Ball, soon-to-be-Peace Corps Director Jack Vaughn, Secretary of State Dean Rusk, and President Johnson.

happen from one hour to the next, and, hence, the Peace Corps staff felt that I would be wiser if I moved to a nearby hospital where I would be a bit safer. I did not want to leave because I felt that my place was with my friends. We had been sharing our lives and work for over a year and a half, and I wanted to share their times of crisis as well.

"I arrived at the hospital on Thursday morning. Already there

and working were some Peace Corps nurses, working sixteen to eighteen hours a day, assisting with the waves of wounded and generally supervising all phases of the hospital operations. Other than the nurses, there were the nonmedical types who performed odd jobs from folding bandages, washing instruments, and carrying water to assisting with the operations. I had never been in a hospital before, much less one faced with a disaster. There was no electricity, short supply of water, few medicines, standards of sanitation were understandably low, and blood literally covering the floors.

"Luckily, during the first days, there was so much to do there was little time to collect our thoughts. I guess most of us were so involved in our work and the real necessity of being there, that it never occurred to us what was happening all around. It was hopeless to do nothing—there was work to be done and we did what we could. As things slowed down though, I began to realize the horribleness of the whole situation. This was not just another *golpe*— but a real war. A war that resulted in sixteen- and seventeen-year-olds dying by the dozens, fourteen-year-old children walking the streets with machine guns, and women and children cut down in the accidental shootings. After five days, I asked for a replacement—I had just had it. A schedule had been established for rest and relaxation, and on Monday, May 3, I left the hospital.

"Shortly thereafter, all the volunteers in the capital moved to a central location within the established security zone. It was from this vacated girls' school that a new phase in Peace Corps activities began. By this time much of the wild shooting had calmed down a bit, and there were definite sectors of control—the United States security zone, the military junta section, and the Constitutionalist-controlled sector. The nurses were continuing their work in the hospitals, but for the rest of

In honor of their departing hero, the Peace Corps staffers and ex-volunteers, many in the costumes of their host country, came by the hundreds to Shriver's farewell party—the Shriver A-Go-Go— which was one of the swingingest affairs Washington has ever experienced. Only local laws kept some enthusiastic ex-volunteers from riding an elephant into the lobby of the Sheraton Park Hotel. (*Above*) Shriver dances with Rosie Santoro, the Peace Corps's favorite elevator operator and something of a legend herself.

Jack Vaughn, the man President Johnson picked to fill Shriver's shoes, said shortly after assuming his new job that "following Sarge Shriver around the Peace Corps was bracing. Following him as its leader is a bit shattering. It's like being Robin all alone with Batman gone from Gotham." (*Right*) Vaughn leaves a Bangkok restaurant, where it is customary to remove one's shoes.

Vaughn prided himself on having visited 3,500 volunteers in more than 500 Latin American villages and towns—even before he took over the top job in the Peace Corps. The first thing he did on assuming his new job was to begin carrying out a plan to visit Peace Corps volunteers in all the 46 countries in which the Peace Corps was then serving. In Tanzania, Musasani Bay, near Dar es Salaam, he does what is expected of him by photographer Carl Purcell by posing in an outrigger with volunteers Jerry Skarbeck and Ray Ellis.

His visits also included appointments with leaders in the developing nations, such as Tanzania's President Julius Nyerere, to discuss problems and let them know that he planned no drastic changes in the Peace Corps operating methods abroad.

us, there was a question of exactly what we were going to do. It was decided in a meeting that we would try to participate in the programs of food distribution. It was felt that we would be able to maintain contact with our work sites, and demonstrate to our friends that we were not going to abandon them as much and as long as possible, that Peace Corps was interested in them—'military' or 'rebel.' We obtained some food from CARE—about 1½ tons per trip—and made three separate trips to the *barrios*. This work and planning involved many of us for the next few weeks while, at the same time, others were helping the Red Cross, transporting medicines, providing manpower for the regular food distribution centers, and baking bread.

"During these few weeks of driving through all parts of Santo Domingo there was a definite degree of

danger. I guess all of us were scared. The problem was not so much that we would be attacked personally, but rather that we might be in an area where there happened to be firing.

"In such an environment within which there was a definite degree of anti-American feeling, the Peace Corps received practically none. It was as though the Peace Corps was an entity separate from everything else that was concerned with the conflict—as, in fact, it was."

Some of the volunteers did not feel quite so separate; they openly expressed their sympathy with the Constitutionalists and criticized United States intervention. This stirred up some editorial reaction back home and started people to wondering if perhaps the volunteers had become so immersed in Dominican affairs that they were more "theirs" than "ours." As the Fourth

Annual *Peace Corps Report* to Congress stated it:

"The question goes to the very root of Peace Corps philosophy. The degree to which volunteers have been able to work effectively in alien cultures where other forms of foreign aid have frequently gone amiss has depended on their ability to shed their identity as foreigners or outsiders, to walk a thin line along which they could be sympathetically involved with the host country people and still be separate; in short, the ability to become 'theirs' without ceasing to be 'ours.'"

There was more than a little evidence that, in fact, the volunteers living at the level of the people in the Dominican Republic had made a total commitment—at least for the duration of their service. And just how deep a commitment became obvious during a completion-of-service conference of volunteers held two months earlier than scheduled. Of 46 volunteers present, 16 elected to return to the Dominican Republic to finish their work. The words of one volunteer may someday emerge as the foundation on which a *spirit of Peace Corps* is built:

"There was one thing that overshadowed practically all the others, the magic of the three words 'Cuerpo de Paz.' If there was even a testing ground for the Peace Corps idea, it was during those terrible weeks. Upon identification as Peace Corps at the various checkpoints, 'Cuerpo de Paz' was universally met with smiles and acceptance. It was a proud time for me as it was for all of us.

"I had a very strong reaction when a rebel soldier came up and called us 'Hijos de Kennedy'—Children of Kennedy—and I think in this situation the universal acceptance really hit me as what I considered the Peace Corps to be. I felt very proud to be part of the organization—of a United States organization—in a situation where there was so much anti-American feeling, and yet we were totally accepted. And I felt 'this was what Peace Corps really means, it really gets to the people.' It's sort of like when Kennedy died no one realized the feeling across the world until he died. And I think that in the situation here no one realized—or I didn't realize—the Peace Corps was so accepted until its acceptance was tested in a situation like this. And that's one reason I can't let them down—they want the Peace Corps to come back, and you just have to do it. You have to do it."

If the volunteers' performance in the Dominican Republic was the Peace Corps' finest hour, perhaps its darkest moments came later in the year and early in 1966, during that awkward period after President Lyndon Johnson appointed Sargent Shriver to head up the newly created Office of Economic Opportunity at home while continuing to direct the mission of the Peace Corps volunteers abroad. Two full-time jobs were too much for even someone of Shriver's seemingly limitless energy. For the first time since the early days, rumblings were heard on Capitol Hill where irritated Congressmen were remarking that if the Peace Corps and OEO were important enough to deserve the money being asked for them, they were each important enough to have a full-time director. There were also grumblings at headquarters which kept popping up in the press—that Shriver was overcommitted; that he could not be reached when important decisions needed to be made; that he was not going abroad to visit the volunteers as often as he should,

By August, 1966, when the 10,000th volunteer returned—Sally Poland of Louisville, Kentucky, pictured with her PCV husband, Al (*right*), as they landed in New York—the Peace Corps was no longer on trial. It was an established, growing organization that seemed to have everyone's support—at home and abroad. By 1970, there will be more than 50,000 returned volunteers. (*Below*) Sally talks with her students during her final visit to the nursery school in Ankara, Turkey, where she and her husband shared their Peace Corps experience.

Although the Peace Corps continues to encourage older volunteers, such as Dr. and Mrs. Virgil Payen (*above*) who taught in Cameroon, figures show that only 46 of 14,216 volunteers abroad in late 1966 were over sixty. And experience has shown that older applicants have special problems: For example:

• They often face major hurdles in receiving medical clearance.

• The Peace Corps seeks only exceptionally skilled persons from the higher age brackets, yet many of the older applicants have nonspecific skills. In the case of married couples, the wife has rarely been anything but a housewife.

• Peace Corps experience has shown that young college graduates are more flexible, more adaptable, and easier to train than older people.

• A study of overseas attrition found that volunteers over the age of thirty-one are more likely to come home before their service is complete than are volunteers in the twenty-one-to-thirty age bracket.

However, recruiters still regularly make special efforts to attract qualified older volunteers. Also, about 150 companies extend rights to employees who take off two years, before retirement, to serve in the Peace Corps. Some companies offer pension credits for Peace Corps service. Many school systems offer reemployment and seniority rights to teachers who take off two years for Peace Corps work.

An estimated 340 men and women over the age of fifty have served in the Peace Corps since it began—only about 1.6 percent of all volunteers.

In a survey of returned volunteers, the Peace Corps found that approximately 37 percent continued their education; 19 percent went into teaching; 17 percent into federal or state governments. Over 300 held staff jobs in the Peace Corps, where they have been especially effective in recruiting and as overseas representatives. The highest-ranking ex-volunteer in the Peace Corps is Chuck Butler (*below*) shown on a return visit to the Venezuelan village of Santa Rosa, where he served for two years.

nor as often as he used to.

This period was finally brought to an end when Shriver resigned his Peace Corps functions to devote full time to the war on poverty. Appropriately his resignation came on the fifth birthday of the Peace Corps—appropriate because Shriver had established a rule at the Peace Corps, known as "the five-year flush," which limited staff service to five years.

The man Lyndon Johnson picked to replace Shriver is Jack Vaughn—an early Peace Corps Latin American Director who went on to become Ambassador to Panama and Assistant Secretary of State for Inter-American Affairs, a post which he

And thanks in part to returned volunteers, who are now doing the bulk of Peace Corps recruiting, Peace Corps applications—mostly from the "A.B. generalists"—are pouring in in increasing numbers. In 1966, more than 40,000 were received.

Even Congress no longer looks on the Peace Corps as impractical and unrealistic. One year it even appropriated more money than the Peace Corps requested. (*Below*) President Johnson signs Peace Corps legislation appropriating funds—and the attitude of some more conservative leaders in Washington was expressed by a former Republican Congressman, Walter Norblad of Oregon, who was quoted as saying, while still in office: "I was one of those who voted against the Peace Corps when it was before the House. . . . It was my feeling that it was not practical and that sending these young people to various parts of the world . . . would be a waste of taxpayers' funds. . . . It is my purpose today to admit I was wrong."

78

Despite its having become an established government agency, the Peace Corps continued its experimentation and innovation. For instance, advanced training programs were developed in cooperation with certain universities in which potential volunteers began their training in the summer of their junior year. The Peace Corps also sponsored a school-to-school program under which the students of United States grade and high schools raised money to help build a school in one of the Peace Corps countries. (*Left*) Workers in Gebileh, Somalia, build a school with materials paid for with money raised by the students of the Senior High School in Upper Darby, Pennsylvania. (*Below*) The finished school. Peace Corps volunteers supervised the construction of the school.

held, ironically, at the time the United States sent the Marines to the Dominican Republic to help put down the rebellion. Vaughn says he is proud to have had a hand in stopping a bloody massacre among the Dominican people, but that he is prouder of having sent the first volunteers to the Dominican Republic when he was the Peace Corps's Latin American Director.

Vaughn also says that when the dictator of the Dominican Republic was killed, "the acting Foreign Minister came to Sargent Shriver and said: 'We've got to have 450 volunteers next week. [This was when we

Solidly established in the United States, the Peace Corps idea continues to grow abroad. "Throughout the world," says William Delano, Secretary General of the International Secretariat for Volunteer Service from 1964 to 1967, "more and more governments are coming to realize that the great majority of young people of this generation want to help —all they need is encouragement, direction, and training." (Above) Delano provides some encouragement for Japa-nese volunteers in training at Osaka. In March, 1967, member nations of ISVS met in New Delhi and elected a new Secretary General—Dr. Michael U. R. von Schenck, of Switzerland (left). Under von Schenck, ISVS continues to experiment in new ways of encouraging and organizing international volunteers, such as regional recruitment. (Below) Volunteers from Central and Latin America serving in the Dominican Republic.

Flanked by volunteer teachers Ray Ellis and Jim Crawford, Vaughn shakes hands with students at Kisarawe, Tanzania, on a recent trip to Africa. Under Vaughn, the Peace Corps's role in the developing nations has crystallized (*opposite page*), but in the last analysis, says Vaughn, "the volunteer should be primarily involved in changing human attitudes. The schools and the roads and the bridges and the eggs are means, not an end. The end we seek is a human one—of people able to cope successfully with their environments, of people who are not prey to disease, demagoguery, or despair."

didn't have 200 volunteers in all Latin America.] We don't want professionals and we don't want technicians. We want young mature Americans to come and join hands with us because we've never governed ourselves and we have a terrible deficiency across the board in our institutions. We don't have any tradition or experience of confidence really to set up a Parent-Teacher Association or a municipal council or a forestry service. We have none of that.'

"Last May I went to the Dominican Republic," Vaughn continued. "The first man I ran into was this Acting Foreign Minister who had asked for the 450 volunteers. He came up to me, threw his arms around me, started to weep, and said, 'You know, Jack, if we had gotten those 450 volunteers, this might not have happened.' And I think he was right."

It had been over a year since Jack Vaughn took over the direction of the Peace Corps, and the most obvious thing that can be said about the organization today is that it has come of age. It has survived its period of trial-and-error, a new Director and several changings of the guards at the upper and middle staff levels. And gradually, returning volunteers are working their way up in the organization, especially in the staff jobs overseas. "The Peace Corps is no longer the *enfant terrible* of the early Kennedy years. . . ." Jack Vaughn told a National Press Club audience. "It has become an effective means of communication . . . [it] has proved itself a practical way of attacking the wants of food, education, health, and recognition which so often drive men down paths of frustration and confusion to rebellion and war. In short, it works. And works well. Better, in fact, than many of us who attended its beginning dared even to hope for."

No longer is the Peace Corps as sacrosanct as motherhood and the FBI. "For the first time our public image of unmitigated virtue is being tarnished," Deputy Director Harris Wofford said in his farewell message

(*Opposite page*) Volunteers are: *upper left*, Cecil Suffler of San Diego, who did community development in Panama; *upper right*, Ann Quinck, Tanzania; *lower left*, Joan Dillard, of Charlottesville, Virginia, who taught in Sarawak; *lower right*, Leslie Gile, Rochester, New York, an agricultural extension worker who served in Nepal.

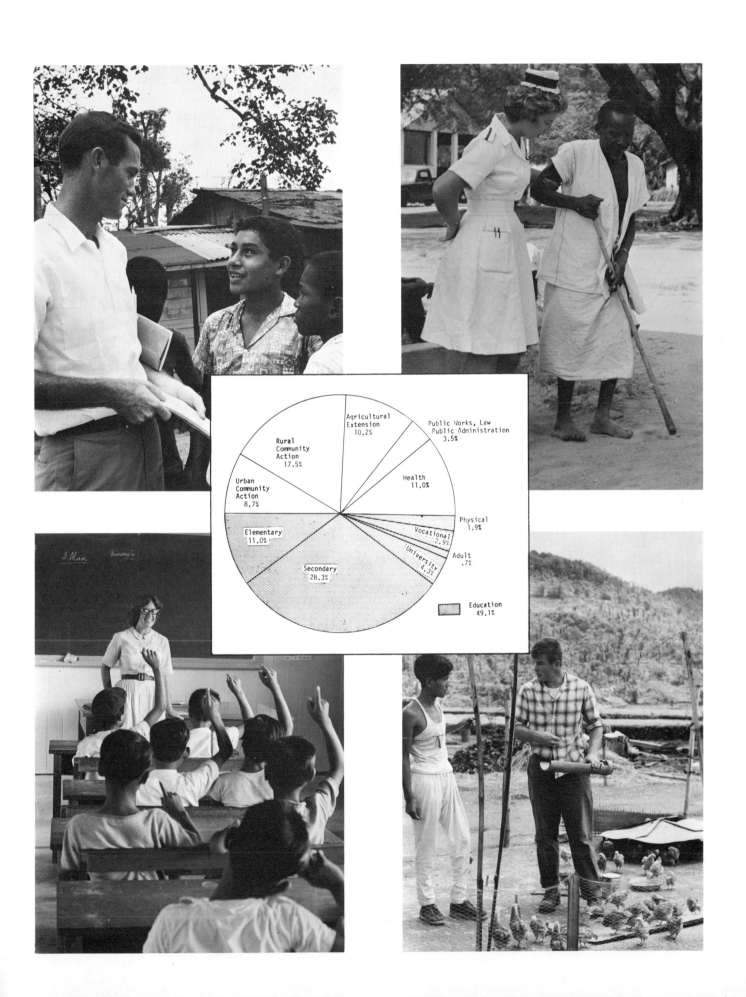

Agricultural Extension 10.2%

Public Works, Law Public Administration 3.5%

Rural Community Action 17.5%

Health 11.0%

Urban Community Action 8.7%

Physical 1.9%

Vocational 2.9%

Elementary 11.0%

University 4.3%

Adult .7%

Secondary 28.3%

Education 49.1%

to the staff: "the protests and letters and literature of volunteers are at last conveying some of the complex reality of the Peace Corps."

William James's gilded youth have been out in the world, have had some of their childishness knocked out of them, and one of the first things they found out was that maybe the Peace Corps wasn't doing all the things Sargent Shriver and his publicists had been telling the American people, and particularly Congress, it would do. "What seemed to characterize the attitude of the volunteers I knew," ex-volunteer Efrem Sigel wrote of his Peace Corps experience in a very critical article for the *Reporter*, "was a new way of looking at the world. From all the evidence, we were great idealists before reaching our assignments and great cynics afterward."

And Arnold and Marian Zeitlin, two ex-volunteer teachers in Ghana, wrote in the *Saturday Evening Post:* "We believe that the Corps has sold the public a bill of goods. We believe it is failing to fulfill its promises and that most of the popular ideas about it are false." But like most of the ex-volunteers critical of

One measure of the new confidence: The Peace Corps's own magazine—the *Volunteer*, edited for volunteers—continually publishes constructive, often hard-hitting, criticism of the Peace Corps operation at home and abroad. Most of the criticism is written by volunteers in the field, or ex-volunteers, and many of the volunteers' brief descriptions of experience abroad which are included in the following pages appeared originally in the *Volunteer*.

the Peace Corps, the Zeitlins were quick to add: "This does not mean we are anti-Peace Corps. We criticize it because we expect more from

the Corps than it is delivering."

The sober realists in Washington are the first to admit that the Peace Corps is not perfect, and that there is a lot more it can and should be doing. But the same could be said of almost any government operation, including some that have been active for several decades. The significant thing about the Peace Corps is that today, after less than seven years in operation, it is a solid established idea, which in 1967 is carried abroad by more than 15,000 volunteers in 53 countries and the U.N. Trust Territories of the Pacific. Another 700 are in training and over 12,000 have completed service and returned home. And after more than six years of experimentation and innovation, the Peace Corps is beginning to find its role in the developing world. Almost exactly one-half of all volunteers abroad today are teaching; approximately 25 percent are involved in community action; approximately 10 percent are working in health programs; 10 percent in agriculture projects; and the remaining less than 5 percent are engaged in a variety of miscellaneous activities.

As I said earlier, collectively the Peace Corps experience is the greatest eye-opening, mind-stretching experience any generation of Americans has ever had. As volunteer Hayward Allen wrote from Ethiopia: "Our original excitement and enthusiasm have been somewhat tempered by a year here. We have come to realize that change comes so slowly that progress, if it comes at all, seems imperceptible. The eagerness is replaced by colder ways of looking at the world, and the youthful vigor and idealism become hardened with a day-to-day job. We can never again become the people we were before we came to Africa. But then, we would not want to."

We hope the following pages will help those of us who stayed at home understand the nature of the experience which is changing a generation.

By 1966, criticism in the press had for the most part vanished. The *Wall Street Journal*, for instance, an early critic of the Peace Corps, reported from Africa that the Peace Corps was making a significant contribution and that the real measure of success was "the fact that almost every country to which volunteers have been sent has requested additional ones." Most of the criticism in the press, in fact, was coming from returned volunteers, such as Arnold and Marian Zeitlin, who wrote in a national magazine that the Peace Corps had sold the public a bill of goods.

Looking to the future, Vaughn predicts that by 1971 more than 100,000 volunteers will have served overseas; over forty nations will have sent volunteers to this country in a reverse Peace Corps program; Foreign Service officers will have had to serve two years as Peace Corps volunteers; volunteers will have served in every developing nation, Eastern Europe, and Vietnam; and that the Peace Corps concept will have become such a way of life that all Americans will be devoting several years of their lives to volunteer service of one kind or another. Vaughn is also emphatic on one point: He will not stay longer than five years as Peace Corps Director—and it is no secret that he wants his successor to be an ex-volunteer.

A trainee at the Peace Corps camp in the Sandia Mountains, New Mexico, gets ready for Ecuador with a course in rappelling. One of the criteria on which the Peace Corps bases selection is: "The physical stamina and emotional stability to maintain effectiveness under the stresses of Peace Corps work."

Chapter 3

Training

*For most volunteers, the Peace Corps experience begins
with the filling out of the famous twelve-page application. Then comes the invitation to join a group going
into training, the training period itself, the agonizing
period during which the Peace Corps "selects out" the*

*trainees who they do not think will stay the course, and
the flight to the host country. All these experiences are
recounted in a very readable reminiscence by Moritz
Thomsen, a slightly older-than-average Californian who
served two years in Ecuador:*

The Peace Corps application is about twelve pages
long, and it takes hours to fill out, requiring of the
applicant (in my case, one somewhat weighted by years)
that he reexamine and record a thousand forgotten
memories, many of them not too pleasant.

You have to disinter and expose to public scrutiny
your entire life, your failures along with whatever
talents you hope to dangle before the Peace Corps people as bait.

I got my application at the post office in Red Bluff,
put it on the table in the kitchen, and walked around
it quietly for about ten days without touching it as
though it were primed to detonate (as indeed it was),
trying to convince myself that at my age the idea of
Peace Corps duty was foolhardy.

All of this happened, I might as well admit, at a time
of real crisis for me. After sixteen years of farming in
the Sacramento Valley I had finally come to the verge

A group of trainees in New Mexico prepare to teach English in Latin America. The trend in Peace Corps training
today is toward smaller classes respecting individual needs
and interests and with trainees participating in some of the
decision-making and evaluation of the program.

of bankruptcy, and with hogs selling at twelve cents a pound, was not making enough even to pay for their feed, let alone my own.

The letter from the Peace Corps which is delivered one day and announces that you are being invited for training is, I am sure, programmed to arrive after your first enthusiasm has died and after you have already committed yourself to some other project.

But there it lay one morning in my mailbox, and I opened it, already convinced that it contained a rejection. I had trained myself to open it with steady fingers and a yawn on my face.

The rebirth of that original enthusiasm from this one-page letter is due to a miracle of technology—for the signature of the Peace Corps Director is so cleverly reproduced that it has every appearance of having been personally affixed to the invitation.

It is the personal quality of this signature that bursts you open. I was flooded with visions of the Director of the Peace Corps, sitting at a desk in Washington studying my application along with a hundred others and finally pointing to mine, while his associates grouped around him nodded in violent agreement and broke into wild yips of joy.

In spite of what the Peace Corps may feel, it is from the moment of receiving this letter that your actual Peace Corps participation really begins. An immediate withdrawal from the scenes of the present commences, and you begin to live in the future.

It is a curious and strangely intense time, since all the things and people you have lived with must sud-denly be reappraised and said goodbye to—the chickens in the yard, the olive trees, the cat, the school kids who comes over on Saturdays, even Mrs. Yeager's guinea hens who sneak across the road to steal hog feed.

They are all observed with a new clarity, and you find that all these things mean more to you than you had thought they could, a sort of drama that is not wholly unpleasant.

But an amazing thing happens to you now in this limbo period between being asked to train for the Peace Corps and the time of actually leaving for that training —this period of storing things and nailing shutters over the window.

Not only are you going through your little reappraisal, but all the people you know are suddenly reappraising you. You have in a sense become public property in a most profound and moving way.

You find friends, almost as though they feel it a patriotic duty, pointing out faults and dredging up from some distant past your more disagreeable qualities and hoping that you can learn to overcome them.

Another curious thing began to develop among the people who were close to me, the friends and family who felt involved on a personal level with my disappearance from the immediate scene.

It was the envy of the average person, living a life of habit, harassed by all the trivialities of a day-to-day existence, growing older under a dim sense of disappointment and loss, who now sees one of his friends about to break out of this trap and become involved in a new kind of existence that holds promise of being

Singing is now an integral part of some training programs. For instance, "singing a song in Spanish," one staff member says, "establishes an identification with the native, particularly the *campesino* (peasant), which nothing else could."

Despite the rigorous program, there is always room for horseplay. This trainee is commenting on the water rations during a three-day trek in the desert.

Training for Micronesia

In an effort to duplicate conditions in the host country as much as possible, the Peace Corps chose Key West, Florida, as its training site for a group of volunteers headed for the Trust Territories of the South Pacific. Volunteers spent twelve weeks in Key West, where part of the curriculum was to learn the customs of the Pacific islands, such as spearfishing . . .

. . . and basket weaving. The training project was organized by the Peace Corps and Westinghouse Corporation. The training staff was made up mostly of ex-volunteers, shown (*below*) gathered for a discussion period in the cafeteria of the Casa Marina Hotel, which was converted to house the Micronesia trainees.

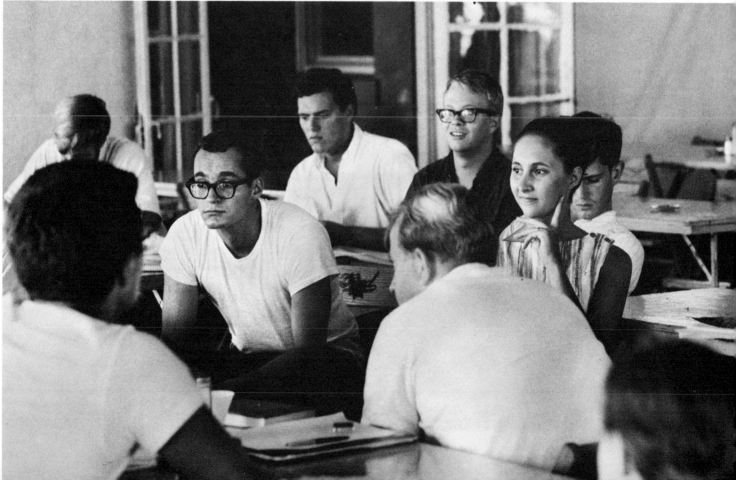

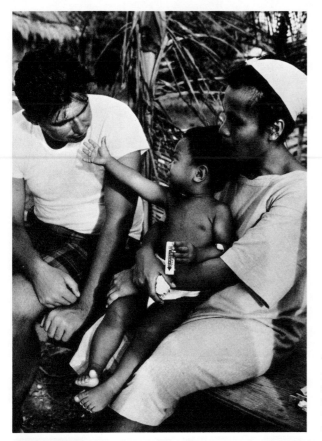

To help the volunteers understand the people of the Pacific islands, more than seventy-five Micronesians, some with their entire families, were brought from the Pacific. They spent many hours in conversation with the volunteers.

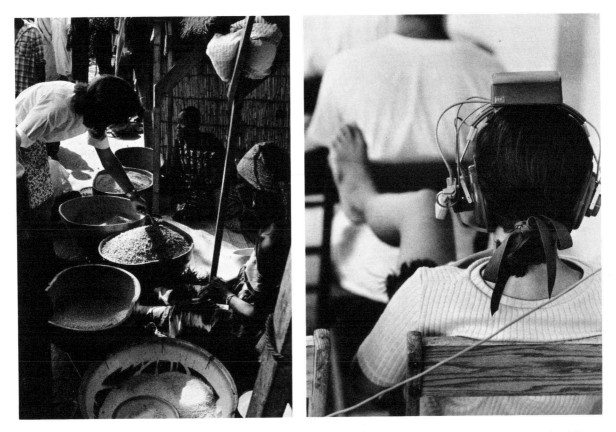

Volunteers also ate the food of Micronesia (*above, left*) and studied, by the oral-aural method, one of the eight different Micronesian languages (*above, right*). More than 300 hours of language training were given.

Lone trainee finds a quiet place to study in the lobby of the Casa Marina.

meaningful, a life that might hold form, pattern, and direction.

Peace Corps training is like no other training in the world, having something in common with college life, officers' training, and a ninety-day jail sentence. What makes it paradoxical is that everything is voluntary; the schedule exists for you to follow if you wish.

At Bozeman, Montana, where our Ecuador-bound group trained, there was only one rule: It was illegal to bring liquor on the campus.

Our schedule began at 5:45 each morning and lasted until 9:30 at night; from 9:30 on, if we so desired, our Spanish instructors were available to work with us.

It was a fantastic schedule. If there were any psychotics in the bunch who had sneaked through the Washington screening, they wanted to find out fast, and if we were breakable, they wanted to break us here in the United States.

They told us the story about the Peace Corps trainee who had come to Bozeman the year before and who had learned the first sentence in the Spanish book, "The students arrive at the door." "Los alumnos llegan a la puerta," and who had become deranged almost immediately from the pressures put on him.

He went around repeating, "Los alumnos llegan a la puerta" in answer to all questions put to him and screamed it all night in his sleep.

We laughed at this story but it was most uneasy laughter because by the end of the first week we too were dreaming horrible stunted things in Spanish and screaming them in our sleep through those short, short nights.

We took psychological tests so long and boring that toward the end we were too punch drunk to lie; we listened in an endless series of two- and three-hour lectures from experts from all over the world who flew into Bozeman and crammed us with information—the

geography, the history, the politics, the religion, the customs, the attitudes.

We began to learn Spanish under a system so intense and concentrated that by the end of the first five weeks we were using a vocabulary roughly comparable to that of Cervantes (1547–1616) and using it practically twenty-four hours a day. We twisted and mauled that beautiful language into a million distorted shapes, and watched in a sort of dumb bemusement our instructors, sensitive and dedicated people all, wither and age before our eyes.

The Peace Corps psychiatrist was the dragon in our lives who evaluated all of the information about us and whose opinion was final. He was the only one in the college, for instance, who ever saw our Civil Service background reports. We did not like the psychiatrist.

In all three phases of our training, we were studied and appraised like a bunch of fat beeves about to be entered in the State Fair. Our instructors watched us and filed daily reports; the psychologist and the psychiatrist watched us; mysterious little men from Washington in black suits whose names we never learned appeared and watched us.

Each weekend we went on camping trips where we were watched by our camp leaders.

The doctor and his nurse watched us; our discussion

But it is not all study. (*Opposite page*) Volunteers headed for 2,000 Pacific islands spread out over 3,000,000 square miles of water obviously had to practice their swimming.

Two volunteers bound for the West African Republic of Guinea practice their vertical welding. They were part of an "all blue-collar" group of twenty-one volunteers who taught Guinean mechanics the operation and maintenance of earth-moving equipment. Left is Mike Connolly, of Chicago; behind Mike is George McCart, from Pontiac, Michigan.

The great emphasis today in Peace Corps training is on involving the volunteer with the host country's culture. (*Above*) Mary Schneider, of California, training to teach in Colombia, practices her Spanish on Spanish children in a rural school in New Mexico.

leaders watched us; our athletic coaches watched us. And even the kitchen help watched us.

The training period for potential Peace Corps volunteers is referred to by its directors as a period of training and selection, but it might more properly be described as a period of deselection. Our group started out with thirty-eight applicants and ended with twenty-four—almost a 40 percent cut.

It was cruel but efficient. And it had its negative aspects for us, since in one sense the aim of the training period is basically not a training period at all, but a period of structured tension, of subtle and purposive torture, in which it is calculated that the individual trainee will be forced to reveal himself.

Because the fundamental purpose of the program is not to change your character but to discover it, not to implant proper motivations for Peace Corps service but to find out what your motivations are, it is probable that a few potentially good volunteers have been eliminated from the program.

In Dallas, those of us who were finally selected were herded into a little office, borrowed for the occasion from one of the airlines, and still tired from the trip, still shaken by the uncertainty of our position, we raised our right hands and were sworn into the service. Talk about emotion. We were Peace Corps volunteers at last.

His students no longer, we said goodbye to our director of training at Montana, and then, having been told to report in ten days to the airport in New York for our flight to Quito, Ecuador, we scattered to our homes all over the country.

Our Peace Corps group, twenty-four agricultural specialists, left New York from Kennedy International Airport one midnight, and awoke eight hours later as we dropped from altitude onto the Quito strip.

Five minutes before disembarking we were all individually and secretly struck with terror, not because of any hardships we might be walking into, nor because of any fear of homesickness or loneliness, but simply because we knew that as part of the welcoming ceremony we were expected to sing as a group the Ecuadorian National Anthem.

Now there is nothing wrong with the Ecuadorian National Anthem except that it is very long, and like our own "Star-Spangled Banner," it contains within it an impossible range of notes, high and low, and the truth of the matter is that we never did get the whole thing down so that we could bring it off with any degree of aplomb.

But as it turned out, our terrors were groundless. We were met at the airport by a bunch of sweet 4-H Club kids who welcomed us with speeches and flowers, greeted by our directors and some high government officials from the Department of Agriculture and by the old group of volunteers who had arrived from all parts of the country to look us over.

And then we all took a deep breath and sang the Ecuadorian National Anthem.

The truth of the matter is that our group knew the words much better than the Ecuadorians whose lips we were trying to read. We were magnificent. Halfway through the song we discovered with a feeling of exultant relief that Ecuadorians were trying to read *our* lips. After that everything was anticlimax.

—MORITZ THOMSEN

(*For Mr. Thomsen's account of some of his experiences in Ecuador, see page 181.*)

On the flight to the host country, volunteers have a few hours to themselves to wonder what the next twenty months will be like. (*Below*) A group arrives in Manila, September 8, 1965.

Many Peace Corps training programs include courses, practice sessions, and special projects in the host country before the volunteer begins work on his specific mission. One of the most interesting such ventures of this kind was the reconstruction of a fort in Taleh, Somalia. The fort was begun in 1910 by Sayyid Mohammed Abdille Hassan, known to the British as the "Mad Mullah." It still had not been completed in 1920 when it was ordered destroyed by Winston Churchill. To reach Taleh, the fifty volunteers who worked on the project drove 400 miles by truck from Hargeisa. The project was planned as an extension of training for the volunteers, who would eventually teach, and as an orientation course for Somalia. They worked two weeks on the fort along with about 100 Somalia police. Other volunteers took up where they left off several months later. The volunteers camped on the desert; the only water was very bitter and came from a small well located some distance from the camp; there was no wood for fires; lack of vegetation made privacy impossible, and rice and spaghetti were the principal foods. On the opposite page is the ruined fortress. (*Below*) In a classroom of a school built by Peace Corps volunteers and the people of Taleh, volunteers gather with the Peace Corps staff to discuss fort-clearing strategy. The plan of attack is outlined on the blackboard.

Chapter 4

Teaching

To the implied question—"What is a nice liberal arts graduate like you doing in a place like this?"—that most people seem to ask when they come across Peace Corps volunteers in faraway places, the answer usually is: "Teaching." More than half of the volunteers going overseas now are destined to teach, and during the next ten years, 50,000 volunteer teachers will be sent abroad —most of them liberal arts majors with A.B. degrees. These photographs and reports from abroad by Peace Corps volunteers help reveal what it is like to be a Peace Corps teacher in one of the developing nations. For instance, Gwynne Douglas, who was an English teacher in a girl's secondary school at Freetown, Sierra Leone, describes below what was for her a marvelous event that occurred in her class one day. Miss Douglas is from Colorado Springs, and received an A.B. in 1963 from Colorado State University where she majored in English and Speech.

Like thousands of Peace Corps volunteers all over the developing world, Ron Kuhl arrives at a lonely schoolhouse in the early hours of every weekday morning—in Kuhl's case, 7:30 A.M. The students, who live in the little hamlet of Tambunan in southern Sabah on the island of Borneo, are cleaning the yard and trimming the hedges. Ron is a University of West Virginia graduate who majored in Education. He teaches forty half-hour classes of English a week at the Government Primary School, and although he does not particularly like the monotonous repetition involved in teaching a language, says: "I'm a taskmaster and really get a half-hour's work out of them."

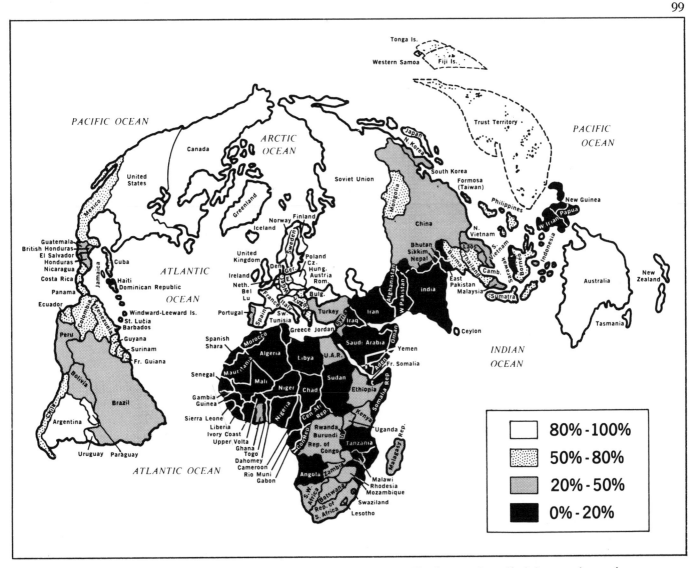

The Literacy Gap: Shaded areas of map show percentage of population able to read and write in each country, according to United Nations studies. Peace Corps education projects are generally concentrated in areas of the world where the literacy rate is lowest.

"No, I didn't build any bridges. I don't know anything about culverts or soil conditions. I didn't organize any clubs, and I haven't started any libraries. I never did much of that sort of thing before I came here, and I probably won't start now. I just go to school every day and try to do my job.

"I have one hundred students that I try to teach every day, and for me, that's a full-time occupation. And I rack my brains. What's the *matter* with the kid in the fourth row? She doesn't say anything, and she won't *do* anything. There ought to be some way, somehow, and I look at her speculatively as she bends her dark braided head over her wooden desk, her blue uniform making her look like any other kid in the room.

"But she isn't any other kid in the room. And she writes platitudes. And clichés. How do I get through to her? Or that one over there. That tall one looking out the window. The smart one. I'm always leading with my chin when it comes to her, Tramping over to her vindictively, 'Finished?' I say, knowing full well she can't be. No one *else* is. She pushes the neat paper toward me, looking out the window, still pointedly bored. I glance down. Perfect. From start to finish. As correct as the nice clean check mark it will eventually get at 2:00 A.M. when I finally get through the stack to hers, knowing it won't be much trouble because it's nearly always right. How can I catch her and not lose the one in the fourth row?

"I walk to the back of the room; my shoes are noisy on the concrete floor. Now all I can see are bent blue backs and moving elbows. Exams. How I always hated them. And I understand the tension in the room, and the remembering three parts to the problem but not the frustrating fourth—and even seeing the page num-

After the Peace Corps was established in 1961, requests for teachers poured into Peace Corps headquarters from the newly independent nations eager to expand their school systems. In Jamaica, for instance, where Myra Ilson, of New York City, is shown above teaching "play" methods in a Kingston "Headstart" class, four to five thousand schools for children between the ages of four and six and one-half have sprung up—in abandoned stores, makeshift bamboo lean-tos, and under mango trees even in the more remote villages.

ber and remembering what the teacher was wearing when she explained that elusive fourth—but for the life of me . . . Yes, I remember. I glance at the board, and gasp. My handwriting looks so *different* from back here. How in heaven's name do they ever read it?

"I visited some other volunteers the other day. She's organized a dramatics club and he's dug a well, is contemplating the village water system, has started a garden, is building a school building out of mud bricks. It's great. But I just haven't done any of those things.

"But I do know that yesterday that girl in the fourth row—the stoic one—smiled for the first time, and timidly handed me a perfectly expressed idea, an idea all her own that she didn't get from anyone else. Oh, it lacked a few commas and capital letters. But I didn't care just then."

—GWYNNE DOUGLAS

One of the distinguishing characteristics of Peace Corps volunteers is self-criticism—they criticize the organization, themselves, and the job they are doing and have done. The Peace Corps magazine, The Volunteer, *continually publishes articles by volunteers sounding off about what's wrong with the Peace Corps and how it can be made to work more effectively. One such article was written by Samuel B. Abbott, who returned to Harvard Law School after teaching in Lagos where he also wrote a television series for the Nigerian educational television network and organized various voluntary service projects. In Abbott's opinion, only about half the volunteer teachers "go beyond their adjustment to an involvement with their situation," and of these only half again are really effective volunteers.*

I returned a year ago from two years' work as a Peace Corps teacher in Africa. The intervening time has brought me some realizations I did not have in the midst of that experience. If I am unhappy, it is not because I mourn the good old days and the fresh zeal of a first generation of volunteer teachers. I'm sure there were Peace Corps giants in Africa in those days, but there are now, too. *What I do mourn is that the best of us could have been so much better and should have been more numerous.* Our goals as volunteers were never really defined beyond job performance; more important, we were not trained to them, selected by them, or supported in them once we were in the field. Nor does our feedback to Washington seem to have sharpened and modified the existing approaches very much, save, perhaps, in training innovations.

I also mourn a failure to translate the initial Peace Corps ideal into action, to make it practical and functional, less of a mystery and banner emblem and more of an approach to working and thinking. Most of us entered with the hopelessly broad notion that we were going overseas to "help" other people. Most of us left with the hopelessly narrow notion that Peace Corps service was teaching our classes and remaining more or less interested in Africa and Africans. The failure to de-

It soon became evident that the Peace Corps could not provide enough experienced teachers to satisfy the demand of the developing nations—especially in Africa. Many of the older volunteers, such as Mrs. Clara Rathjen, sixty, a Ph.D. who had taught at Trinity College in Washington, had had teaching experience, but they were too few in numbers. Mrs. Rathjen is shown with her class at the Mary Leakey Girls Schools in Nairobi, Kenya, where she was the oldest volunteer in that country.

fine and refine and implement was pardonable, perhaps, in the first years, but now it suggests an organization that has never understood its business.

Our secondary education project was recruited in early 1963. By the time we entered training, the first returning volunteers had brought home a blue note which began to sound officially: that all was not glamour. *We were proper recruits, then: idealists without illusions. We were also two-thirds amateur; only 31* percent had taught school previously. We had joined the Peace Corps to serve, and were assigned to teach. Beyond our devotion to the ideal of service and the idealization of Africa, we were, for better or worse, pretty much *tabulae rasae*.

We certainly weren't ten weeks later. We had gone through a super cram course *which left us with sore posteriors and dizzy minds. The components were weighted according to staff availability and interest, but*

Faced with the alternatives of either no teachers or nonexperienced teachers, the developing nations agreed to give nonexperienced teachers, such as Peter Oppenheimer seen above teaching a science class in the government's secondary school at Mzuzu, Malawi, a chance. Oppenheimer has his A.B. from the University of Chicago and did some graduate work at Stanford. He also teaches math and history—and after five years the Peace Corps still cannot supply the demands of the developing nations for unexperienced teachers such as Peter Oppenheimer.

As a result of the worldwide shortage of experienced teachers, a new kind of teacher has appeared in the schools of the developing world—a college graduate with an A.B. in science or the humanities and who, before Peace Corps training, had never taught a class or thought of spending two years of his or her life teaching. Good examples are Marylee Meyers (who taught English and biology at Belize Tech, a secondary school in British Honduras. Marylee is from Seattle and received her A.B. degree from the University of Washington) and . . .

this has since been remedied. What has not is the training rationale. No one seemed to know what a Peace Corps volunteer really was, and yet everyone was determined to produce them. The assumption, I gathered, was that a Peace Corps volunteer was a composite of competent, if amateur, Americanist, well briefed if slightly practiced teacher, articulate spokesman for the American Way, and healthy mind in sound and flab-free body.

At the end of ten weeks they were ready to select us. As the training program had worked out, they had discovered we were intelligent, healthy, and cooperative (or should I say, obedient?), which they already knew when we arrived at training. Only now they were more certain. They did "select out" two, one who was a tiny bit too shy and one who was a good bit too loud. The rest of us were qualified, presumably, as Peace Corps volunteers. But what a Peace Corps volunteer was or how he functioned was as unclear to me as ever.

As a result, my Peace Corps training continued throughout my first year of service. I don't know whether I was slow or who was to blame. I do know that I conducted my training myself. Although I was five miles from headquarters, the staff never came. I

. . . Stephanie Dawson of Richland, Washington, a 1964 graduate of the University of Washington (Stephanie teaches English as a foreign language at the Zarghoonah Lycée in Kabul, Afghanistan) and . . .

harried them a good deal by phone and in person, but as far as on-the-spot support, none. You may say I was too close, but the bush volunteers rated one to two visits in their twenty-four months.

There were a few language courses, but no conferences to cope with volunteer problems or opportunities or my school subjects. In another part of the country a regional director of prodigious energy and devotion gathered his flock regularly, but most staff, despite ability and dedication, were oppressed by administrative procedures and the logistical problems which arose from doubling the number of volunteers during my two years. Also the staff was coming and going and

going and coming with a frequency bound to sap effective leadership.

What issued from staff in the way of goals, guidance, definition, or resources was largely limited to negative fiats against sloppy dress on formal occasions, political utterances, public drunkenness, vehicles owned by Peace Corps volunteers or given by the Peace Corps, and saving money on living allowances. Oh, yes. *For* bicycles. This definition by negation, like training, yielded a murky and curious composite to answer the question: What is a Peace Corps volunteer?

A staff concern was for us to "get off the compound and into the community." No case was made for the incompleteness of compound life to teachers who considered themselves full-time employees, and no good case was made for following the suggestion. Vacation projects were required, and endless subterfuge resulted. Peace Corps volunteers simplified the issue to, "Isn't teaching enough?" and indeed it was all they had clearly been trained for, oriented to, or practiced in. Those who had never graded a paper before the Peace Corps felt free to rejoin that they were dedicated professionals engaged in a demanding full-time job. And in the pit of some stomachs was anger that the Peace Corps, having agreed to send secondary teachers to Africa, was now telling them that they were out of step with the rest of the Peace Corps and somehow not true blue until they used their teaching job as an excuse for community development.

This quarrel between staff and personnel, which had its beginning in a childish and irrelevant training experience, was a disaster. Conscientious staff became policemen trying to enforce policy edicts; they could not escape being "them" in the minds of Peace Corps volunteers. And volunteers, alienated from effective staff leadership and support, and very clear on what they were against, lost interest in finding out what they were for.

Peace Corps volunteer gatherings, in my experience,

. . . George Fries, of Fresno, California, who teaches English at the Mwanza Lake, Tanzania, secondary school. Fries has his A.B. from the University of California at Berkeley.

told horror stories of their cross-cultural snafus, talked of home or Africa in general, or complained of the staff and Washington. But seldom, if ever, did they deal positively with problems in volunteering, conceptions of volunteering, or how to translate ideals into action. It would not have been taken seriously. Seldom were we a corps of anything but transplanted Americans, certainly not of peace.

It might be easy to dismiss the foregoing as needs now being met, a rough period of policy implementation now smooth, or growing pains now eased, and point with pride to low attrition rate, higher average trainee I.Q.'s, increasing host country requests, or increasing applications. This is not enough because this

is not our business. What is lacking is basic definition, communication, and implementation. What is the job of a Peace Corps volunteer working as a teacher? What is job effectiveness? What qualities and skills predict success? What support is needed overseas? What criteria for selection? What training? Answer these questions well, and apply the answer consistently to every part of the Peace Corps experience from the recruiting poster to the termination conference, and I will be satisfied. Here is one answer.

Being a Peace Corps volunteer, and here I speak in the African teaching context, is manifestly *not* limited to careful lesson preparation, classroom teaching, and staff duties as assigned. I say this with the certainty that

No matter what else might be said about them, by virtue of sheer numbers the Peace Corps teachers have already made a tremendous impact on the developing nations. For example, more than half of the degree-holding teachers in six African nations are Peace Corps volunteers . . . such as Ann Bell who teaches science at the Kirimara Secondary School in Kenya, and . . .

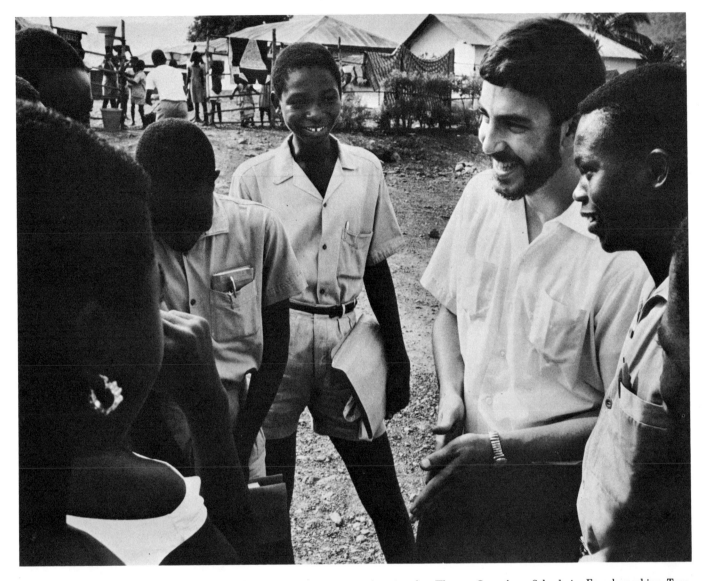

. . . Peter Lefcourt, of Flushing, New York, who is a general arts teacher in the Woame Secondary School in French-speaking Togo.

the African secondary school is, in some sense, a charade. Historically, colonial educators placed a student in a school compound whose atmosphere, discipline, classes, organization, uniforms, and ideals resembled, as closely as possible, those of a European school. In what better way, it was thought, could European values, concepts, and skills be imparted?

The danger for the Peace Corps volunteer today is that he will perceive the surface similarities, which he may at first embrace with the joy of discovering familiar things in a strange place, such as textbooks, the language, syllabi, or even surnames, and miss the tremendous difference between his own and the indigenous culture. The adaptation of African mind to European educational mold is not often achieved by the student alone, and it is difficult to see how a Peace Corps volunteer can function as a teacher, leading his students out to new skills and concepts, if he lacks a firsthand experience and understanding of the student's culture. The meeting place is halfway, and the Peace

Corps teacher must go his half by involving himself in the society in which he proposes to educate.

"The job as defined" is insufficient in a more general sense because the job is defined in a variety of ways or not at all. It is clear what subject is to be taught and how often. What is not always clear is content, methods, relation to students, and role in the school and the community. Peace Corps volunteers often feel different pressures and demands on them from students, headmasters, colleagues, Ministries of Education, and Peace Corps staff. These conflicts can be resolved only in "the job as *I* define it," and (given teaching competence as basic, but also given doubts about the needs for secondary education and whether the Peace Corps's mission is to a 5 percent elite, and whether a teacher can teach only in a classroom and out of a book) the volunteer may range as far afield as his judgment and mobility allow.

Finally "teaching is enough" is not enough until the Peace Corps volunteer experiences the total context of his assignment sufficiently to permit an intelligent decision as to where he can best apply himself. Far too often he finds himself checked or frustrated in his teaching but will not recognize wider and more imaginative opportunities for service. I defend the right of any Peace Corps volunteer to decide for himself the job in his situation, but that right follows the responsibility to explore his situation thoroughly. Otherwise it is a denial of growth and adaptation, and the question arises, "Who is serving whom?"

Having said some things a Peace Corps volunteer is not, I had better get on with what he is. Growth and adaptation are most of it—or flexibility if you prefer. But for what? To help other people meet needs. This is

(*Below*) In Ethiopia, the number of degree-holding secondary school teachers was doubled by the first 280 volunteers. Among them was Floyd Davis of South Norwalk, Connecticut, a graduate of Virginia Union University. He teaches chemistry and biology in Gore.

(*Right*) In Nigeria's nearly 300 secondary schools there are more than 500 Peace Corps teachers, such as Lucy Wallace of Mound, Minnesota, a graduate of Smith who teaches French at the University of Ife extension class in Ibadan.

PCV Bill Shurtleff, who taught physics in Nigeria, wrote after his first year:

"The most stimulating and rewarding hours here are those spent in the classroom; if my goal were to teach facts about physics this would surely not be true.

"But attempting to develop the ability in students to THINK, both analytically and creatively, and to find the real excitement in the process is far more of a challenge and in the long run, I feel, a much sounder way to approach the subject.

"Providing motivation to learn is no problem: every boy struggles to be at the top of his class in the school. Furthermore, they must pass the stiff West African School Certificate Examination.

"When I came here, the younger boys expected me to dictate notes to them which they would then memorize. The older boys were in the habit of writing down rough class notes and then recopying them after class, a very time-consuming process. Both habits had to go. With the younger boys, this meant letting them begin to work with their hands at simple experiments. These we would discuss and the boys were encouraged to ask and answer questions. The response was truly refreshing and most enjoyable for them."

By far the greatest number of Peace Corps teachers have been sent to Africa to teach in the government's secondary schools—equivalent to United States junior and senior high schools, like the Secondary School in Benue, Nigeria, where Willie Blair (*below*), of Humboldt, Tennessee, teaches. Willie has found that the biggest problem facing the students of the developing nations is their commitment to rote (*see above*).

And it is pretty much the same everywhere—in Katmandu, Nepal, where Dan Pierce (*above*) teaches physics, or in Jesselton, North Borneo, where volunteer Jesse Zellner (*below*) teaches. The volunteer teachers must overcome the students' reliance on outdated learning techniques.

what a volunteer is, isn't it? Where would the volunteer fireman be without any fires? Or the hospital volunteer without any bedpans the nurses can't get to? You say "I will" to a need when you think there is a chance you can help to meet it, and when you agree that it needs meeting and has priority for you. But in saying "I will" among strangers you must reconcile these two with a third consideration: what needs they want met. If you are in a strange situation, you will require a new understanding of what you are able to do and what the needs are—these may be different from your own familiar situation. So that in forming the Peace Corps, a modern, industrial nation has assumed that in the abundance of its trained manpower are individuals who can help to meet needs in underdeveloped countries, given their goal of industrialization and modernization.

Most Peace Corps teachers made the adjustment in Africa.

But of the Peace Corps volunteers I knew, I would say one-half had gone beyond their adjustment to an involvement with their situation in real friendships, projects, or a lively curiosity about local politics, art, or religion that brought them out of their jobs, their culture, and themselves.

And of this group, half again were sufficiently involved that they could be of service: that service which came from their own assessment of what they could do, what was wanted and what was needed in the situation. This assessment was the only way to balance all the various deprivations, duties, and diversions which were around them asking for their time. These were the effective volunteers. Whether they were successful depended somewhat on circumstance. But service attempted without this assessment was not service at all, but invariably things imposed, begun and unfinished, finished and unused, tried and abandoned, given up, wasted.

Extra classwork on the binomial theorem may be needed or it may not. A camera club may be needed or not. A latrine in the village may be needed or not. Or better staff relations, or flowers in the compound, or assistance at the dispensary, or basketball introduced, or a clean-up campaign. A specific activity can't be prescribed for volunteers in general. But in his own context, the volunteer will have priorities for service if he is sufficiently adjusted and involved to make an effective assessment of needs.

The question is not what a volunteer must do, but what he must be to serve.

Language proficiency is important. So are classroom and subject competence, and comprehension of local society. But beyond these, the volunteer's sensitivity, persistence, flexibility, and mature judgment in the situation are crucial to the possibility of service. The latter can atone for a lack of the former. The reverse, unfortunately, is not true.

Since most Peace Corps volunteers enter a new culture and a new job as green Peace Corps volunteers and young adults, they need to grow. The process of adjustment and involvement takes time, and the best volunteers cannot begin their service at once. The capability for growth is essential if Peace Corps volunteers are not to give up, hang on, and merely wait out their two years.

It is clear that training cannot. hope to make Peace Corps volunteers. Only growth in the overseas situation will make volunteers, and the situation cannot be anticipated. Training can try, however, to orient them to goals in acquiring skills and concepts relevant to overseas service, and to assess their resources for meeting these goals as a prediction of their performance overseas. The prediction can be valid only if their growth during training is in a context similar to that required overseas, generally speaking, a context where their motivation, resources, and support come from themselves. Set reasonable goals with the trainees' consent, and then force them to take responsibility for their own time and energy in meeting these goals, for the choice and use of resource materials and personnel. Only in this way can a training program bring out the sensitivity, persistence, mature judgment, and flexibility which, along with the potential for growth, are the crux of volunteering.

The selection process is then reversed: selecting people *in,* determining which of the intelligent, healthy, and obedient applicants have the additional resources necessary for being Peace Corps volunteers, instead of passing through an entire group with the exception of teaching incompetents or serious psychological cases who are selected *out.*

The overseas support given the resourceful volunteer is crucial. If the emphasis is placed upon his own assessment of the situation, he will need the stimulus of other experiences and wiser heads. A Peace Corps volunteer needs desperately to talk about what he is doing and explain the choices he has made. Contact with others through conferences, visits, or even reports will help him and stimulate growth in the difficult early months.

I do not feel that projects can be given this kind of field support by staff. But then I don't think this kind of training and selection process would result in large projects. If I am anywhere near right in my estimate of effective volunteering and effective volunteers, we are missing the boat 75 percent of the time. The hard truth is that we do not have an experience here for almost any college graduate with some motivation for it and no serious physical or mental handicaps, but one requiring special skills and qualities not, I fear, too common in this culture and this age group—nor probably in any.

—SAMUEL ABBOTT

PRETTY GIRLS:
The Peace Corps Has Its Share

Everybody remembers "falling in love" with the pretty young teacher at one time or another in their school days, and the boys who have Peace Corps teachers will no doubt face the same hazards—at least those who are taught by Lucy Wallace in Nigeria . . .

The News

Yesterday a new nurse came,
Today we have a visitor.

. . . or Ann Schmidt in northern Malaya . . .

. . . or Eva Ingle in the Philippines . . .

. . . or Mary Jo Dudley in North Borneo . . .

. . . or Carolyn Dukes in the Ivory Coast . . .

. . . or Natalia Forsyth in Nigeria . . .

. . . or Nancy Tanner in Santiago, Chile . . .

. . . or Judy Danielick in Iran . . .

. . . or Barbara Wylie in Katmandu, Nepal . . .

. . . or Charlotte Bailey in the Philippines.

117

Although most Peace Corps teachers teach the conventional subjects—especially math, general science, and English as a foreign language—they have taught everything from "Art to Zoology," as the Peace Corps recruiting brochure says and as the photographs on these next few pages confirm. In fact, the subjects the Peace Corps has taught, in addition to the ones mentioned above, are: commercial skills, physics, biology, chemistry, engineering, geography, history, home economics physical education, sociology, psychology, arts and crafts, literature, law, music, political science, teacher training, literacy, vocational education, French, library science, agriculture and animal science, drama, geology, geophysics, social studies, business administration, accounting, radio/TV, and electronics.

Bennet Oberstein tells what it was like to teach drama in Bahia (Salvador), Brazil.

When I announced my plans of becoming a volunteer, I got responses like:

"You're going in the Peace Corps to teach drama? You mean they need this? What's the Peace Corps coming to, anyway?"

It's well they asked. And believe me, everyone asked, from my fellow students and teachers to my family and friends, who, in the back of their minds, still nurse the hope that I'm using my job as a teacher of drama in the Peace Corps for something more socially practical and significant to the Brazilians.

Students of drama learn that action is a verb—"to win," "to convince," "to conquer." The Peace Corps has its verb of action, too, which I think is "to develop." Along with helping communities to develop better methods of agriculture, sanitation, and nutrition, we know that a truly developed nation is a nation that can express its ideas and has found its voice—a nation that has an art of its own. We are not here to "bring" art, but, in our own fields and in our own ways, to help develop the arts in Brazil.

Here in Bahia, it isn't as if art were a new concept. The oldest city in Brazil, Bahia, founded in 1549 as São Salvador de Bahia de Todos os Santos, could be

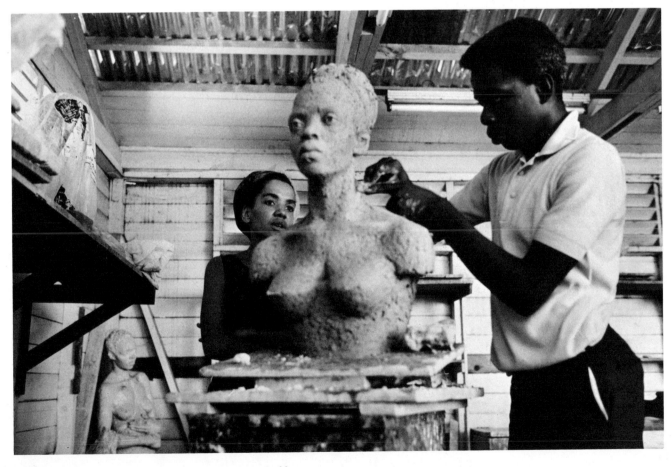

Requests for teachers to teach almost every conceivable subject have come into Peace Corps headquarters, and the Peace Corps has fulfilled as many of the requests as possible. For instance, at the Jamaica School of Arts and Crafts in Kingston, Volunteer Juanita Ballinger, of Indianapolis, taught a course in sculpture . . .

118

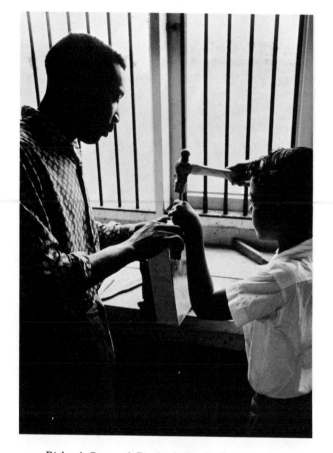

an art-lover's paradise. Heavily spiced with an African flavor (it grew prosperous through plantations worked by slaves) the city is characterized by the beat of *Carnaval* drums, the blazing blue of the sea, and the vivid colors of Bahiana *caraje* street vendors, which all serve to stimulate a regional art wholly spontaneous and as yet unstudied by American university art departments.

As for the local theatre, there seem to be more splinter groups in the area than in the Rye–Westchester–White Plains crowd. Each day I hear of another group —no director, no theatre, but somehow they want to do plays or pageants, or some other kind of dramatization. The dramatic instinct in Brazilians runs deep.

I came here as part of the Peace Corps university-teaching program. In my initial (and probably last) interview with the vice-rector of the University of Bahia, I discovered that he was a nutrition expert— that is his field and main interest, and I was started on my university theatre-teaching career with the inspiring words, "Send me a nutritionist!"

Since I had arrived two months before school was to start, I thought I had a good chance to find out about my courses and classes, meet students, and submit lesson plans and plays for the year. I learned my first big lesson: Nothing is done before *Carnaval*, or during *Carnaval*, or for a while after *Carnaval*.

When school did begin, I found nothing suitable for a Peace Corps poster: a beautiful white building with

. . . Richard Coger of Pineland, South Carolina, teaches metalwork in Belize, British Honduras . . .

. . . John Donohue, of Janesville, Minnesota, and a Mankato State College graduate, teaches music appreciation in Ethiopia . . .

... (*Above*) Muriel Michaud, a St. Joseph's College graduate from Lewiston, Maine, teaches secretarial training in Libreville, Gabon ...

... (*Below*) Joe Brown, of Tewksbury, Massachusetts, teaches an electrical class in Shiraz, Iran ...

polished marble floors, statuary, photographs of the Comédie Française, and a large stage (with no lighting equipment).

There were only forty students enrolled in the drama department. They go to school for three years, receive diplomas, and are automatically "actors." While this might amuse those in United States theatre, in Brazil, actors are really needed. It is not nearly as difficult to gain a foothold as an actor here as it is in New York, and the stages of Rio and São Paulo are filled with students who have been lucky enough to go to school, but who are neither trained nor, for the most part, talented.

While my efforts at Bahia are not exactly Actors Studio, I find a great satisfaction in watching students grow and make connections between things, just as there would be for teachers in any subject. However, they have rarely performed plays here. At times, there has been one in a year. Everyone talks wistfully about a production of *Romeo and Juliet,* which was rehearsed but had to be cancelled at the last minute because of a severely overextended budget. As for my question of why they didn't go ahead and do the play without em-

... (*Below*) in Jimma, Ethiopia, Casper Carlton, from Penns Grove, New Jersey, and Union College in Kentucky, teaches business administration ...

... (*Above*) in Ghana, Susan Bartholomew of Minneapolis, teaches classical ballet to the Obadzeng National Dance Company ...

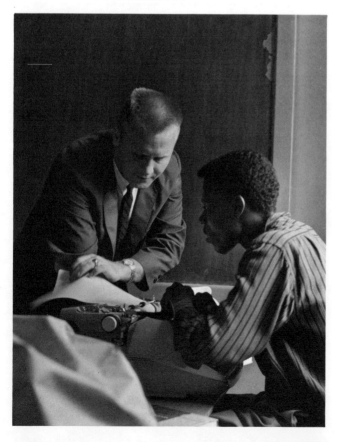

bellishments like costumes and scenery (Shakespeare doesn't get any royalties any more), I might just as well have asked why the school didn't sprout wings and fly to Greece. While waiting for manna from heaven—money from the *deus ex machina,* the rector, to do a complete production—they have done nothing at all. The students had no place to put into practice the things they were learning in class. Theatre, like anything else, can remain theoretical only so long. "The play's the thing."

This lack of a workshop, plus the abundance of people who seem to want to do something, has led me to what could be the successful blending of Peace Corps and community drama in Bahia. Against the objections of the school, which didn't want to keep the building open at night, and against the scorn of the splinter groups, which were supposed to loathe the theatre school, I have invited them all to participate in a grand studio theatre, spending exactly nothing and using no

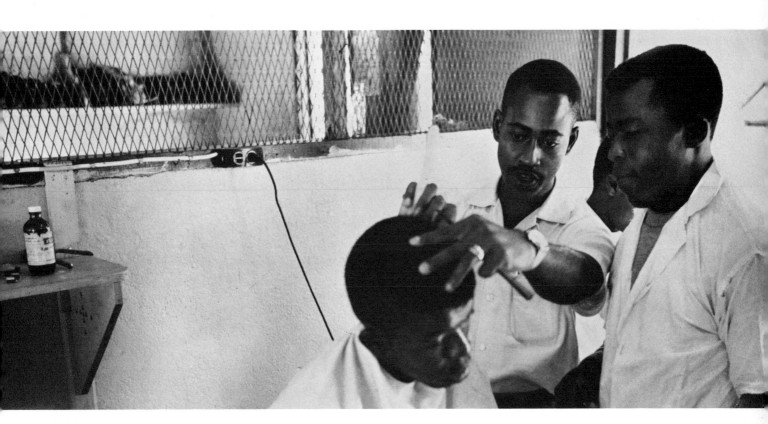

. . . (*Above*) In addition to barbering, Oscar Williams teaches cobbling and tailoring at a vocational training camp in Jamaica . . .

. . . (*Below*) in Malaysia, Hubert Jones, Dallas, Texas, teaches industrial arts and agriculture in a boys' school at Sungei Mangis . . .

costumes or scenery other than what they can dig up. We are rehearsing in classrooms or houses or whatever is available, whenever we can.

There are to be two evenings, repeated for a total of four; one will be *The Glass Menagerie* directed by me, and the other an evening of one-acts directed by three different people, two students and a member of one of the other groups. After this first project is over I intend to do less directing, since I am highly dispensable ("A Good Volunteer Is Never Indispensable," remember?). At least I hope to show that one doesn't need a mammoth and impossible budget to do theatre.

I have introduced some revolutionary concepts— among them grades, and, in courses about dramatic literature, examinations and work projects. Theatre usually comes under fire from administrators who are not devotees as being "unacademic." My attempt to reinstate drama as an academic subject at the University of Bahia has been greeted by various groans and protests,

. . . In Guinea, Linda Mintener (*above*), taught the flute at the National School of Music, and David Thurston (*below*) taught at a shoe repair school in his December vacation. He regularly teaches at the College of Commerce in Blantyre, Malawi . . .

mostly from the students, who complain of a lack of time—to work at outside jobs, visit the local pubs, and lie on inviting beaches.

In my work, I run up against the same sort of frustrations that are encountered by volunteers working in other fields, and use the same words to describe my problems in the theatre as volunteers in other occupations would use. My observations of the semantic gulf are no different from those of someone working on a farm in Mato Grosso or breeding chickens in Alagoas. The problem concerns words with an implicit value judgment. How far apart two people can be using the same word in a given situation—who is to say what words like "soon" or "now" or "clean" or "quick" or "slow" or "comfortable" mean? They mean something to me, but very likely something different to someone raised in another culture.

And I come in for my share of criticism. After all, I'm not teaching in the primary grades. The students are mature, many older than I am. Recently one said to me, "Have you come here to change our lives?" My mind went back to something I read in a Peace Corps recruiting brochure in the "days when": "No, not to change your lives; but not to leave them the same, either."

—BENNET OBERSTEIN

. . . Ruth Burns, sixty-four, of Lake Charles, Louisiana, taught home economics in El Salvador . . .

124

. . . Frances Butsavitch, from Detroit, taught square dancing at the Nakhom Patom Teachers' Training School in Thailand . . .

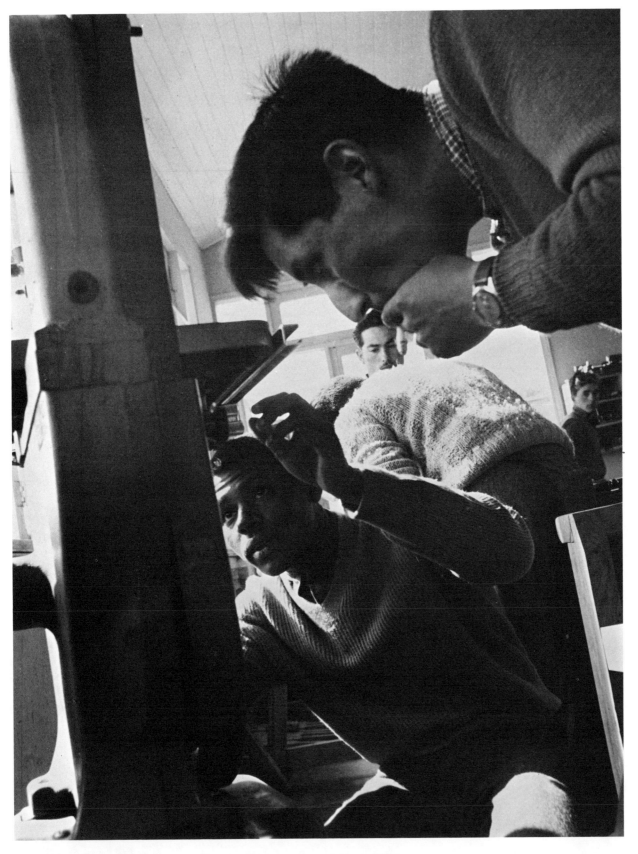

. . . and Wendell Gorum taught carpentry at a boys' school near Osorono, Chile.

Teaching with the Tube

One of the most exciting Peace Corps teaching experiments has been the Educational Television program in Colombia. Colombia was picked as the test country for Peace Corps ETV for several reasons—there is a national curriculum which every teacher has to follow; the Colombians all speak Spanish; there is a long-established system of free public education; also, the educational system needed reform. With ETV, it meant that a poorly prepared teacher would have the help of one of the best teachers in the country, and a good teacher would have access to a new, stimulating visual aid.

Although there have been problems, they have not been insurmountable, and the Colombian program has been considered a success. Today, eight geographic departments receive the broadcasts; the school audience exceeds 250,000 children in grades one through five. Subjects taught are social science, natural science, new math, language arts, and music.

Future plans are ambitious: Classes in literacy, public health and physical education will be offered; eventually the program will be expanded for the secondary schools. It is also hoped that someday the Colombian ETV program will be the training ground for all of Latin America. Pilot programs are already operating in Peru and Jamaica.

Volunteer Charles Ewing, from Tennessee, helping in a rehearsal of an ETV broadcast in Bogotá.

(*Above*) Volunteers Dan Acuff (*l.*) and Davil Murello install a television set in a rural Colombian school. Nancy Earle (*below*) an ETV "utilization" volunteer, from Youngstown, Ohio, shows Bogotá students how to use TV. Dean Gottehrer, a volunteer who worked in ETV in Colombia, said: "ETV has proven a number of things. A highly technical device can be used to gain entry to a society and an education system for the purpose of initiating reform. That reform, however, cannot be effected simply with the introduction of TV into a school; it must be followed up, and new teaching habits must be established. . . . Where the circumstances are right and the initial support is present, the road is open for deep and profound changes in educational methods."

And, of Course, Sports

Most of the developing countries are anxious to encourage sports as part of their public health program. Consequently, the demand for Peace Corps physical education teachers has been heavy, and as the following pages show, volunteers have taught just about every conceivable sport. The volunteers have found, as one of them put it, that "nothing communicates like sports—it's an international language."

Tex Lee Boggs, checking out a candidate for Thailand's Olympic team, teaches track at the College of Physical Education in Bangkok. Tex is from Pulaski, Virginia.

130

(*Above*) Daryle Russell, of Portland, Oregon, was athletic director at the Hailie Selassie University in Ethiopia.

(*Right*) David Merchant was a physical education instructor in Tanzania. He reports that of all the sports he taught the Africans, football was the most difficult for them to learn. They often confuse it with soccer, and try to bounce the football off their heads.

(*Opposite*) Karen Pederson teaches swimming at the Jubilee Children's Home in Malaysia. Many of the children are mentally or physically handicapped, and swimming is taught as a physical therapy.

(*Above*) Bob Gallagher of Orange, New Jersey, taught the national basketball team in the Ivory Coast.

(*Opposite*) Soccer is the most important sport in Afghanistan, where PCV Philip Needham of Weston, Connecticut, taught physical education at Kabul University.

And every American overseas is supposed to teach baseball! (*Opposite, below*) Bob Bartlett, of Salem, Oregon, shows the proper stance at the summer camp in Rabat, Morocco, where he taught.

(*Below*) Frances Winzurk, who taught Physical Education at the Meta Upper Primary School in Mbeya, Tanzania, measures the performance of a high jumper. As one ex-volunteer says: "Nothing communicates like sports—it's an international language."

Although more than 400 volunteers have been sent abroad to teach physical education, of the more than 12,000 volunteers who were overseas in 1966, more than half devoted at least a portion of their time to sports and recreation. And the reason is not hard to find. "My actual assignment was as a teacher of English as a foreign language," one volunteer wrote from Senegal, "but the director was convinced that all Americans are sportive, so I was drafted into teaching physical education."

Back home, in America, the job is over for the average teacher when the bell rings. But for Peace Corps vol-

unteers, their most important work is often just beginning when classes are over. "The job of the Peace Corps volunteer," says Warren Zeigler, a former regional director in Nigeria, "is to go in deeper and out wider; it is to be much more than a classroom teacher. . . ."

Naturally, the volunteers found sports to be one of the quickest ways to go in deeper and wider. "Sports is the best way I know to work your way into the community," says Chuck Butler, a former Stanford quarterback who served in Venezuela.

School may be over for Janet Bing of Kearney, Nebraska, who taught English in Baghlon, Afghanistan. But her job was just beginning.

Ray Brodeur, a physical education teacher in Venezuela, definitely found that baseball was the best way into the community. He played with four Venezuelan teams, including the *Penitenciaría General de Venezuela* nine. Above, he poses (*top row, left*) with the San Juan de los Morros squad.

Raymond Brodeur from Plainfield, Connecticut, received a B.S. in Mathematics from Central Connecticut State College in 1961 and an M.S. in Physical Education from the University of Colorado in 1962. He was a three-letter man in college—baseball, football, and basketball. Here he tells what it is like to play baseball with a Venezuelan prison team:

On Sunday morning, I rise at 8:30 and dress in the cleanest of the four baseball uniforms hanging in my room. They represent the four teams I've played with in the past year.

A short walk takes me to an Italian restaurant where my typical Sunday morning breakfast is served.

Two eggs, two chunks of white cheese, a bun, and two Pepsis later I'm ready to face the two-mile walk to the Penitenciaría General de Venezuela.

Once through the iron gate, I hand over my *cedula* (identification card) to a guard, put my hands over my head while another guard frisks me. A third guard leaning in a chair against a wall fondly handles his machine gun. Past the second gate, a walk leads me through a courtyard, then a lobby, through a third gate, and into the main area of the prison. I acknowledge the wishes of good luck from the prisoners clad in bright yellow uniforms as I continue toward the field.

As I move on to my left, prisoners surrounding a bingo table listen intently to the caller yell out the numbers. Another prisoner has a coffee stand in a corner. One prisoner selling popcorn thrusts a bag in my way; others hold up lottery numbers still available. A prisoner selling pool tickets on today's ball game moves through the crowd shouting.

I cut through a courtyard where several chickens and pigeons are pecking away at the ground. On one side, the small dingy cells can be seen through the screen enclosure. Underwear, towels, mirrors, calendars, innumerable items clutter the screen. One prisoner is shaving, another is making *alpargatas* (shoes worn by the poor), while a third is eating breakfast. A long row of communal sinks line the opposite side of the courtyard. Here women are busily washing their babies. As I approach the end of the sinks, three women nursing their latest children are sitting on the ground.

At the baseball diamond most of the players come over to exchange *abrazos*. My arrival is at game time, 10:00 A.M. This allows me from an hour to two hours of fielding and batting practice. The opponents,

136

whether from near or far, are always late.

During the wait, I take time out to bet two *bolivars* (44 cents) on the cockfight, which takes place punctually along the left field foul line. The prisoners, encircling the ring, watch intently, some complaining about their choice being a *flojo* (lazy one), and roar vigorously when one *gallo* (fighting cock) critically wounds the other. The owner of the loser appears close to tears as he walks away with his lifeless *gallo*.

Finally the game gets under way. I take up my position—a seat on the bench. Even though I am considered the prison's ace pitcher, the only other pitcher is a prisoner and has seniority rights. He is a short, dark-skinned, toothless, bushy-haired bank robber, who has failed to go beyond the fourth inning in fourteen consecutive games. My entrance, with our team anywhere from five to ten runs behind, is cheered by the captive audience, especially the announcer, who is the Mel Allen of the prisoners.

Possessing an enormous imagination and great love of his own voice, he has matter-of-factly blatted that I

played three years with the Pittsburgh Pirates as a pitcher and shortstop. He probably got this idea from the uniform I was wearing. On the back was written "Piratas," the name of the team I had been playing for in San Juan de los Morros. He increased my age by at least fourteen years when he said I fought during World War II. He also mentioned I was a personal friend of the late President Kennedy.

Since he found the pronunciation of my last name difficult, he replaced it with Brown. In one game I struck out seven batters in a row. He raved about this for the next three games.

His remarks are not confined solely to Raymond Brown. He describes players not statistically but by their physical appearance. He quickly points out that the batter is too fat, has very poor eyesight, and thus far has been playing a terrible third base. If a base runner is thrown out, he calls him a slow-footed mule. When he thinks the prisoner-umpire has made a bad call, he announces that the umpire has sold out to the visitors. In spite of all the jabber, he still finds time to

Michael Bailkin, of Philadelphia, teaches English in a neighborhood settlement house in Bombay, India—but he also teaches track.

plug "Gillette Super-Blues." He does this simply to identify himself with the professional broadcasters.

Needless to say, no game is complete without arguments. Venezuelans, like most Latins, argue for the sake of arguing. There are the usual number of arguments where both teams are shouting, waving their arms, and stomping their feet at each other. By the time the dispute has ceased, practically the entire audience—little kids, mothers, and passersby—have all managed to form a circle around the arguing players to get a closer view of the action. You would think only the team who received the raw end of the decision would argue with the umpire. Wrong again. The other team shouts at the umpire as if it were they who received the bad decision. They also argue to convince their rivals that the umpire is right.

The manager, who also plays, is decidedly the most interesting person to watch. His reasons for shifting and exchanging players are so intricate, they would baffle the greatest baseball minds. He's a scorer's nightmare. A typical managerial maneuver goes something like this:

Says "Chuck" Butler, former volunteer in Venezuela: "You can carry a soccer ball down the sidewalk of almost any Latin American town, and in no time you'll be followed by twenty kids who want to play," which Gene Adams found to be as true in British Honduras.

The third baseman makes an error on an easy ground ball, allowing a run to score. Immediately, the grandstand managers begin shouting "*Sacalo!*" ("Take him out!"). Now the shortstop yells at the third baseman for such a stupid error, waves his arms, threatens to quit if he isn't removed from the game. As is the Latin custom, the third baseman begins shouting back that it wasn't his fault. He points at the ground indicating a stone, or at his glove exhibiting a defect, so everyone can see. He's quite apt to blame the right fielder for his blunder.

During the noise the manager is already in action. He calmly walks over from his first-base position and ejects the completely innocent shortstop. He then gestures he will assume this strategic position, believing himself the most capable. His face now gives the impression that his next decision will be the most important of his lfe. With careful scrutiny, he selects a

Homer Brawley, from Morresville, North Carolina, learned to speak Thai, which was helpful. Not only did he teach agriculture at the Village Institute in Chombung, Thailand, he also coached basketball and refereed the games.

Bill Miller, of Portland, Oregon, teaches English as a foreign language in a secondary school in Rasht, Iran. After school he also teaches boxing.

140

bench warmer, pointing him to left field. Then with a wag of his finger, he has the old left fielder putting on the catcher's gear, the catcher trotting out to center field, the center fielder replacing the second baseman, who assumes the manager's former position. Why? *Quien sabe!* Content with his generalship, he proudly reports the changes to the umpire who then announces them to the wincing scorer.

My chances of winning games are meager. Nevertheless, I still look forward to the trips to the *penitenciaria* on Sunday mornings. As a diversion from my daily teaching, I find baseball, Venezuelan-prison-style, matchless.

—RAYMOND BRODEUR

But athletics are not the only way to go in deeper. (*Below*) Volunteers Stephen L. Allen (*extreme right in white shirt*) and Carl Olson (*left rear, wearing glasses*), two English teachers in Ceyhan, a town in southern Turkey, drop by the local coffeehouse every day for a chat and a game of backgammon. (*Opposite page*) Merry Lee Corwin of Hingham, Massachusetts, who teaches on Leyte Island in the Philippines, uses a guitar, music being every bit as good an international language as sports. (*Opposite, below*) Marion Hornbeck, a graduate of George Washington University in Washington, D.C., plays the harmonica for some students at the Mahasarakham Teachers' College in Thailand where she teaches English.

(*Above*) Elaine Opriska taught history, music, and drama at the Kachonag School in Uganda. Here she cheers her team along at a track meet, but she said, "the thing I need most here is a piano." (*Below*) Ernie Fox (*right*) and Sam Fisk, two volunteers who teach in Addis Ababa, Ethiopia, found that Bach seemed to appeal to their young friends in a Leprosariam, where they work in their spare time.

(*Above*) Bill Ilson, a teacher in Jamaica, used whatever was at hand, and (*below*) John Lavella, in Liberia, developed a certain renown as a fixer of minor wounds.

(*Opposite, above*) Marianne Fearn, who teaches in Ethiopia, goes in deeper with drama. She and another volunteer, John Coe, wrote the words and music for musicals which were put on at Jimma. Here she helps patch up a lion for use in Shaw's *Androcles and the Lion*. (*Opposite, below*) Murlene Dowding, of Farmington, Michigan, goes out wider with a folk dance with some of her students at the Mzuzu Secondary School in Malawi.

Ron Kuhl, who said that he didn't like the monotony and repetition of teaching English, also says that after school is when he really gets to know the people. Usually his house is overrun with children, and during the afternoon he usually drops by one of the Chinese *kadai* (general stores) where most of Tambunan's social life takes place. Here he pauses for the most universal ice breaker of them all—in this case, *tapai*, a local drink made from fermented rice.

146

Softball helps Ed Voirol, who teaches commercial subjects at a girl's parochial high school, establish contact in Belize, capital of British Honduras.

(*Opposite page*) And there is nothing like a walk on the beach after school. Ask Lois Fenzl, who taught in Chimbote, Peru.

African checkers does the same thing for Stephen Hirst of Miamisburg, Ohio, who teaches in Liberia.

(*Below*) But all is not fun and games. Jack Thomas, Theodore Rideout, and Steve Frantz, three volunteers who teach in the Somalia schools, help build school classrooms during their summer vacation; (*opposite page*) a group of volunteer teachers in the Philippines study Cebuano, the most widely used of the Visayan languages, in special classes held during the Christmas holidays.

(*Below*) Ron Kuhl, who opened this chapter, arriving for his 7:30 A.M. class, prepares for the next day's lesson. Being a Peace Corps teacher is hard, and, to Kuhl, sometimes boring work but he says it is worth it. "People who used to ignore me are beginning to talk to me about personal things," he told Peace Corps photographer Paul Conklin. "Now I'm just another person around here—nobody stares." This is the goal most Peace Corps teachers strive to achieve . . . this, and friendship.

(*Opposite page*) Volunteer Mary Hamomn with one of her young friends at the school for retarded children in Guatemala City, where she teaches and gives psychological tests.

Chapter 5

Community Development

In the opinion of many Peace Corps staffers, Community Development is the name of the game. Only one-fourth of the volunteers abroad today are engaged in projects specifically tabbed as community development—or action. But many volunteers who are in what the Peace Corps calls "structured" jobs—that is, teaching, health, agriculture, and so forth—are also considered to be community development workers. The Peace Corps has had difficulty coming up with a concise definition of Community Development primarily, it says, because the function itself is still in a stage of development. However, one Peace Corps publication attempts to define it as follows:

"Community development is a matter of convincing people who have never controlled their environment—and whose cultures haven't had the luxury of such control for hundreds of years, if ever—that they in fact can run the show.

"It is a process of bringing together people who live near each other and having them articulate their problems, choose solutions and implement them."

Despite the fact that it is a relatively new activity in the field of social development, more than 5,000 volunteers have gone abroad as community developers. And the letters back from some of the first volunteers reflect the extent to which the Peace Corps and the volunteers were feeling their way in the early days of community development. Here are two good examples:

From Louis Rapoport, who was in Masingbe, Sierra Leone:

During my childhood, the thought occurred to me

The early volunteers sent to Colombia were pioneers in community development. (*Below*) Volunteer Dan Dobbin of Lawrence, New York, works on a Barranquilla housing project in which 150 families eventually contributed to the construction of their own homes.

Community Development worker Winifred Boge of Denver, Colorado, serves in the school lunch program in Hyderabad, India. As one official in the Peace Corps's Far East Division says: "We have the conviction that every volunteer, whether in teaching malaria eradication or environmental health and sanitation, is a community development worker. Every volunteer is trained for CD and is expected to work at it while in the field."

that I didn't know how to do anything. But somehow, my shoelaces always got tied, my bed got made, and I survived in this practical world.

Then I went to the university, where I took subjects like Scandinavian Literature, History of Historians, Modern Slavic Literature, and Philosophy of Literature.

When I joined the Peace Corps, I was classified as a "generalist." As a man who could do absolutely nothing of a practical nature, I was slightly amazed when I met my fellow trainees for the Peace Corps "R.C.A." program in Sierra Leone. I honestly thought I would be working with computers or television sets before I learned the initials meant "rural community action." There were carpenters, masons, geologists, an architect —people you read about in books, unreal people, people who can (shudder) do things.

I tried to fake my way by dropping words like "hammer," "cement," and "wrench." But somehow, my clever plan failed, and I feared and trembled on Selection Eve. But I look like a very Sincere Friend of Man, and it's hard to get selected out of the Peace Corps if you're sincere.

In Sierra Leone, I was given a road project in Bombali district. I *Kriolized* (after Krio, the English-derived lingua franca of the country) my technical words —amma, c'ment, 'spana—dropped them expertly and waited for cheers and applause from my workers. Meanwhile, I read something called "How to Build a Bridge," and I built one (I'm still laughing).

When a new Peace Corps program was proposed— chiefdom development instead of specific construction projects—I was asked to begin a pilot program for the Northern Province. The director of the CARE–Peace Corps rural development program patted me on the back (after feeding me) and told me to go out and develop a chiefdom. It's easy to see why I was chosen for this mission: No one really knows what community development entails, and who is better qualified for an undefined project than an undefined person?

I packed my bags and moved to Masingbe, a town of about 2,300 people and headquarters of Kunike Chiefdom. Immediately after my arrival, I went to the highest point in the town to survey my new home: the huts of mud, wattle, and burlap; the fragrance of lilac, frangipani, and purple-tasseled flowers filling the heavy air—ah, sweet life. While I was gone my house was robbed.

In the weeks that followed I worked hard, dropping new words such as "cooperative," "social center," "adult education," "dispensary," and so on. I even pretended

Putting it the other way round, community developers can end up doing almost anything, such as supervising a school project in Souk el Arba, Tunisia (volunteer Lowell Sykes of Idaho Fall, Idaho) . . .

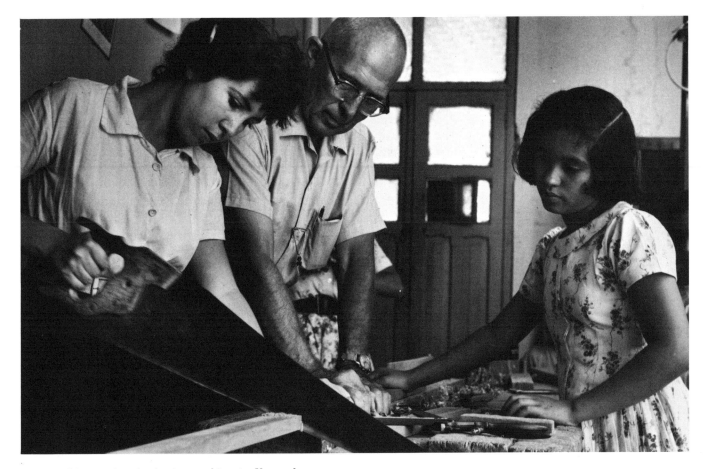

. . . teaching a class in furniture-making in Venezuela (*above*, 52-year-old volunteer Charles Pell of Grand Rapids, Michigan, and his wife, Hazel) or a kindergarten class in Panama City (*below*, Paulette Di Yanni, of Pittsburgh, who could pass for Lauren Bacall) . . .

to know the Temne equivalents: *kaw opaneh, nseth nim atui. . . .*

The number of projects I had going was ridiculous, and I would have needed to be a Renaissance Man to handle them all. But I bluffed my way; and my ingenious word-dropping scheme convinced at least some people that I am possessed of virtue, that I am a true "generalist" (that is to say, generally good in everything). And just as my shoelaces got tied, my projects, somehow, were completed.

—LOUIS RAPOPORT

From Tom Clark, one of the first Peace Corps volunteers assigned to Community Development. He served in Peru:

Let me tell you about what I do down here. I'm involved in a program of "Urban Community Development." I live in a giant slum, or *barriada,* on the edge of Chimbote, a city of 120,000 people. The movie *Black Orpheus* showed another *barriada,* more colorful but otherwise similar to mine.

My neighbors have come down from the mountains, attracted by the money and in hope of a better life. Because of a lack of marketable skills (for generations they have known only farming and grazing), they find it hard to get a job, and end up in unbelievable slums, with disease and starvation rampant. Largely illiterate,

and sometimes speaking Spanish only as a second language after their Indian tongue, they get almost no public service, and many of their rights aren't protected. The slums around Chimbote stretch for miles and miles, staggering the imagination.

My job is to get these people, my neighbors, organized, to make them better able to compete in the city for their rights, and to try and get them to raise their standard of living back to the human race.

I teach in the local school during the days, and I teach carpentry to adults at night. Both are important jobs but I consider them only a front. Teaching kids, while fun for me and hilarious for the rough housing students, is only an excuse for being in the *barriada.*

For example, our school has no roof. It would be a ten-dollar project and about one day's labor for two or three Peace Corpsmen to build that roof. Yet we don't do it. If we gave my school a roof, it would always be that—a gift, the *gringo's* roof. When it needed fixing, no one would fix it.

If it takes me a year to talk my neighbors into putting on that roof, it will be worth it. Because it will then be their roof on their school. It would be a small start, but in the right direction. Maybe then we'll take on a little harder project, and step by step build up a powerful organization that is interested in progress and strong enough to do something about it.

. . . working in the rural slums of Brazil (*opposite page*, Marie Hornbein of Kent, Ohio), or the urban slums of Caracas (*right*, Jerry Page of Denver, Colorado) . . .

It has to be an organization that doesn't need me, however; otherwise it would collapse when I leave.

In another *barriada* in my town, there are two schools side by side. One is a several-thousand-dollar complex with classrooms, meeting halls, and a medical clinic. It was built, brick by brick, by Peace Corps volunteers, laboring day and night for six months. Architects labored with social workers, pouring cement, laying concrete blocks, putting in lights and plumbing. It is now completed and in partial use. Peruvians call it the *"gringo* school." Not one Peruvian ever lifted a finger to help build that school, and it will crumble back to dust before one Peruvian will lift one finger to repair it.

Though highly touted in the United States press as another example of the Peace Corps in action, this school is an utter failure. Yes, there is a school there, and now kids can go to school, but what has it really done? Nothing. The building is just another example of Uncle Sugar with a great big Alliance for Progress sticker on it.

Next door to this complex stands a two-room school built of grass mats, without windows or lights, and with a dirt floor. It was built because the *barriada* grew and because classroom space was needed. The teacher, a Peace Corps volunteer, talked the parents of the stu-

dents into building those two rooms. The school was put up in one day. Volunteers only gave limited aid in construction. I consider the grass-school a success, and ten times more valuable to the community than the big complex it sits next to. Now the grass school is being replaced by another massive school, with Alliance for Progress money, but without Peace Corps help.

Even with the grass school gone, I still think it will remain a symbol to the *barriada* people of what they can do—working together.

A volunteer has to be careful, however, and not become too much of a leader. I have said, if I stir up all the action, what will happen when I leave? I hint at things and let my neighbors come up with the ideas, and I let them lead the action.

A really good Peace Corps program receives little credit. Keep that in mind when you read Peace Corps success stories.

This then, in short, is what I try to do in Barrio San Pedro. I have a lot of failures, few tangible successes, and a great deal of frustration. (I was a dreamer once, too, and my fall was hard.) Now, all things considered, I think I'm doing something worthwhile. I don't think I'll sign up for another stint, but you couldn't drag me away from this one!

—Tom Clark

. . . coaching a girls' basketball team in San Gregorio, Chile (Ida Chambliss of Reba, Alabama) . . .

. . . working in a slum housing project in Costa Rica (John Proctor of Richmond, California) . . .

THE CULLS IN MALAYSIA. While community development means many different things to different volunteers, depending on where they are serving, it also means many different things to individual volunteers in their particular community. Bill and Carol Cull, two Peace Corps volunteers in Malaysia, have learned the hard way what community development means in Asia.

Bill and Carol met while they were students at the University of California in Berkeley, and were married in 1962. Bill was graduated in 1963, with an A.B. in anthropology, then went to work briefly for the United States Public Health Service in San Francisco. Carol was graduated the following February with an A.B. in political science. They applied for the Peace Corps and were invited to train for a Malaysian village-development project at the University of Northern Illinois. They spent ten weeks at Northern Illinois, another month at the Peace Corps training camp in Waipio, Hawaii, then departed for Malaysia in May, 1964. They were assigned to Kampong Sungei Seluang, a small village of about five hundred people 15 miles inland from the island of Penang, near the northeast coast of the Malay Peninsula.

"Some days I just sit and talk . . . talk all day long. And I feel as if I've gotten somewhere if these people understand their own problems better."

Bill watches as two villagers construct a water-seal toilet.

(*Opposite page*) Bill and Carol with some of the men of Kampong. "I decided when I came to Malaya that I was not coming here to sell American culture, and I was not coming here to bring American values," Bill says. "I was coming here to help these people solve any particular problems they might have. . . . But we found the culture of the industrialized world is creating all kinds of problems and new values—so it amounts to the fact that the culture is changing anyway. What we are trying to do is help the change. We are generally using two approaches to community development here. One way is to have my wife and me do something, like building a model privy. Our neighbors see it, think it's a good idea, and try it themselves.

"A much better way is to find an 'innovator,' a villager who is willing to try something new. If his project is a success, his friends see it and realize that *he* did it—that the Peace Corps 'outsider' didn't have anything to do with it—and realize that they can do it too."

(*Opposite page*) Carol spends much of her time calling on the women of Kampong. "'Why are Peace Corps volunteers so big?' a housewife asked me, mentioning that Bill was a full head taller than any other man in the village.

"'One reason,' I said, 'is that mothers in the United States begin to feed their children solids when they are four months old, instead of waiting until they are a year old as you do here.'

"The conversation passed on to another subject. But within six weeks two mothers had started to feed their infants solids at four months. It was a miracle."

(*Above*) The Culls' metal roof house in the *kampong*; kitchen is at rear.

"A lot of the *kampong* kids come to the house after school to use our paperback library. I've been working with them on their English." Behind Carol is a life-size wooden statue of a Malayan man.

(*Opposite page*) "About six months ago we took a villager to a neighboring town to see a chicken cooperative. The one condition we put on the trip was that he would tell his friends what he had seen.

"Three days after the visit he came to our house to tell us that seven families were interested in starting a chicken cooperative, and that each was willing to invest $25. Now there are ten families in the project. They have built a hen house and a brooder. Another hen house will be started in a few weeks, as they already have too many chickens for the first one.

"The families really have become a working group capable of developing projects on their own—this is the important thing, not the chickens. The group feeling has already expanded into several home improvement projects like the construction of waste drains for kitchen water.

"That cooperative developed a spirit so strong that when the *kampong* headman asked if he could invest in the project he was turned down. The members said they wanted people who would work in the project, not investors.

"The next step," he said, "will be to carry the ideas started in this village to other neighboring villages in the district."

Carol became "the local nurse by default. It's all for minor cuts and bruises—the type of thing anybody would take for granted in the United States. But our medical kit gets depleted pretty quickly." (*Above*) The patient arrived at 6 A.M. for treatment of a cut thumb. Carol's other jobs include introducing nutritional foods to buttress the rice-based diet, and talking to village women about family planning.

166

Community development can also mean simply sewing. Marian Cast is from Beaver Crossing, Nebraska, and was graduated from the University of Nebraska the year before she went off to Morocco to work in a community development home economics project. With volunteer Marlene Mansk, she works in one of Morocco's eleven Women's Centers developed to improve the status of women in the country's modernizing Islamic socity. The project is a joint Moroccan–United States–United Nations venture. Marian's job is to teach home economics to about twenty teen-age girls. She also teaches in a nursery school.

Marian also visited the women in their homes because many "are too busy to come to the *foyer* (*center*), or their husbands may not permit them to come."

The homes are usually paper-covered wooden one- and two-room structures with a straw house next door for a kitchen. There are few cement buildings in Ain-el-Aouda,

where she works. "I try to feel out the community's needs and problems and pass them along to the *caid* (mayor)," she says, "And I tell the women to come to 'Ladies' Nights' at the village television set." (Marian was one of three persons in the town who had permission to turn the set on or off—a position of great respect.)

"Making clothing is one of our basic jobs. Since there are no printed clothing patterns in Moroccan villages, I have made literally hundreds of patterns ranging from dresses to underclothing, men's shirts and slacks.

"Fortunately, Moroccans aren't too particular about fit. The material may be old or new, and many times measurements are made by mere guess from descriptions—fat, thin, tall, short."

A-frames in Sierra Leone

In Africa and to some extent Asia, Community Development volunteers are more likely to end up working on specific, organized projects, such as the construction of roads and schools, which are part of the national government's own development program. Below, volunteer Truman E. Howell, Jr., of Raytown, Missouri, tells how Peace Corps community developers helped solve Sierra Leone's shortage of schoolrooms.

When Group V volunteers (generalists in construction) arrived in Sierra Leone in May, 1964, several of us became involved in trying to help solve a pressing problem: shortage of primary schools.

The need was to build schools, build them quickly, and at a low cost.

What was required was a school-building design that could be reproduced throughout Sierra Leone. After traveling over the country and studying the local buildings, we struck on an idea based on the farmer's *shimbek*.

The *shimbek* is a temporary structure that is placed in the fields for the farmer and his family to live in while farming that plot of land. It is made of bush

Norman Tyler, Benton Harbor, Michigan, helps to build Sierra Leone's first A-Frame structure, a school near Kenema. It was patterned after the farmer's shimbeck, a temporary dwelling the farmers use when they move to the fields.

Mike Bradbury, New Milford, Connecticut, helps mix cement. The rough stone walls had to be completely smoothed over with cement because the Sierra Leones did not like the rough surfaces.

poles lashed together and erected in the shape of a pup tent, then covered with palm leaves to keep out the rain. With this as a start we designed an A-frame building (after a design often used in United States churches and vacation homes), confident that the design would not be a radical departure from what was already a common structure here. The model was 32 feet wide at the base by 40 feet long, with the apex about 25 feet above the ground. The sides, at a 60-degree angle, were covered with corrugated metal on 2-by-12 timber frames 8 feet on center and purlins (horizontal roof beams) at 4 feet on center.

Every eight feet along the sides an opening of 4 by 6 feet was designed to provide ventilation and light. Above each opening was a sheet of 2 by 6-foot corrugated fiber glass to give additional light. Ventilation was increased by a raised section of metal at the apex. We had two basic concerns about the design of the structure—both had to do with the large amount of metal that would be needed. First, would the large area of metal cause overheating inside the building? Secondly, would the metal amplify noises caused by the torrential rains of Sierra Leone? Both worries proved unwarranted, as we had designed these problems out of the building. The extra-large openings on the sides for ventilation solved our heat problem, and the steep

slope of the metal allowed the rains to hit at such an angle as to make the noise minimal.

To finish the building, we would place local stone on the end walls up to a height of 10 feet; above the stone, bush-boards (rough-sawn wood) would be placed in a board-and-batten fashion. The side openings were also to be given shutters made of the local bush-boards. These final touches would give a textural and color relief to the stiff and somewhat monotonous metal.

When the design was completed, it was shown to all the local men of note, from area-government officials to the paramount chief of the chiefdom in which the building would be constructed. All of these men showed great enthusiasm for the first A-frame in Sierra Leone. A great future was predicted for the building. Other structures were envisioned using this same design—schools, hospitals, dispensaries, and warehouses. An immediate start on construction was urged. The town of Naima, in the Eastern Province, was selected for the first building.

Two volunteers, Mike Bradbury (New Medford, Connecticut) and Norman Tyler (Benton Harbor, Michigan), were given the job of supervising construction, which began early in June, 1964. The voluntary labor force was large; about two hundred people came to the site daily from the surrounding villages to help with the school. Within two weeks the people had put in the foundations and the footings for the entire building.

A shortage of materials delayed work periodically, and we failed to meet the self-imposed two-month deadline. Still, within ten weeks the main structure was completed, and stones were gathered for the walls at the ends of the building. Bill Atkins (Rockland, Massachusetts), a volunteer bricklayer, moved in to give our helpers a few lessons in stone masonry. In two days he helped put up a good portion of the wall, and then returned to his own project. Suddenly we noticed the labor force was getting smaller and smaller. It was necessary to have the chief remind the people that more workers were needed. Finally, after three months under construction, the stone walls were completed and the board-and-batten started above the stone. Without notice, one day we were without workers. Even the prodding of the chief became ineffective. All of us, including the chief and other local authorities, were completely baffled. A week passed, then another. Still no workers. Finally, the chief called for Mike, Norm, and me, and explained the difficulty. To the people, the end walls of stone and wood were distasteful. Their complaint was that the walls were too rough, quite unlike the smooth surfaces of the mud on their homes. The board-

and-batten also met a similar fate. The appearance to the people, instead of being a textural and color contrast, was one of untidiness. Though we talked and talked and proved and reproved the structural soundness and economic advantages of using these local materials, as well as explaining our aesthetic reasoning behind using the stone and wood, we could not change their ideas. Objections had not come from the "big men" of the area, but rather from the workers on the project. We were surprised and deflated.

The board-and-batten was removed to be replaced by metal, and the stone walls were covered both inside and outside with cement, making a smooth wall. The building is now completed at a cost of about $1,100 ($300 over the projected cost) and ready for occupancy.

In retrospect we find that we have learned a great deal both from a construction-technique standpoint and from dealing with different aesthetic values. Specifically, we have found that it is imperative in a project such as a school to get the construction done rapidly so that interest can be maintained, to have materials on the site to make this goal possible, and to make sure that the materials and the design of the building are suitable to the people involved.

—TRUMAN E. HOWELL, JR.

Former Boston bricklayer, Bill Atkins, who worked on the Sierra Leone school buildings, sits out a cloudburst with some of the villagers working on the project.

Bradbury helps nail the last few sheets of metal on the roof. The volunteers at first were worried that the metal roofs would make the rooms too hot, but side ventilation solved that problem.

Latin America: Where the Community Action Is

The most typical, and the greatest concentration of Community Development programs are in Latin America, where the people of the barrios *and urban slums are often cut off from their government. Here volunteers work with community leaders trying to get them to define and recognize their most immediate problems, then providing the spark which will hopefully initiate a community solution. If successful, the end result of community development in Latin America will be to make a community out of a group of people who formerly just happened to live near one another. And once people see what they can achieve acting together, who can say where such a revolutionary—to them—idea might lead?*

Throughout the world, but especially in Latin America, the community developers are working with the roots of social change. Below, two volunteers, in describing their Peace Corps experience, tell what community development meant to them. William Krohley, who is from Huntington Station, New York, and received his B.A. in philosophy from the University of Rochester, wrote from Brazil:

Sooner or later someone is certain to puzzle out a formal definition of urban-community development. Out of his garret and into the sun he'll come bandying his sheet of convoluted prose only to be greeted with a recent erasure in *Webster's New Collegiate.* Exactly what he'll find where urban-community development once stood is hard to say, perhaps something like "better burg breeding" or "coached community commotion" or any one of a thousand possible locutions which would shed an aura of respectability on an undertaking whose very nature suggests a lurking, sleight-of-hand presence. In short, to define a phrase which expresses the workings of an idea in the hands of hundreds or perhaps thousands of people is to ignore one of its most salient features—mysterious happenings—and commit it to an orthodox fate.

Brasilia Teimosa, with a population of about 10,000, is a *barrio* of Recife in the northeast of Brazil. One of its perennial problems is the ruin of its roads during the four-month rainy season. During this period, from

May to August, the rain becomes a way of life, often falling continuously for several days. Fishing becomes sporadic, and all but indoor workers are forced to sit and do little but watch the steady downpour turn the sand and dirt roads into rivers of mud that settles in low spots and is churned into black muck by traffic.

Jim Lail (Lexington, Kentucky) and I talked with many of the local citizens about the roads and found a real desire to get something done. Several informal meetings were held to discuss the problem, and it was decided to see what a group of residents could do working in conjunction with the city government. The people were willing to perform necessary labor if the government would supply the equipment needed. The planning took about six weeks, and what started as a small group of ten men turned into a nebulous affair involving suddenly revived organizations dedicated to *desenvolviment das ruas* (street development), an unlimited supply of idea men, well-wishers, and skeptics and the prompt attention of an incumbent councilman running for reelection who arrived with trucks and work crews, and began spreading sand with a flourish. This latter measure worked well on the less-traveled streets where the sand wasn't pushed out of the holes, but the widely used streets and intersections remained impassable. The situation worsened daily as the families living on these streets shoveled away the few remaining high spots to build dams to keep mud out of their homes.

Somehow the mud had to be drained and the particular stretch of road leveled and then covered with a packed layer of sand. We worked with some of the families concerned and suggested that they petition the city for a small bulldozer that could work in the narrow streets. The city didn't have one. There were, of course, a number of firms in the city which sold just the machine needed. Money was no object; there wasn't any. So maybe we could borrow a bulldozer and advertise some company's product. We thought it was a good idea. Most of the firms didn't.

After a series of conversations with incredulous salesmen, which usually ended in helpful directions to the offices of nearby competitors, we finally got a machine

The day begins for community development volunteer Elizabeth Plotkin in a hillside slum outside of Rio de Janiero, Brazil. The city can be seen in the distance below.

and a driver who could come out to Brasilia on the first rainless Sunday. The men lived on the job site, so getting them together was no problem. But it always rained on Sunday. One Sunday in mid-June, however, Brasilia Teimosa reposed under clear skies; it was not raining. It was urban-community-development time.

First: Drain the mud before the arrival of the bull-dozer. There was one family which had a front yard large enough to dig a drainage pit in. The *dona da casa* (woman of the house) thought it would be all right. The hole was dug along with a trench to the mud; the trench was opened and the mud began to flow. Enter *don da casa*: "What is going on here?" It was obvious. His yard was being filled with black mud. He had been away, out of touch, and thus the logic of urban-com-munity development was a complete mystery to him. The ensuing confusion ended the moment the mud ceased to flow; what can one say to a yardful of mud?

The project proceeded and was eventually completed as the dozer came to level the road, and the councilman came to dump two truckloads of sand for the workers to spread and tamp. The drained mud dried in the sun and was covered with sand, and urban-community-de-velopment gained another adherent. Sunday came to a close. The workers congratulated themselves on a job well done; the councilman busily shook hands, and the Peace Corps volunteers went for a beer.

The following Sunday, we would tackle the next stretch of road, rain permitting. It didn't.

—WILLIAM KROHLEY

Ed Cheira, of Lakeville, Connecticut, and a graduate of Hobart College, wrote from Bolivia:

The old city of Sucre, the constitutional capital of Bolivia, is a community of 60,000 people located in a subtropical region of this Latin American republic. I arrived here in January, 1964, ready to go to work.

After a few weeks of being shown around the city by departing volunteers, I realized there was no job wait-ing for me to take over. Remembering that training maxim which holds that volunteers must be resourceful and imaginative, and that often they create their own jobs, I arrived at the idea of starting a community-education program in the neighborhoods of Sucre, pat-terned after that of the Puerto Rican Department of Public Instruction, which I had worked with during training.

One day I was introduced to Angel Paniagua, a medi-cal student at the local university, who helped me make initial contact with people in Villa Charcas.

As we walked up to the *barrio,* Angel told me its brief history. It was a newly inhabited area; the people of the neighborhood were mainly masons and day la-borers; they lived in one-room adobe houses; a family's average annual income was a hundred dollars, and so forth. What I found especially interesting was that sev-eral years back the people had formed a neighborhood council on their own initiative. They had started on community-development projects, relying solely upon their own voluntary efforts and cash contributions. Even though this self-help project failed, after the ini-

174

tial burst of enthusiasm waned, at least they had tried, and that was an encouraging sign.

Don Román, president of the neighborhood council, greeted me warmly. When he heard that I had come to Sucre to work with the people of the *barrios,* he said: "We have many problems, *Señor.* The people are indifferent. But with your guidance, we can overcome this."

After Don Román had showed us around the neighborhood and explained its problem, I accepted his invitation to attend a council meeting that was scheduled the next week. Angel and I then walked back to the center of town and stopped at a sidewalk café for a cup of Bolivian espresso coffee. As we sat down at a small table, some of Angel's friends came over to meet this new *gringo.* They were amused at my *barrio* development plan.

One student argued, "You're wasting your time, Eduardo. Those people don't know what their problems are and don't care. Of course, you're an American

with a lot of money, so perhaps you can build them a better community."

These words infuriated me, but I controlled my anger and told him, "These people do know what their problems are, and they care. Naturally, they don't view such things as the lack of latrines or poor nutrition as problems as we see them. But if these people are going to take pride in their neighborhood, they will have to deal with these needs as they themselves sense them. The right to decide what is 'good' for their community is theirs, not ours. Furthermore, as an American, I will not obtain outside aid. If the people cannot resolve their problems with their own material resources and with their own hands, the task will not be done."

The student laughed, saying: "You *gringos* are too idealistic. No one can work with those Indians."

Maybe I was too idealistic, but I had to prove him wrong.

For months I attended council meetings in Villa

En route to the clinic where she spends her mornings, Elizabeth pauses to talk with some of the children in her *favela.*

Charcas. The neighbors discussed and planned how they would improve their community, but nothing came of it. I patiently guided them toward discussing one small project, the installation of a first-aid station. Monica Shutts (West Palm Beach, Florida), who also attended those meetings, suggested that they have a raffle to raise money for the drugs and medicine cabinet. The neighbors accepted the idea and decided to hold the raffle on the saint's day of the *barrio*. The first prize was a baby pig; other prizes were a few hens, some household brushes that a blind man in the neighborhood made in his small shop, and some ceramic pictures.

Everyone in the *barrio* bought chances, and on the day of the raffle they anxiously awaited to see who would win the pig. The blind man's son won the first prize, and with a big grin, he carried the squealing

animal back to his father's adobe hut.

The raffle was a big success, not only because the neighborhood had raised twice the amount of money that was needed for the installation, but primarily because a new community spirit had arisen. After a short while the first-aid station was completed. The result was that Villa Charcas had accomplished its first self-help project.

About that time, two new volunteers, Art Hansen (Clinton, Iowa) and Tina Hughes (Culver, Indiana), joined us. Art started work in San José, a *barrio* mainly inhabited by carpenters and their families. In a few months, he got the people to solve their principal problem, the lack of public water. Feeling the competition from Villa Charcas, which had now completed its second self-help project, the installation of public water faucets, and had started on its third project, the con-

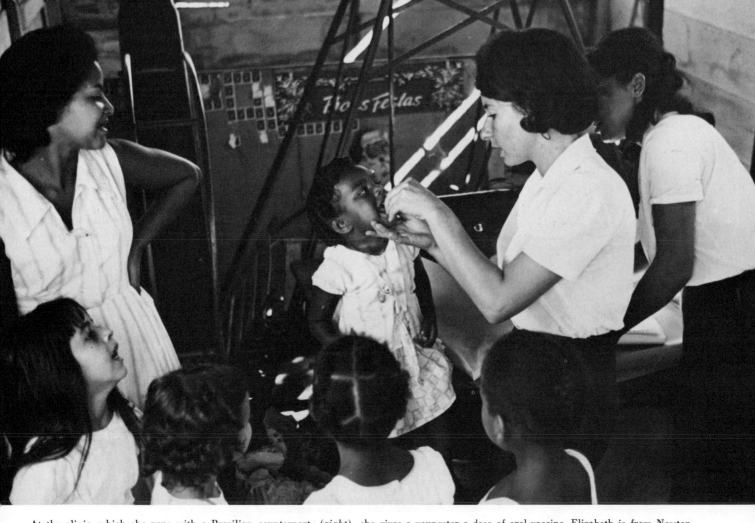

At the clinic, which she runs with a Brazilian counterpart (*right*), she gives a youngster a dose of oral vaccine. Elizabeth is from Newton, Massachusetts.

struction of a public showers building, the residents of San José raised funds among themselves to buy pipe and install a water system. Other *barrios* followed suit. After several months of meetings that were conducted in the Quechua dialect, the citizens of Avenida de Ejército united to repair a small chapel. San Cristobal built a well to supply all of its thirty-two families with water.

Our work was countering the skepticism shown by the aristocratic sector of Sucre's society. The community-education program had grown to include many Bolivian organizations. We now had public-health classes, recreation, credit unions, 4-H clubs, community-development films, and literacy classes. All of these were being integrated into the daily lives of the *barrio* people. We may have been idealistic *gringos*, but it is possible to work with "those Indians."

ED CHEIRA

Joan Marasciulo was a volunteer in Jamaica before she went to Brazil as an Associate Peace Corps Representative. Below she tells about a group of women volunteers who worked in the slums of Brazil:

In August, 1963, twenty Peace Corps volunteers, all

women in their twenties, arrived at the Brazilian state of Guanabara to take up duties as health and community-development workers in the *favelas* (slums) of Rio de Janeiro.

At last count there were 232 *favelas* in Rio, and approximately 25 percent of the population of the city, or more than a million people, live in these *morros* (hills).

When the volunteers arrived there was much speculation as to whether they would be able to work and live in the *favelas*, since they were said to contain the largest segment of the criminal population of the state. A Brazilian woman official objected to the volunteers' request for housing in the *morros*, since "only two kinds of single women live in *favelas*—nuns and prostitutes."

Brazilian doctors, nurses, social workers, and other hospital and health-post personnel with whom the volunteers were working raised their eyebrows and voices in horror at the prospect of female volunteers going in these "dens of iniquity." The Brazilian families with whom the volunteers had their initial home stays refused to accept even the idea of such a possibility.

Nevertheless, the volunteers—undaunted by the fears expressed by all—managed after two years not only to work in the *favelas* in their areas of assignment, but obtained or had built for them, houses in Parada de Lucas, Borel, Salgueiro, and Tuiuti.

• In Borel, where the Association of Laborers was predominantly leftist, and where no organization or group had ever been accepted, the association presented to the United States Embassy a petition, signed by almost every literate member of the community, asking that the two volunteers who had lived and worked there during their tour be permitted to extend for another two years.

• In Parada de Lucas, two of the volunteers who lived there were appointed to the Association of Laborers' Council.

• In Salgueiro two of the volunteers who lived and worked there danced with the Escola de Samba during *Carnaval*. The Escola in this particular *favela* constitutes a governing body of the community. . . .

Sub-health posts were established and conducted by volunteers in a number of the *favelas*. The first group of dental assistants was trained by a volunteer, and a manual for dental assistants translated and planned for use throughout all of Brazil as a result of her work. A

In the afternoon Elizabeth works with recreation groups. Here she talks with a young boy making a kite out of some hillside debris.

177

purse industry was organized and is still operating as a result of the efforts of another volunteer. The first Girl Scout troop was established in a *favela*. These are but a few of the many accomplishments of the volunteers.

At a recent meeting of regional administrators, doctors, nurses, and other supervisors, the Peace Corps liaison officer for the Secretary of Health of the state of Guanabara stated that two years ago, when the Volunteers of the Guanabara Health Project arrived in Rio, the Brazilians never realized so much could be accomplished through the work of the Peace Corps. He went on to say that the volunteers had proved their potential and possibilities, that they went way beyond the host-country agency's expectations. This had all been

accomplished through tremendous spiritual, cultural, and physical strain on the part of the volunteers.

All of this sounds like an unqualified success story. It would take too many pages to list the failures, disappointments, and frustrations suffered by the volunteers; and the details of heat, garbage, open sewers, mud, knifings, robberies, rats, fleas, and sweat. The original group of twenty volunteers has departed Guanabara, after a job well done. A group of thirty-four new volunteers is continuing the work, and has branched out into other areas of the state. Although everyone said it couldn't be done, these volunteers of the *favelas* proved it was possible.

—Joan Marasciulo

A soccer game is under way in the background as Elizabeth talks with some of the mothers in her *favela*.

178

"Apathy, ignorance, and disorganization are the things we want to eliminate in cooperatives, community development, education, and in all of the areas in which we work. Clearly no volunteer can hope for absolute success, nor can he even expect limited success to come easily. In many ways the life of the volunteer who sincerely seeks to effect progress is miserable. That may not seem to be a very hearty recommendation for the Peace Corps, but if we as enlightened people ignore the moral and economic poverty of the unenlightened, we really slight the challenges and needs of the modern world."

—Robert Rupley, from a letter to a friend, January 28, 1965. Rupley, a former volunteer who became a staff member, died February 19, 1965 in Caracas, shot by police who mistook his vehicle for one driven by terrorists.

Late in the day she and co-volunteer Marcyanna Orzelek of Watertown, New York, stop in at the neighbor's to visit and play with the children. But the day still isn't over for Elizabeth. In the evening she gives classes in adult literacy.

Chapter 6

Agriculture

With the world's population increasing at the rate of over 2 percent a year, 10,000 people dying every day of starvation or malnutrition, and with more than half of the world's 3.2 billion people living on the brink of hunger, it is not surprising that the Peace Corps has a great demand for agriculture workers. As with the other "technicians" that the Peace Corps had hoped to provide the developing world, volunteers from the agricultural colleges or with farm backgrounds did not materialize in great enough numbers to meet the demand. So, although a good many volunteers do have a background of 4-H club, childhood on a farm, or agricultural college, of the more than 1,500 agricultural volunteers either overseas or in training at the beginning of 1967, the great majority were liberal arts graduates to whom the Peace Corps, as one of its brochures put it, provided "the green thumb free of charge." Having developed the technique for training generalists in agricultural extension, and in light of the great demand for farm technicians, officials are now predicting the number of agricultural workers in the Peace Corps will equal the teachers and Community Developers by 1970.

In general, the "hunger fighters," as the Peace Corps public affairs department calls the agricultural volunteers, are not word men and women—they do not write

In most countries where they are active, Peace Corps agriculturists are not there to teach highly mechanized, American farm techniques. Rather, they attempt to make local farm techniques more efficient. At the Kolo Agricultural School in Niger, Philip Westra, of Randolph, Wisconsin, organizes and directs all fieldwork done by students, including how to care for oxen and the use of oxen-drawn equipment.

180

One of the main objectives of the agricultural worker is the changing of centuries-old attitudes. (*Above*) Willie Douglas, from Tampa, Florida, talks about up-to-date cultivation methods with his agricultural students at a rural "pilot high school" in Katlang, Pakistan, near the Afghan-istan border. (*Below*) Stuart McKenzie talks with Bedouin farmers on an experimental farm on the edge of the Sahara in southern Tunisia. Stuart is from Grandview, Washington. He and his wife, Connie, both agricultural extension agents, live on the 11,000-acre farm called Ouled M'Hamed.

long, sensitive letters home about their experiences, as the teachers and, to some extent, community development workers are likely to do. But there have been some who have attempted to put their experience in words. Moritz Thompsen, for example, whose account of his Peace Corps training experience appeared in Chapter 3, wrote of his experience as an agricultural worker in Ecuador: "I had one secret reservation: 'Dear God,' I prayed, 'don't let them send me to a country where I have to eat dogs.'" They didn't.

About six days after arriving in Ecuador as a new Peace Corps volunteer, I finally got to see a real live volunteer in action, and began to get some small idea of what was involved.

I lived for ten days with Byron Dahl, an old volunteer from Iowa, in the town of Cariamanga just north of the Peruvian border. I followed him around as he worked in the town and in the small rural centers in the hills where the farmers gathered together at the church or in a classroom on the days when they were to meet with the agricultural extension people.

We inoculated pigs against cholera, introduced and planted new types of vegetables in community gardens, gave talks on sanitation and animal nutrition. We visited small farms on the rocky slopes above Cariamanga.

There we showed the farmers how to delouse pigs with old crankcase oil, and how to treat sick baby pigs

with penicillin. We hauled coffee out of one mountain valley for a farmer who had neither a wagon nor a mule.

We spent a morning outside the town at a community garden that Byron had started after months of the hardest kind of sell. Finally, not because they believed in a garden or saw the need of one, but simply because they were tired of the pressure and because they liked Byron, the farmers planted a small plot of onions, lettuce, radishes, tomatoes, and cabbage at the bottom of a piece of steeply sloping communal land.

Everything grew beautifully; the farmers were delighted to have a change from the steady diet of corn, rice, yucca, and potatoes.

They had tripled the size of the garden at the next planting, and the day we were there bringing them new seeds, there were about twenty farmers working in the beds, staking tomatoes up or weeding, and another group was breaking sod to make the garden even bigger.

They were very excited and proud; now they planned to raise enough cabbage so that they would have a surplus, a cash crop to sell in the market at Cariamanga. Byron, listening to them, decided that they were on the way at last, and instead of giving them the seed this time, he charged them for each package.

Strangely, now that they had to pay for the seed, they even bought packages of a new type of lettuce that they had been unwilling to try when the seed was free. Byron

In most emerging nations, the farmers lack the equipment and management necessary to develop efficient dairy herds. (*Right*) In East Pakistan, volunteer Bob Taylor, of Oakdale, California, set up a model dairy farm at Comilla and worked to increase milk production.

In many areas of the world, diseases which have been under control for years in more advanced agricultural areas still take a staggering toll among farm animals. (*Above*) Harold Detrick, of Horsham, Pennsylvania, works with his El Salvadorean counterpart vaccinating a team of oxen . . .

turned the money over to one of the newly formed boys' clubs.

But the most exciting was the day we delivered two feeder pigs that Byron had picked up in Quito from our Heifer Project[1] organization for a group of farmers who lived about ten miles out of town. Before the pigs were delivered, the group had been coached in a series of weekly meetings on the necessity of a balanced diet, and a warm, dry place for the pigs to live, and the farmers had agreed to build a proper shed.

They had done a beautiful job, constructing a two-room building with an outside pen, all of it of adobe and tile, complete with a cement feeder and waterer.

We drove out one morning with the extension agent in his jeep, the two pigs each tied in a gunny sack, and both of them furious at the indignity of the situation. About forty families were waiting for us at the pigpen.

It was not a town we went to but simply an open

[1] Heifer Project, Inc., is a nonprofit organization maintained by private donations in the United States. It is a plan to get pure-blooded animals onto farms and into the hands of farmers all over the world. The aim of Heifer is not only to get animals of fine breeding into the countryside but to emphasize that without proper sanitation, proper management, and proper nutrition, the finest of animals will go to pieces and end up looking like hell.

place on the slope of a great mountain—a one-room schoolhouse, a "futbol" field slanting badly away toward the valley floor ten miles below, and a couple of farm houses.

What excitement! What exclamations of delight and disbelief as we poured the pigs into their new home! Eighty-pound pigs at four months? Unbelievable!

The two pigs were being loaned jointly to the members of the community; they had agreed to feed them a properly balanced diet and to give them proper care; the pigs were to be paid for by replacing pigs of equal value after the gilt had farrowed.

These pigs in turn would be turned over to another group or another farmer under the same conditions.

When Heifer is most successful, it expands into the areas of human welfare also. A *campesino,* for instance, who feeds his hogs a ration that more closely meets the needs of that animal than the diet he is feeding his children, will be more ready to accept the idea of proper nutrition for the formation of strong bodies and the building of resistance to disease.

The stunting of children through protein starvation may not show up for months or years, but the stunting of animals is quick and dramatic.

I had thought that I could move into a completely different culture and, if not loving it, at least accept it

Twenty-year-old Ben Brackin, from What Cheer, Iowa, helps rope one of the semi-wild Bolivian dairy cows which will be tested for TB.

184

to the point where I could do the job I had been trained for.

It came as an ego-shriveling shock to discover after the first couple of weeks that I wasn't doing much of anything but reacting naïvely and highly emotionally to the poverty around me.

Then slowly, slowly, I began really to become, however superficially, involved with the life of the town. The president of the colony, who was old and jolly but with whom I had never been able to work, was one day voted out of office.

The new president, a much younger man, called on me one evening and asked me to come to the next town meeting and explain what I was doing living among them. "What *are* you doing in the town?" he asked me. "Is it true that you are a technician from the United States and that you wish to aid us?"

The next day, very nervous and speaking very badly, I was introduced to about sixty farmers at their Sunday meeting at the schoolhouse. I explained it all again— that I was with the Peace Corps, a representative of the government of the United States, that I wished to live in the village, make friends, learn their language and their customs, and that I wanted nothing from them except their friendship and, if they wanted, a chance to

(*Opposite page*) The Peace Corps's "hunger fighters" in action: (*left above*) Jim Portman, Coraopolis, Pennsylvania, feeds the ducks he bought out of his own pocket for his 4-H club in Tonacatepeque, El Salvador; (*right, above*) in Nepal, Larry Wolfe, from Garrison, Kentucky, teaches horticulture to Katmandu agricultural extension students; (*left, below*) Herb Clauson started a rabbit farm in Paispamba, Colombia; (*right, below*) Bill Hundley of Cle-Elum, Washington, and an agricultural graduate of Washington State University, travels from farm to farm on the island of St. Lucia helping farmers solve their soil erosion problems.

Jim Dungan, of Casper, Wyoming, works with Indian farmers in Chile, teaching them how to increase the yield of their land.

help them create a school garden and to organize an experimental nursery for growing new crops; also that I wanted to show them some new ways of raising pigs, chickens, and cattle.

I sat down, trembling, and suddenly everyone was smiling; *all* the faces had softened. Old farmers, sitting behind the tiny fifth-grade desks, turned to catch my eye and smile and nod their heads. The president made a formal speech welcoming me to the town.

It was my town, now, he said. If you need land for a school garden, just tell us how much you need; we are completely at your orders.

My relationship with the town changed quite suddenly after that first meeting; it was as though I had to acknowledge publicly an intention to live twenty months among them before they could believe it or take me seriously. The last couple of weeks that I was there I had actually become so busy that I had to make appointments three or four days ahead of time with the farmers.

At night, a steadily growing stream of visitors began to appear; they wanted to talk about life or the United States or about John F. Kennedy. Some of them, many of them, could not talk about Kennedy without weeping.

—MORITZ THOMPSEN

Next to production, the greatest agricultural needs in the developing countries are for new markets and the improvement of existing ones. Below, Ronald Venezia of Spring Valley, New York, writes about his experience with a Guatemalan cooperative. Ronald attended Fairleigh Dickinson University in New Jersey and Kent State University in Ohio, where he received his B.S. degree in marketing. He went to Guatemala as a volunteer in 1963. He calls his experience a "profitable waste of time."

The atmosphere for co-ops in Guatemala is rarefied. The government contributes with a small but dedicated and competent staff which is seriously hampered by lack of material support. Procedure for chartering co-ops takes from three to six months. (A new law has been under discussion for three years.) In addition, during a previous regime, cooperatives were used for political purposes and thereby tainted with *communismo*.

Add to this thirty-five Peace Corps volunteers, ill trained in "marginal efficiency" and then sent as cooperative "specialists," and the situation becomes explosive. Somehow a measure of success was attained, but at a terrific cost of time.

When we arrived, the cooperative movement in Gua-

Volunteers Mike Conlin (*left*) from Arthur, Illinois, and Bill Bryant from Birmingham, Alabama, carry supplies into the Kasungu Consumers Cooperative in Malawi, which they manage. The co-op specializes in the marketing of ground nuts (peanuts), maize, and beans. Its commission on ground nuts alone in 1965 was about 2,000 pounds sterling (about $5,600).

Harvey Sims, of La Habra, California, established a fishing co-op in Sanchez, on the northeastern coast of the Dominican Republic. His wife was a volunteer nurse in the village.

temala had its focal point in the mountainous northwest Indian region and was spearheaded by the Maryknoll missionaries. In central Guatemala, a small number of Indian agricultural associations had been initiated by our host agency but were handicapped by the problems of untrained personnel and short-run ideas. There was a lack of farm machinery, and few agricultural supplies were available. In the northern part of Guatemala, cooperatives had not penetrated at all.

After two years, the steps in official processing have not changed substantially. There has been some progress: the Credit Union National of America (C.U.N.A) now has a Central American mission and is slowly increasing the number of credit cooperatives. As for the Peace Corps, the so-called "cooperative specialists," our major effort has been to force the issue. We have accomplished the legalization of three associations and the creation of five new cooperatives with government charters, and in addition we have initiated the beginning of several new groups. In so doing, we have created the precedent of free publication of the statutes in the official paper, a paid-for requisite before that time.

We have induced the government credit agency, heretofore represented largely on the coast, to enter other regions in force, and have requested and received over $40,000 worth of cooperative loans, plus additional credit capital for individual farmers. These loans are now represented in the form of tractors, threshers, insecticides, seeds, and other farm equipment and supplies.

In conjunction with the Grange, we have introduced, through the cooperatives, purebred pigs and goats to improve local bloodlines. We have expanded the function of the Agency for International Development to include more small rural-development projects as a supplement to its large-scale programs, and received from it small grants from a special-development fund for the building of warehouses (three are now finished, two are under construction), office machinery, and foot looms for weaving of native cloth.

We have shown that *co-operativismo* is not synonymous with *communismo*. Indian blankets and pottery are now being sold in the United States, a result of volunteers' efforts with craft cooperatives. In Cobán, animal feed will soon be made from local products and sold at a fraction of its former prohibitive price. In Rabinal, a new building will soon house the ceramics students brought together into a cooperative by a volunteer. We ourselves were caught up in the idea and formed our own credit cooperative—Co-op de Paz—voluntarily contributing $10 a month from our personal funds and using it for seed capital on small projects. And through it all, I guess we also had a lot of fun.

As for the future, cooperatives in Guatemala have a good chance to succeed if certain conditions are faced. Most important, one must realize that the development of co-ops is often discouraging and usually fruitless when the programs are imposed from the top, whereas approaching the problem at grass roots will bring quicker results. It means training volunteers to be, in reality, cooperative specialists. It means taking advantage of the C.U.N.A. program for credit cooperatives. It means creating regional federations which will in turn create a favorable political environment by which resources can be attained. It means, in effect, beginning the effort wholeheartedly with the conviction that cooperatives provide one of the stablest bases for community development.

"Wasting time profitably" was the theme of my service, because I know that if we had been better trained in cooperative organization and management, the job would have been smoother and what we accomplished would have been done in a shorter time.

—RONALD VENEZIA

Emory Tomor, of Calabasis, California, helped establish a grain co-op in the Indian community of Galvarino in southern Chile.

By far the greatest Peace Corps agricultural effort today is in India. In early 1967, there were more than 1,600 volunteers in India, the largest concentration of volunteers in any country in the world. Most of them are agricultural workers. India's population is increasing by 12 million every year. Its farm land totals about one-third of America's, and its antiquated agricultural methods produce about half as much an acre as United States farmland. As a result, much of India faces starvation, a crisis which President Johnson has promised to help meet with grain shipments to India and increased agricultural aid, including "an expanded Peace Corps." Under Director Jack Vaughn, the Peace Corps has launched an elaborate program of agricultural aid to India which is pioneering in developing the role of the generalist as a middle-level conveyor of knowledge about food production. However, the Peace Corps cautions that its expanded Indian program will probably not have an immediate effect on the food crisis, but volunteers are showing Indian farmers how to increase their crops in the future. (*Above*) Volunteer Wayne Thurston and an Indian farmer inspect a new Formosan rice variety on a demonstration farm in West Bengal.

Of all the agricultural projects initiated by the Peace Corps in India, the one that has created the most impact has been in poultry production.

Until the arrival of the first contingent of Peace Corps

volunteers nearly five years ago, poultry production in India has seldom been a profitable farming enterprise. Most flocks were maintained as loose backyard operations with little or no management. But, with the coming of the volunteer, chicken and vegetarian (nonfertile) egg output has made dramatic inroads on both the diet of the Indian people and the economic welfare of the farmer.

For example, a poultry cooperative in southern India had eight farmer-members early in 1965 when a Peace Corps volunteer was assigned to the area. The cooperative collectively owned 2,500 laying hens which produced less than one egg per bird each week.

In May, 1965, a new egg marketing program was started by volunteers and Indian cooperative members in Delhi. By July the demand for cooperative eggs had increased to a point where the store could not meet the demand. Daily home deliveries and over-the-counter sales have jumped to 11,500.

In Calcutta, volunteers used a different marketing approach. There they assisted in securing contracts with hotels and large restaurants, ensuring cooperatives of a year-round market and price. The emphasis in marketing in Calcutta is now on wholesale dressed broilers.

In Bombay, marketing programs sometimes present problems due to the high cost of shipping poultry products by rail from rural areas. However, with the aid of volunteers,

poultry cooperatives are now sending and marketing their commodities collectively, thus qualifying for reduced freight rates.

While volunteer poultry efforts have moved in the direction of improving feed production and marketing of poultry products, the development of farm flocks with 100 or more layers continues. At the same time, many volunteers are experimenting with reestablishment of profitable small-scale backyard poultry operations of ten to sixteen birds for home use and sale within the villages.

One volunteer in Uttar Pradesh developed a poultry house for fifteen birds at a cost of $3. The frame is bamboo, thatch roof, and wire mesh encloses the entire building, including the raised floor.

In some villages, volunteers have helped build ten brick poultry houses for fifty birds each with the use of welfare funds which had been largely unexpended for poultry projects in the past.

(*Left*) Volunteer Larry Tadlock, of Addy, Washington, shows an Indian how to debeak a chicken with a hot, sterilized screwdriver. Tadlock worked on a poultry project in Habra. (*Below*) Greg Brown examines eggs produced by the poultry project he organized in Barapur.

Land Settlement in Kenya

Phil Schaefer (*left*) and Amherst graduate Art Schoepfer of Wellsley Hills, Massachusetts, bargain for a goat with a new Kenyan landowner.

One of the most interesting and significant agricultural projects in which Peace Corps volunteers are involved is the Kenya land settlement scheme which Barbara Ward has called "the most important social experiment in the world today." For centuries land in Kenya was divided between "scheduled" and "unscheduled" areas. The former belonged exclusively to white settlers, who cultivated the fertile areas extending north and west from the capital, Nairobi, into the Great Rift Valley. The area was known as the White Highlands. "Unscheduled" areas consisted of the land left to tribal ownership and not claimed by white settlers. They generally provided a meager living for their African inhabitants. The struggle for control of the fertile highlands was a key factor in the independence movement in Kenya. When colonial rule ended, agrarian reform had political and economic priority.

The Kenya Land Settlement Board, with loans from the World Bank and the British Government, purchased one million acres in the "scheduled" areas. Shambas (small farms ranging from seven to seventy acres) in each settlement scheme were then sold to African families who were financed by thirty-year loans for the purchase of land and ten-year loans for initial agriculture and production needs.

Each scheme has a cooperative which sells the farmer's produce and assists him in paying his farm and production loans.

Schaefer reaches into a primitive threshing machine on the Uaso Nyiro Settlement where he was an assistant settlement officer. With him are two other Peace Corps officers, Art Schoepfer (*right*) and Lanie Wiig (*behind Schaefer*) of Honolulu. The Kenyan on the left was a Mau Mau fighter who spent several years in detention during the Mau Mau skirmishes of 1952–1960.

192

At first, the schemes are administered by a settlement officer and his agriculture assistant. The officers keep production going until the land has been completely turned over to the farmers. A study of some of the larger farms in the new schemes showed that farm output is at least 50 percent higher than it was before settlement, and that all but 10 percent of the farmers are on time with the repayment of their loans for development and land purchase.

The Peace Corps volunteers assigned to the Kenya schemes help administer them as assistant land settlement officers. Philip Schaefer, an A.B. generalist from New York City who graduated from Antioch College, was one of them. Below, Schaefer gives a brief description of his work in the historic Kenya program:

When I arrived on Uaso Nyiro Settlement Scheme, located in the heart of the Aberdare Valley of Kenya, I found myself in an old house, the scene of a famous Mau Mau battle described by Robert Ruark in *Something of Value.*

I discovered 127 settlers on the scheme, many of whom were leaders in the so-called Mau Mau revolution, and who are now among the most progressive settlers. (Mau Mau General China is one of our plotholders.) It is my job to assist in the difficult transformation from landless worker to successful entrepreneur. At first I thought that this would be beyond my abilities since I am a New York City "farm boy" whose agricultural experience was previously limited to a tour of fruit and vegetable stands on the Lower East Side of New York. But working in close cooperation with the trained agricultural and veterinary staffs which are assigned to each settlement scheme, I soon came to realize that "Catcher" and "Fanfare" were varieties of wheat and

Schoepfer and a Kenyan land settlement officer inspect the drying flowers of the pyrethrum plant. The plant, used in the manufacture of insecticides, is a major cash crop in Kenya.

George Owen, one of the sixty Peace Corps volunteers involved in the Kenya land settlement schemes, is from El Dorado, Arkansas, and was graduated from Baylor with an A.B. in psychology. "To understand the African," says Owen, who worked in two schemes at Kinangop, "whether he's a Kikuyu, Kamba, Nandi, Luo, or a Kipsigis, you have to realize that his hopes, dreams, future, past, present: all he is and hopes to be, is linked to the soil. It was the need to own a plot of ground that precipitated Mau Mau, and the fulfillment of that need, by settlement, that has brought stability to Kenya."

not terms to describe the action on the baseball diamond.

At the heart of the settlement scheme is the marketing cooperative society which markets all of the settlers' produce and represents collective purchasing power for the settlers. Recently, after much painstaking discussion and persuasion, the settlers took two major steps to improve their wheat production. (Wheat is our major cash crop. Although the scheme is on the equator, the altitude is high enough for wheat to thrive.) First they decided to pool all the profits from the previous crop in order to purchase their own *tinatinga* (tractors) and plows, thus eliminating the need for private contractors. Next they developed a plan to consolidate their *shambas* (plots) for the purpose of growing wheat on a large scale. This has met with the hearty approbation of the "experts." The people have also taken the initiative to negotiate a contract with East African Breweries and will become one of the first settlement schemes to grow barley for use in beer production.

Dashing around on my *piki* (motorcycle, which, unfortunately, not only stops when the ground is wet but when there are clouds in the sky) with the cooperative chairman making arrangements to harvest the wheat or to purchase cattle has been hectic and exciting. But ordinary life on a settlement scheme can be pretty dreary. On Uaso Nyiro we have tried to create an exciting sense of community. We have started our own scheme newspaper, an idea which is catching on with other settlement schemes. But we are most proud of our recent water show which helped to raise nearly $4,000 to bring needed water to the scheme. The Minister of Lands and Settlement opened the show; major companies from Nairobi donated exhibits; and 127 settlers, old and young, carried branches and built the showground. Of course, *Mungu* (God) works his mysterious ways, and just as the Minister opened the show, there was a torrential rainfall.

The people have begun to work together in the spirit of *harambee* (pulling together) as preached by *Mzee* (the old one) Jomo Kenyatta, the President of Kenya. To be a small participant in positive change is probably the most exhilarating and satisfying experience of my life. To leave General China and his 126 compatriots and return to the wheatless streets of New York will not be entirely painless.

—PHILIP A. SCHAEFER

Chapter 7

Public Health

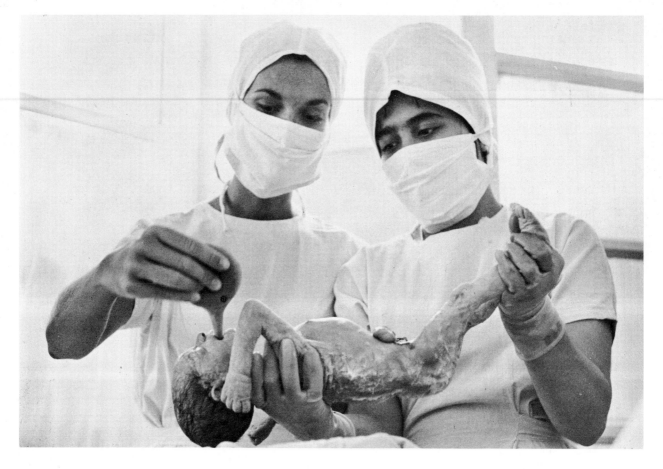

Because of the shortage of medical personnel, even in the United States, public health workers will probably always remain the fewest in numbers of the four main categories of volunteers the Peace Corps sends abroad. But the need and demand for them is almost overwhelming. In India, average life expectancy is forty-two; in South America, the number of children who die before they are six years old is twenty times the United States figure; in northern Brazil, one out of every two babies is likely to die before his first birthday. In a large part of the world, millions of people continue to die of smallpox, tuberculosis, cholera, dysentery, and nutritional deficiencies—enemies of man which most of the advanced nations of the world conquered long ago. In some of the developing countries, there is only one doctor for 100,000 people. And the problem continues to increase in almost direct ratio to the world's population increase. Obviously, Peace Corps nurses, doctors, dentists, and laboratory technicians are a welcome sight in the countries struggling to gain their

national health as the first step toward economic independence and progress. To help meet the demand for health personnel, "the Peace Corps has pioneered abroad in designing health programs without doctors," says former Peace Corps Deputy Director Warren Wiggins. "We are using the generalist with short-term training—combining him in large numbers with the specialist in few numbers. We are still learning, still experimenting, but we are showing some progress—in the fight against TB, malaria, and other diseases which can be brought under control with organized public health programs."

In the following pages, a few of the volunteers who have gone abroad to help make the world a healthier place to live tell about their Peace Corps experience. Patty Schwartz was a registered nurse from Minneapolis before joining the Peace Corps. She was assigned to Bolivia, and worked for a year in La Paz, the capital, before being asked to help set up a twelve-bed hospital in the village of San Borja with another Peace Corps

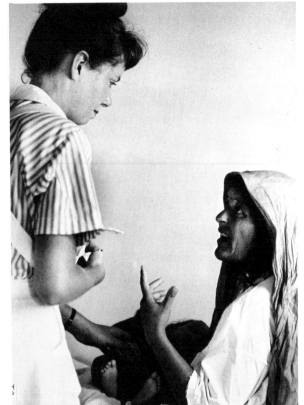

Infant mortality in many countries of the developing world is appalling by Western standards.
(*Opposite page*)   Lou Barfield (*left*) of Goldsboro, North Carolina, and Barbara Eck of Milwaukee, Wisconsin, deliver a baby in the Zaishgah Sherara Hospital in Kabul.
(*Right*)   Judy Vielhaber, of Doylestown, Ohio, talks with a mother in Sousse, Tunisia's third largest city.

nurse, Prudence Ingerman, and a Bolivian nurse and a Bolivian doctor. Patty's account is extracted from letters home to her parents:

I returned safely from San Borja sitting among alligator skins and beaver hides in the back of a cargo plane, holding oxygen to the nose of a man whose appendix had ruptured some days ago and was being flown up here for surgery. Due to a wet landing strip we were stranded there 2½ days but enjoyed it thoroughly, walking on the mud streets, slapping mosquitoes, smelling roses, and drinking papaya juice. We rode down to San Borja standing in the cockpit of a meat plane, standing, mind you, as we flew over the high Cordilleras and finally down down down from the height of 20,000 feet to about 1,000 feet. San Borja checked out wonderfully, and Prue and I will be going back on the 19th, with some hospital equipment, we hope. The twelve-bed hospital that the townspeople are just now completing has absolutely nothing in it. The Minister of Health has made wonderful promises, and now all we can do is wait and see.

You'd be wild about San Borja, especially in this season. It's hot, flat, a small cattle town looking as though it were dropped in the middle of this great flat grassland, the "pampa." It is a town of three to four thousand, not including the outlying population or the Chimani Indians near the river. The people are beauti-

ful and dress primarily in whites and light prints, and all go barefoot. There are no paved streets, no telephones, one movie a week, no school building, though school is held in an open-air-theatre sort of structure. The atmosphere is that of our Far West a century back, with emphasis on bravery. The only medical personnel in town is a young doctor on his year of provinceship, very bright and with a good concept of public health, so I'll have at least his backing in this matter. . . .

San Borja

I have gained weight here, about five pounds, I think. I am eating virtually mountains of food which is mostly starch, but feel good and am taking a vitamin pill every day to sustain me. Every day I am served at least six small cups of coffee, so black and so thick that it is unbelievable. It hangs to a spoon like axle oil but the aftertaste is nice. I love fried bananas. . . .

This has been a wonderful week. So many good things have happened that we're just on clouds. The doctor has not come back from La Paz yet, so we've been the only medical people in town. Several people have come rapping asking me to go see someone with some ailment or other. This in itself is nice, but what is really nice is sitting down with them afterward and getting to know the family—from great-grampa down to the newest baby sleeping peacefully in a hammock. Friday we started the polio vaccine program, begin-

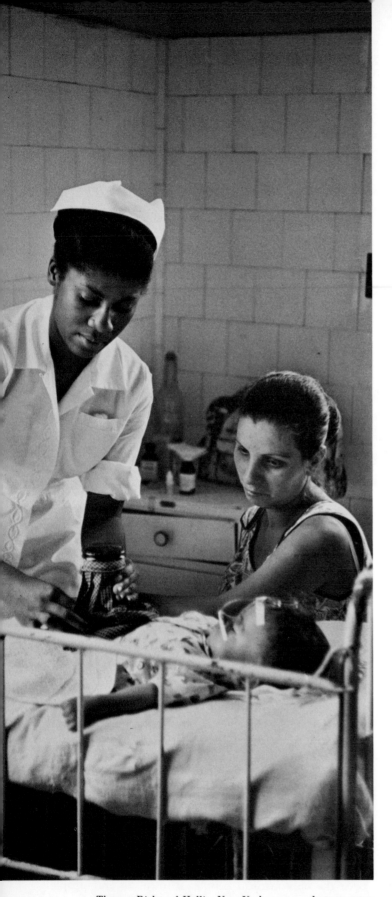

Theresa Ricks, of Hollis, New York, was a volunteer nurse in Rio. In parts of Brazil, one out of two babies will probably die before his first birthday. One volunteer took a coffin to a baby boy's baptism. "We knew he could only live a few days . . ." said the volunteer. "I was the godmother, and the gift I took was a coffin because I knew the family could not afford it."

ning with the schools. It is only for kids six months to twelve years, because there is just not enough vaccine for everybody. We announced on the loudspeaker at the movie (which the whole town hears) and put a poster on the church door. It worked for Martin Luther and it's working for us. So far I have poked over 500 kids, and we have two days left. Prue prepares and I poke. Yesterday when we asked the mayor for the use of his place of work, he just gave us a key to the place, a big smile, a word of encouragement, and now we have the run of the place. He is really the finest man and doing a wonderful job in the town, progress-wise. I think I told you that there is a stress here on being brave. I'm sure that rarely has a group of kids been vaccinated when so few cried. It was amazing—they would tremble and gasp and stop breathing altogether, but cry? Not a peep. . . .

We have been so busy that I have literally not had time to bathe for three days. Bathing is done only in daylight, and these have not been my free hours, so I snatch a midnight sponge bath from a half tutumba shell which is like a gourd only bigger and circular. We use it in the kitchen for scooping rainwater, washing hands, etc. Our cooking has been minimal—bananas and fruit juice and water for breakfast, fried bananas and milk for supper. People have been giving us chicken, bread, fruit, etc., so it's been a whole lot easier.

Since Monday I've been working with Dr. Miranda at his house and on home visits. I've made up five clinical record forms, and the priests are dittoing them tonight. The poor guy has only paper notebooks for record-keeping, and had time neither to make nor keep good records.

Tuesday night Dr. Miranda came flying by, shouted "follow me," and we splashed through the mud to see a man who had just arrived by oxcart from 120 kilometers away with a serious bowel obstruction and in terrible shape. Fifty-five years old. He was lying on a dirt floor on a cowhide in the lean-to part of a house. There were two more cowhides strung from the roof to the ground to keep out the rain. So in this mess we started IV's (intravenous) and kept watch. The man's *patron* had sent a note putting two of the town leaders here in charge of him. The man had peritonitis, quite advanced, and the obvious thing was surgery. But—

(1) The *patron* was not here to say he'd pay for a trip to La Paz.
(2) Landing strip soaking wet—plane cancelled.
(3) Man's condition so bad that he'd probably die with or without surgery.

So they waited. And waited. And waited. All day Tuesday, Tuesday night, and Wednesday. He got worse and worse. Wednesday at 6:00 P.M. the two men in charge told Dr. Miranda to operate—here. No operation has ever been done here. We had planned on several simple operations for next week with absolute certainty of a favorable outcome. But this! And I'm the only darn thing in town that faintly resembles an anesthetist. At 6:00 Dr. Miranda said "we will operate at 8:00. Go home, get food in your bellies and I'll see you at 8:00." The two of us went into a near state of collapse. Prue had been studying the names of instruments in Spanish and how to thread surgical needles, and all of a sudden it all slipped her mind!

At 8:00 we sterilized everything in pressure cookers over an open flame, moved the doctor's examining table to the middle of the room, borrowed a 100-watt bulb, and then scrubbed. Then in came the patient in a hammock suspended from a pole carried by four men.

In the waiting room were the mayor, the priest, the man's family, the two put in charge of his care, and the two sisters of his *patron*. This the doctor demanded, with the understanding that the man had only a 5 percent chance of living, and that if he died it was *not* because of the doctor's decision to operate at all.

So at 10:00 we proceeded, with a spinal anaesthetic (which did not take—the medicine was potty) and local. He would not have tolerated general anesthesia—nor could I. What I had to do was take the blood pressure every two minutes and keep it up with Levophed by means of an IV drip.

All went very well— At 11:15 the lights blinked, indicating another 15 minutes of light before they're out for the night, so I dashed into the other room between B/P's and told the mayor to race to the *alcaldia* and tell the mechanic not to shut the motor for a while. At midnight he was put in his hammock and sent home— alive and much improved. We all just sat dumbfounded looking at each other.

This morning at 8:00 he was talking, moving well, and the wound had drained a good deal. It's almost too good to be true. Time will tell. . . . (The patient recovered.)

Yesterday was the big dedication of the hospital, and the Minister of Health, senators, and a lot of bigwigs came down in a military plane for the ceremony. For three days we had scrubbed, rearranged, disinfected, and made the beds, so that it looked pretty swish. A recent graduate Bolivian nurse on her year in the province arrived. She will be living with us.

It's really been fun—biggest thing to hit San Borja since the town existed. There was a big parade to the airport, then all the kids lined the road to the airport in their little white school coats and clapped continually while the important people rode by. The inauguration itself was short but with enough speeches to satisfy protocol. And last night there was a big reception dance.

—PATTY SCHWARTZ

Judy Hoenack, of Bethesda, Maryland, was a *sanitadora* (visiting health worker) in Rio de Janeiro, Brazil. She carries a medical kit over her shoulder as she climbs a steep cliff to her slum area, which has a beautiful view of Rio, but little more.

To Eliminate Malaria, You Must First Eliminate the Mosquito

In December of 1965, I was given a special assignment in the Ministry of Education—as technical aid to Dr. Helen Bailly-Choumara, director of the entomological laboratory, attached to the national university at Rabat. The work of the department is primarily directed at research on the various species of Culicidae or biting gnats and, more specifically, mosquitoes. Research on mosquitoes included studies of their environment (season, type of nesting place, vegetation, hours of feeding and feeding source); development (age of captured mosquitoes, time taken for each stage of their development, physiological characteristics); general classification and identification of all mosquitoes in all stages (egg, larva, pupa, and adult); various research on trapping and preservation of each stage. Part of this research was on the request of the World Health Organization.

I was to collect the specimens. (My laboratory duties also included dissection of mosquitoes, mounting of specimens for preservation [adults were impaled on pins and mounted on small cardboard rectangles; larvae were mounted on microscope slide or in alcohol], secretarial duties, and occasional draftsman, cartographer, and translator.) Usually with a Moroccan technician from the laboratory, Thami Lacheb, or on several occasions as part of a World Health-sponsored malaria control team, I would go out on an assignment to study a particular area. These excursions ranged in length from several hours to several weeks, from the Mediterranean to the near-Sahara/Wadi Dra basin. In all, I traveled over more than three-fourths of the country. Our trips were well prepared in advance; it was often necessary to carry food supplies and always a fresh water supply with us. (Once on a mission to the edge of the desert, we went to the once-a-week market of a large village to buy a few staples. The only things available were a few tomatoes and oranges. We ate macaroni with tomato sauce for two days, and afterward were more cautious to bring along a large quantity of produce.) The condition of much of the terrain surveyed required the use of a jeep (Peace Corps supplied), often traveling on roads that existed only on the dotted blue lines on a forestry map.

When we arrived at a possible site near a swamp, stagnant pond, or river bed, we spent the day collecting larvae with soup ladles or a seine, or searching for adult mosquitoes that passed the heat of the day in the shady interiors of huts, stables, or caves. Any animals in the area were observed for horseflies or tics, and this once

(*Below*) Gerald Patrick, seated at the field table, was assigned to the medical laboratory in the provincial hospital at Marrakech, Morocco. With a laboratory technician, Thami Lacheb (*standing*), Patrick made many trips throughout Morocco gathering mosquitoes and other insects to be studied in the lab. Here he tells of his experience in the project the Peace Corps called "Morocco I, Public Health."

included part of the five hundred camels of the Moroccan Army's camel corps. As evening approached, we would make our camp, sometimes staying in a forester's cabin or ex-Legion post, but most often pitching our two-man tent. While Thami prepared an appetizing Moroccan stew (*tagine*) over a small gas burner, I prepared the day's catch for preservation (often specimens were brought back alive—the adults for dissection and larvae for raising—to the laboratory in an insulated box, refrigerated with ice bags), or I caught the early mosquitoes with a net.

At night we would distribute our light traps (a device designed with a flashlight-sized light bulb to lure mosquitoes into an inescapable pocket, distributed to the

"Once we found a location where a species lived in abundance that had been discovered only a dozen times in the whole world, and had never been described in its early development."

"... it is not surprising the number of discoveries we made, especially in species previously unknown to North Africa."

With the large number of unclassified insects suspected to be in Morocco, the number of discoveries we made is not surprising, especially in species previously unknown to North Africa. Once we found a location where a species lived in abundance that had been observed only a dozen times in the whole world and had never been described in its early development. The area not only offered a source for this mosquito, but a number of other insects whose species are still being determined.

During these missions, we were always received with the greatest hospitality by the villagers. They opened their homes freely to our inspection, trying to be of as much assistance as possible. Often seeing us catching the larvae in ladles, they would huddle around and try the same thing with their hands. Usually our tour of a village ended with refreshments of milk and warm bread, often with honey and rancid butter (a delicacy), or at other times an invitation to share the family meal. One evening our caravan arrived in a town in the desert (an oasis) where we were informed that the *caid* (governor) was disturbed that he had not been informed of the name of the American who was traveling in the group, because he wanted to invite him to dinner. While passing through the High Atlas Mountains we came across a celebration of a national holiday. We approached a crowd of spectators to catch a glimpse of the dancers; but as we got near, an official opened the circle and led us into the center, seated us, and served tea before returning to take part in the events.

—GERALD PATRICK

Institute by the World Health Organization to study its efficiency), in areas where a large quantity of mosquitoes could be expected. The human bait was laid out in similar areas as we rolled up our trousers and waited for a bite; the mosquito was then gently taken in a glass tube for collection. (Catches were often abundant; one night, we took over two hundred mosquitoes this way in less than two hours. There was little danger of catching malaria, as the Peace Corps supplied continuous preventive treatment.) The night would be passed this way with results marked according to the hour and location of the capture. A last-minute catch was made at daybreak with the net, as the mosquitoes returned to cover for the day.

"Any animals in the area were observed for horse flies or tics ..."

(*Above*) "A last-minute catch was made at daybreak with the net as the mosquitoes returned to cover for the day."

(*Left*) "While Thami prepared an appetizing Moroccan stew (*tangine*) . . . I prepared the day's catch for preservation . . ."

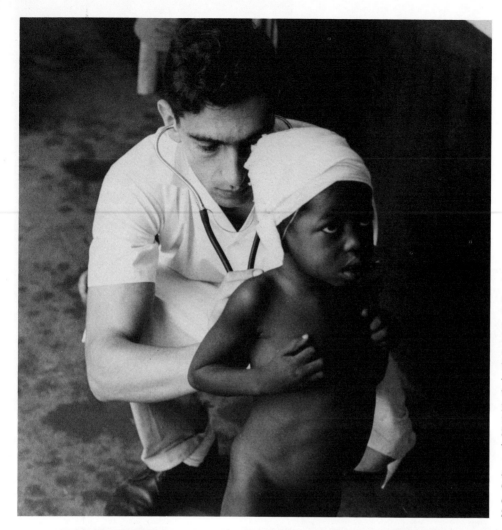

Unlike other volunteers, doctors and dentists volunteering for the Peace Corps are permitted to have dependents under eighteen years of age, and the Peace Corps will support the dependents overseas. There is no pay, although their readjustment allowance is larger —$125 for every month of duty. All wives must participate in the training program. Peace Corps service does not fulfill his obligations for military duty. Still, many doctors and dentists have volunteered for Peace Corps duty. (*Left*) Dr. Merton Koenigsberger examines a child in Togo; (*below*) Dr. Carroll Hibbard was one of only three qualified dentists in the entire state of Sabah in Malaysia.

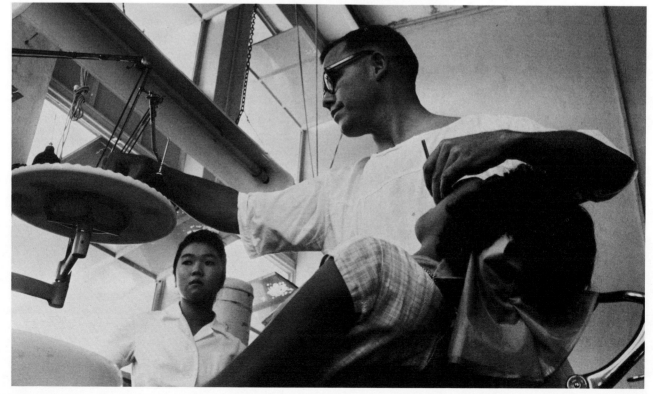

If eliminating the mosquito is the key to malaria control, decreasing the birthrate is the key to controlling population growth in the developing nations. Fifty-five volunteers in India pioneered work in the field of birth control, and the programs have extended to other areas. (*Right*) Volunteer nurse Beth Halkola gives the wife of a local teacher some birth control pills.

It's a Discouraging Business

Carole Watkins was a volunteer nurse in Paraíba, Brazil. She asks whether Peace Corps nurses have realistic goals:

We nurses in the Peace Corps have to take a second look at ourselves—and our reasons for joining in the first place. After reading the results of the report ("Volunteers Rank Problems"), I begin to wonder just why the nurses have the largest "drop-out" rate and why the majority are dissatisfied with their two-year service.

It stated that this may be due to our "higher professional expectations that are not matched by realized accomplishment, and hopelessness about the health needs of a growing population." Granted! But why do we arrive in the first place with higher expectations? What do we in the health field consider "accomplishments," and why this overwhelming feeling of hopelessness?

In training, we are told that there won't be the hospital situation as we know it—or any hospital at all—no health post or bandages or medicines, cooperation or interest. But when we do start working—from doing dressings to teaching first aid—we start looking for those "little rewards" that we went into nursing for in the first place. Those indefinable somethings called "gratitude," "recognition," a "feeling of being needed," or whatever. And when we don't find them—or when we don't recognize them for what they are, a part of another culture—we begin to lose our perspective of our whole purpose of being here.

What do we consider accomplishments? This, of course, depends on what our expectations are, realistic or not. Before we set our sights for the horizon, let's be sure we see it clearly. Let's evaluate the total situation, not as it was given to us in training and not by what we learned of the area before we arrived, but as we

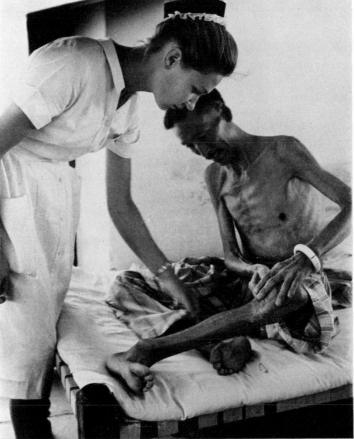

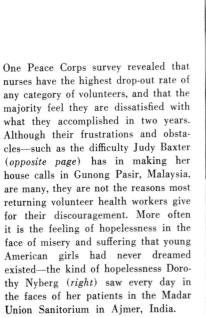

One Peace Corps survey revealed that nurses have the highest drop-out rate of any category of volunteers, and that the majority feel they are dissatisfied with what they accomplished in two years. Although their frustrations and obstacles—such as the difficulty Judy Baxter (*opposite page*) has in making her house calls in Gunong Pasir, Malaysia, are many, they are not the reasons most returning volunteer health workers give for their discouragement. More often it is the feeling of hopelessness in the face of misery and suffering that young American girls had never dreamed existed—the kind of hopelessness Dorothy Nyberg (*right*) saw every day in the faces of her patients in the Madar Union Sanitorium in Ajmer, India.

Despite the discouragement, as every nurse knows, there is a fundamental satisfaction in helping those who need it—just ask Barbara Sims (*left*) who was a nurse in the village of Sanchez in the Dominican Republic, or Bernadette Pieza (*opposite page*) who worked in a hospital in Sousse, Tunisia.

ourselves see it right there in the site. Then we must decide what is most important. What can one person do in just two years?

When my partner and I arrived at our site, a town of three thousand people, there was neither a furnished health post nor medicines, and no trained medical person. Approximately 50 percent of all the newborn babies die before six months of age, and adult mortality rates are high; the houses are filthy, and the small children left naked; animals feed in the dusty streets, and even the so-called "upper class" has no concept of preventive health measures and basic hygiene. Heavens! What can one person do? The people are far from that "point of readiness" to begin to grasp ideas of health and sickness. I doubt if there will be any drastic physical changes in the next two years, but sometime, maybe five years from now, some volunteer will see something happen and marvel at his or her community development. This will be only part of the process, a process someone has to start somewhere. Getting this learning process off to a good start would be a realistic and realized accomplishment for this area, this country, at this time.

Why, then, a feeling of hopelessness? There is a phrase we nurses learn in school: "Attitudes are caught, not taught." Reversed, this can be applied to our relations with people of developing countries. They are born, live out their lives, and die surrounded by these conditions. They have never seen anything change and never expect it to. The Peace Corps calls this attitude "apathy." I call it hopelessness. It's a very contagious disease. It can eat away at your determination day after day until there is nothing left and you finally succumb.

Nurses who have "high expectations" are especially susceptible and have to take preventive measures. I suggest simple, but serious, second looks, reevaluations of your original goals. Were those goals realistic in the first place? Were they based on the facts as you found them at your site? Are your goals flexible (that magic word!) as you learn more about your site, its people, and their way of life?

So, all I've done is raise more questions, and haven't offered any solutions. We have a problem, and I have a feeling it isn't just the nurses' problem. Reevaluation is important in any kind of job, but in the Peace Corps, I don't think it can be stressed enough. I'm not saying it will solve any or all of the problems we run up against, but it will help us to know ourselves better, and this comes first before we can understand others.

—Carole Watkins

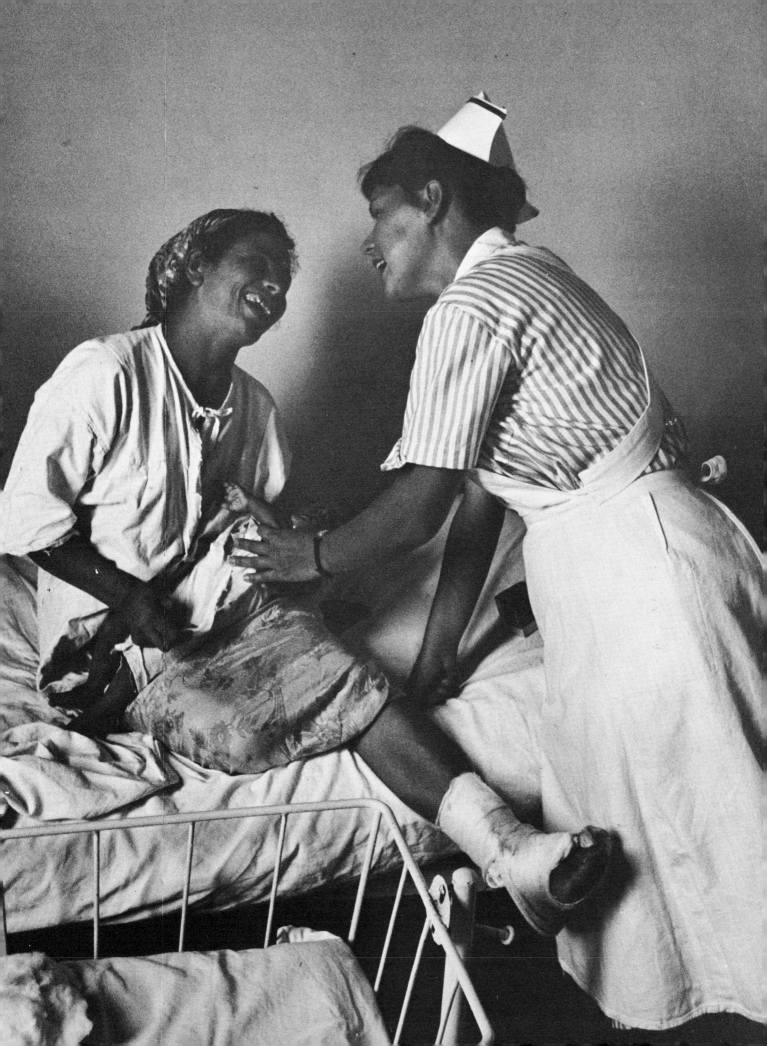

Chapter 8

Miscellaneous Missions

In addition to the four major categories of Peace Corps activities, volunteers are engaged in more than two hundred different skills. Many of these, of course, are skills that volunteers with a conventional teaching or community development assignments practice as part of their regular assignment or on a part-time basis in the afternoons, evenings, or on weekends. But there are or have been several hundred volunteers engaged in specific skills, trades or professions, and although these volunteers total less than 4 percent of the volunteers who have gone abroad, their assignments have included some of the most interesting and unusual in the Peace Corps's brief history. Roger and Ellen Watson, for example, who were married while in the Philippines, did not imagine when they joined the Peace Corps that they would end up working with the Philippines Commission on National Integration. But they did. Roger is

(*Above*) Roger Watson with Dumagat men and boys. (*Right*) Ellen Watson, wearing a lip guard to protect her lips from the sun, on an excursion trip up the Anibawan River on Polillo, in search of Negrito groups.

from Levittown, Pennsylvania, and was graduated from Union College in Kentucky; Ellen is from New London, New Hampshire, and was graduated from the University of New Hampshire. Below, they recount their experience in the Philippines.

The Philippines is not a homogeneous nation, though the majority of the islands' 31 million people are of the Indo-Malay race and follow the Catholic faith. There exist, often in isolated regions, more than 3 million people of other races or religions.

In Mindanao there are 1½ million Muslim Filipinos, completely apart—in Christian Filipino eyes—from the mainstream of national life. Elsewhere, on most inhabited islands, are pagan groups of a few families or many thousands. Some of these groups are Negrito or Papuan racial types; some are Indo-Malay; a few possess Caucasian characteristics. Nearly all retain age-old cultures and styles of living.

In 1957 a Commission on National Integration (C.N.I.) was created by the Philippines Government, charged with responsibility for the integration of these cultural minorities into the body politic of the country.

In October, 1964, this agency asked the Peace Corps for help. The project seemed to be a challenging one that would contribute to the development of the country in an important area, by helping to bring about the

Fortunately, Rae Ann Wright, of California City, California, did not join the Peace Corps to get away from American advertising. Her Peace Corps experience consisted of doing art and sales work for the advertising agency run by Afghanistan's Ministry of Press and Information. Ann poses in front of one of the billboards she designed, urging Afghans to visit Russia, which is the ad agency's largest client. Ann graduated from Brigham Young University in Provo, Utah.

peaceful integration of a potentially useful portion of the population. If the project was successful, it might by its own simplicity encourage other Filipinos to support it too.

First, however, the Peace Corps had to learn more about these cultural minorities and the C.N.I.

As it happened we were available, having just extended for a third year after teaching for two in the elementary school of a small *barrio* in Mindanao.

Since last November we have visited tribes of a racial group generally classed as Negrito, in six provinces in central Luzon, to find ways the Peace Corps might work with C.N.I. to help the minority groups. We have learned a lot about the problems and ways of life of these people.

A description of one encounter might serve to illustrate our experiences:

After a five-hour jeep ride from Manila, and a four-hour hike, we arrived in Limutan Valley, thirty miles east of the capital. Here, in the heart of a rain forest, was the home of a group of people called Dumagat.

"Dumagat" is a Filipino word meaning "people of the sea," an apt term for these former coastal dwellers. They fled from Spanish slave merchants and the more aggressive Tagalog tribes centuries before. Their refuge was the dense jungle of the Sierra Madre Mountains in Quezon Province. Here they remain relatively unchanged to this day.

It is only recently, because of the encroaching farms of the lowlands, that the Dumagat, or Agta, as they call themselves, are beginning to feel the confinement of their self-imposed imprisonment.

In the past, with each new thrust of the lowlanders, the Dumagat were able to retreat farther into the forest. There, wild game and roots could fill their needs from one skimpy harvest to the next. The nomadic cut-and-burn agriculture which they practice is barely sufficient to meet their food needs at times, for they have been slow to adjust to ways of farming more advanced than simple hand cultivation. Now, however, the outside world is closing in. The forest is disappearing, and few wild deer or boar are to be found in the diminishing wilderness.

As we came down out of the thickly forested ridge which bounds Limutan on the west, we could see evidence of the Agta people. Here and there on the hillside, etched against the brilliant greens of the jungle, were ravaged black areas newly burned over to permit planting. Here the Agta would stay only long enough to plant one or two crops of corn and *camote* (sweet potatoes) before moving. Lacking plows, they are unable to cultivate this land after one or two harvests.

On the rocky banks of the Limutan River, running clear and cold from the mountains, were three small huts, with six or eight posts and a roof of pandanus leaf, a broad fanlike plant that grows wild in the tropics. The bare ground formed the floor, and the sides were open. Seated in the shade of one of these huts was a grizzled old man. He wore only a simple loincloth, and his possessions were few: spear, bow and arrow, and betelnut box. However, he had great dignity and, through an interpreter, welcomed us and related some facts of his life.

He said he could not remember his name, for that is something given at birth and rarely used by his people. Nor could he remember his age. His family had been the first to settle in Limutan Valley when he was a small boy. His life since then had not changed much, for nomadic agriculture and wild game and plants were still important for survival. He was married and had teen-age children when the Spanish forces were defeated in Manila Bay (1898), and most of the people of the valley, nearly fifty families, were in some way related to him.

He could even remember when they took the heads of the few Spanish soldiers who ventured into the valley seeking gold or slaves. During World War II, American soldiers encouraged his people to resist the Japanese forces in the area. Now, however, the Dumagat are a peaceful people.

At the southern end of the valley a struggle of a different kind was building. There lowland settlers were beginning to claim land and establish farms. The old man spoke disparagingly of their ways and of their desire to clear the area of trees. To him this was an affront to the Dumagat god of the forest.

Evidently his criticism of the settlers was more an ode to the past than any real antipathy toward their way of life, for he admitted that life as he had known it was hard.

Luckily for him and his people, though, there was living in the valley a man who was trying to help them bridge the chasm between the past and present. This was the son of a lowland father and a Dumagat mother. Because he had married a pure Dumagat woman from Limutan and had settled there, he was accepted as one of the group. More important, he knew how to plow land and work it so that one could live there permanently, and he was sharing this knowledge with his neighbors.

The C.N.I., recognizing this man's potential, supplied him with a carabao (water buffalo) and plow, and with these tools he now serves as demonstration farmer. Some of the men of the valley, including one of the old man's sons, have begun to follow his lead. However, establishing permanent farms is not the end point of development. To understand titles, so he can hold his land, a man must learn to read and write. To benefit from the land now legally his, he must learn when and how to plant certain crops, and how to market his goods. And, in order that this growth and improvement not go in vain, he must learn modern health and sanitation methods.

These problems, of course, are not confined to the Dumagat. Many other cultural groups, most of them with much more complex and sophisticated societies, face the same frustrations. But the conditions are not impossible to cope with. Here in its rawest form is community development through basic education.

Peace Corps involvement will probably take the form of furnishing field workers who will teach basic literacy in the dialects, and teach basic agriculture and health. The commission has also asked for assistance in an anthropological census of the non-Christian groups, which in addition to a mere head count would involve recording the languages and obtaining fairly extensive social and cultural information.

Until the Peace Corps can determine what kinds of qualifications and training are desirable for this sort of project, volunteers who have extended will be the primary source of field workers.

—ROGER AND ELLEN WATSON

(*Above*) Nicholas Napoleon, of Trenton, New Jersey, was a surveyor in Iran where he helped build feeder roads.

(*Below*) John Bird (*center*), San Jose, California, and William Grubber (*right*) from West Seneca, New York, are part of an industrial management team in the Kampur-Andreapredesh region of India. Their assignment was to help Indian small industries become more profitable.

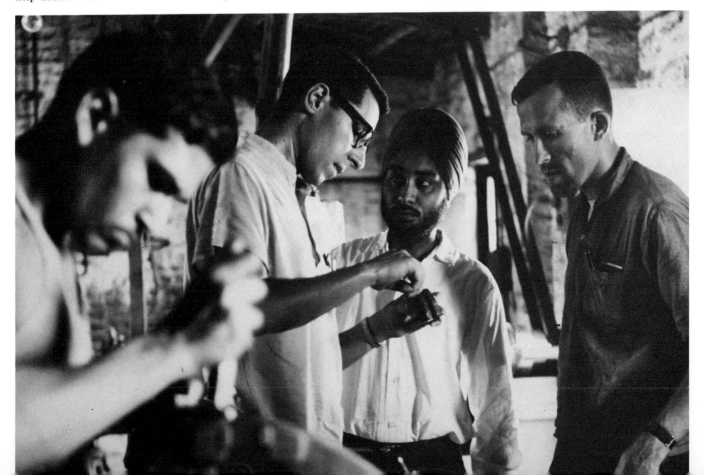

Although their jobs are usually defined, the professionals in the Peace Corps often find this is more of a handicap than advantage. Brooke Baker, a city planner who served in Sousse, Tunisia, tells why. Baker has two degrees in architecture—one from Princeton and one from the University of California at Berkley.

I am a city planner: professional, coat and tie, telephones, letter writing, conferences, designing, secretaries, office cars, just like in the United States. I have never dug a latrine; I have never even *seen* a latrine (dug, that is).

I wasn't always a planner. When I came I was an architect, but there was no work, so I took up planning, where there was work. I am about to finish a complete set of plans for the land use, street layout, and real estate policies of this city of 60,000, a master plan for Sousse, something the city needed badly and never had before. Its primary function is to avoid the urban chaos inherent in the present burst of hitherto uncontrolled

growth, to let the whole be something more than just a pile of houses. So much for what I do.

There are almost no physical problems for me here in Sousse. I have the nicest living and working conditions I've ever had—hot water, gas stoves, balconized apartment, maid service, movies, and so on. *But,* that's not what I joined the Peace Corps for, and therein lie the considerable mental problems which are part of my situation. They may be summed up in three words: Who needs me?

The problems we (the city Peace Corps volunteers here) attack are not the basic ones of health, food, rudimentary education; not the ones which give visible results per hour spent; not the ones the ads told us about. We're farther up on the curve of diminishing returns; the stuff we deal in is more sophisticated, less essential to the life of the body, much less visibly rewarding, and thus we are often bereft of that visible achievement (however small) which keeps other volunteers going over the rough spots. I would prefer physical privations

Most of the Peace Corps architects in Tunisia were assigned to the Ministry of Public Works. However, Bob Mabry, of San Antonio, Texas, was assigned to the National Institute of Archeology in the Ministry of Cultural Affairs. One of his jobs was to work on the restoration of the Grand Mosque in Kairouan—one of three architects assigned to assist a well-known Italian authority on restorations. Al-

though it proved a fascinating assignment, Mabry could not help having a guilty conscience. Like Brooke Baker in Sousse (*see above*), Mabry found it hard to see where he was making a contribution. How did restoring the Grand Mosque help the development of Tunisia, he wondered. (*Below*) Mabry and two Tunisian fellow workers test the strength of the Mosque foundation.

Mabry gives volunteer teacher Kay Elquist a guided tour
of the Grand Mosque. His biggest frustrations on the job
were the tourists who continually swarmed throughout the
Mosque and even into his office, despite a sign on his door
in six languages which said "Private Office. Do Not Enter."

to this constant effort at justifying one's presence as simply a money-saving convenience for the host government.

My own presence saves the government $4,000 a year —the difference between my pay and that of foreign technicians who do the same job. That's nothing, considering that the United States pays that same $4,000 to train, heal, ship, staff, and readjust me. The host government gets along without these luxuries fairly well, with little apparent discomfort on the part of the other foreign technicians.

The basic problem is that we must keep trying to convince ourselves that the information-exchange objectives of the Peace Corps are enough to carry on, even in the absence of the objective of work which has fundamental utility. Either the Peace Corps has to enlarge its advertising image from the present latrine-digging one, or else it has to abandon these more sophisticated jobs. The conflict between the fact of the sophisticated job and the advertising which attracts a person with promises of more fundamental jobs is es-

sentially harmful. Many good, hardworking, sensitive Peace Corps volunteers consider themselves inadequate and useless because they're never able to dig a latrine. This is a direct result of misleading representation, and the major problem of city life in Tunisia.

I am sorry that the Peace Corps itself is the source of most of our problems in Sousse. Almost everything else is quite good: host relationships, work in sufficient quantity, cultural activity. But I always have the feeling that a proper employment agency could do the same here. And we would not bear this dual albatross of being "poor relations" vis-à-vis the other technicians and "rich relations" vis-à-vis the Tunisians.

The effect of this article is, I hope, reformist. Things could be good, but the Peace Corps will have to change to make them so. My own adjustment to the conflict has been to forget that I'm a Peace Corps volunteer, and behave entirely as a foreign hired hand. I feel better that way.

—BROOKE BAKER

PLACE EHOUHADA

Another one of Mabry's assignments was to prepare a series of sketches for architectural changes which might be made in the old part of the city. His plan is to preserve the traditional elements of the medina, such as Arab doorways and balconies; he sees the medina street as a progression of closed vistas, short turns and surprise views. (*Above*) A Mabry sketch for a proposed plaza in Kairouan.

"You're a What?"

Most Peace Corps headquarters offices abroad have volunteer secretaries. As Magdalena Tapia wrote from Costa Rica: "You're a volunteer WHAT?" Miss Tapia is from Los Angeles, where she attended the Metropolitan College of Business.

"You're a what?"

As you hear that familiar question again for the fifth time that day, you smile and start over again—"I'm a Peace Corps volunteer secretary."

"But how can you be *both* a secretary and a volunteer?"

By this time, you begin to wonder how you *can* be both.

The life of a volunteer secretary is easy only in the fact that it is probably the most structured of all Peace Corps programs. Like secretaries around the globe, you work an eight-hour day, five days a week (unless that ten-page report you're typing just *has* to go in tonight's mail). During this eight-hour day your site is a Peace Corps office overseas, your *junta progresista*—the Peace Corps staff in that country. Your working tools are not a shovel nor an English teaching manual but a typewriter and a dictation pad.

You're a walking encyclopedia with ready answers to the countless number of questions asked by volunteers and staff. You're an amateur psychiatrist listening to the problems of your fellow volunteers. You're the local mailman stuffing envelopes with the latest memorandums from the staff or perhaps the latest issues of *The Volunteer* and *The New York Times* to volunteers all over the country. You're a file and index clerk trying to keep that filing basket empty and all communications in order in the endless number of files that must be kept up-to-date. You're the office messenger girl running to the embassy or the local post office for the long-awaited letters from home.

If you have worked as a bilingual secretary before entering training, it certainly would be a blessing, for one of your many tasks is to arm yourself with a Span-

Looking like a harassed secretary almost anywhere, Peggy Duncan of Dayton, Ohio, sits at her office desk in Enugu, Nigeria. Peggy was a volunteer secretary for the Associate Director of the Nigerian Peace Corps contingent.

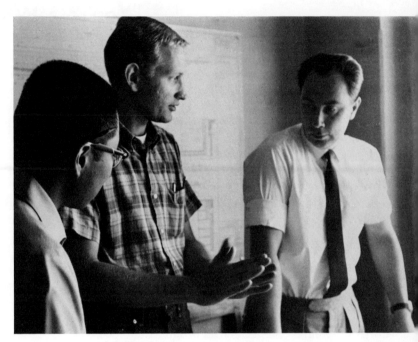

Peaceful coexistence: Robert Hall (*left*) and Donald Gregory discuss plans for a new bridge near Kabul with their Russian boss, a U.N. technical adviser. They were members of a rural development team in Afghanistan. Hall was graduated from the City College of San Francisco's School of Engineering; Gregory received his degree in architecture from the University of Illinois.

ish-English dictionary (if in Latin America as in my case) and *struggle* to answer the foreign correspondence that crosses your desk. These are but a few of the tasks that await a volunteer secretary when she arrives at her site each morning.

As for any volunteer, her first month overseas is perhaps the hardest. Along with the usual adjustment come the puzzled glances when she enters a room with other volunteers. She begins to wonder if her slip shows or maybe she forgot one earring. Then comes the night of the first party. Someone is sure to pull her aside and want to know why so-and-so left the country or exactly what's in his file. They'll be wondering if she has a tape recorder hidden in her purse. Will she tell the Director everything that's said? We'd better be careful and not say too much or let anything slip. After a month or two of being in the country, all this wears off, and you stop checking in the mirror every morning to see if you really have two heads. Some volunteers will always think of you as a staff member but, to the majority of them, you're just another volunteer in a new kind of program.

Like all volunteers, we go through a training period. I trained with four other secretaries last summer at Georgetown University with a group of volunteers who are now teaching in Colombia and Chile. Our training was almost the same as theirs—we also ran around the track (all the time wondering, "Just what are these Directors like, that we have to run a timed mile?" After all, how much running can you do in an office?) We participated in community development projects so

that we would be capable of undertaking such a project overseas if the opportunity arose.

Our area studies were somewhat different because we did not know where we would be stationed until the day before training ended. For the first few weeks of training, we all thought we were going to Chile, and my roommate and I were beginning to wonder why they needed five secretaries in Chile. Our technical studies consisted of two weeks of instruction in teaching English as a foreign language and several weeks of orientation at the Peace Corps office in Washington, the last few weeks of which were spent performing secretarial duties in the Latin American Regional Office.

When I arrived overseas I was anxiously awaiting the day that I could start some type of community development or health project. However, I soon realized that all such projects are full-time jobs, and that nights after work and Saturday afternoons and Sundays just weren't enough time to do a satisfactory job and still fulfill my secretarial role. Yet I wanted to do something during my nonoffice hours to feel more like a volunteer. I have put my English-teaching practice to work and have started an English class comprised of a few neighborhood women three nights a week. In addition, I find that I have enough time to tutor a local student a couple of hours a week. Maybe this doesn't exactly fit the Peace Corps image but it's my way of fulfilling my role as one of those strange animals in that crazy new program—Peace Corps volunteer secretary.

—MAGDALENA TAPIA

Chapter 9

Peace Corps Life—and After

The job the volunteer is sent overseas to do is only part of the Peace Corps experience. The other part —and perhaps the most important—is the volunteer's day-to-day existence in a strange new world. In the long run, his effectiveness as a volunteer usually depends on how well he can make the adjustment to the new world, and how successfully he settles into the host country community. It is not an easy transition. Some volunteers make it more easily than others; some sooner, or later, than others. But, surprisingly, most of them do make the adjustment. The drop-out rate in the Peace Corps, for reasons other than such things as illness or a death in the family, is now less than 3 percent. It is a remarkable record.

Describing what it is like to live abroad as a Peace Corps volunteer is not easy; rarely do any two volunteers have identical experiences, even in the same country, let alone on different continents. However, taken

The lonely volunteer in a strange new environment. Elizabeth Halkola, a volunteer health worker who served in Sabah, Malaysia, makes a house call, balancing her way along rice paddy dikes.

Clyde and Eva Ingle talk with neighborhood children in front of their house in Zamboanga in the Philippines. Living quarters for the volunteers vary, depending on the country, nature of the program, and whether the volunteer is assigned to an urban or rural project.

together, the photographs and the accounts the volunteers have written of their daily life abroad reprinted on these pages may offer some idea of what the Peace Corps life is like. Charles Kratz, who taught English and social studies, discusses life in the Philippines. Kratz received his B.A. in journalism from Fresno State College in California and worked as a reporter and photographer in San Francisco before joining the Peace Corps:

Trying to describe living conditions of volunteers in the Philippines is like trying to describe snowflakes—no two are alike.

A roof is about the only thing that volunteers' living arrangements have in common, and even these range from nipa thatch to Spanish tile.

Volunteers live with Filipino families, with other volunteers, or alone. They live in houses, apartments, and dormitories. A volunteer may have a four-room house to himself or only half a room. His house may be made out of bamboo and nipa, wood, concrete or cement block, or a combination of these.

Bob Wise (Narberth, Pennsylvania) and Barry Parks (Mason City, Iowa) shared an apartment in Paco, Manila, with running water, electricity, a flush toilet, window screens, a fan, and even a refrigerator.

Ralph and Elinor Foulke (Hillsdale, Michigan) built their own bamboo and nipa house with fellow teachers. They had electricity but no running water. One special comfort they claimed was an ice chest. They lived in

Barotac Nueva, Iloilo, Panay.

George Ricketts (Park Ridge, Illinois) lives with a well-to-do family in Santa Cruz, Laguna, Luzon, and has television.

Gerry and Suzanne Hanberry (Denmark, South Carolina) are proud that their wooden house in Malaybalay, Bukidnon, Mindanao, has an indoor john (bucket-flush type).

After a few months in a *barrio,* many volunteers find they are not as ascetic as they thought and are grateful for small comforts, and an occasional trip to Manila, Baguio, Davao, Zamboanga, or smaller cities nearby.

One of the real pleasures of such a trip is a hot shower. Another is food. Manila, for example, has many restaurants serving American and European food. An occasional steak makes the volunteer's usual diet of fish and rice, pork and rice, or just rice and rice more bearable.

Cooking ararngements and facilities vary almost as much as housing for Philippines volunteers. Those who live with families, of course, eat with them. Others cook for themselves, have a houseboy or maid who cooks or helps, or eat in restaurants.

Few volunteers have access to a refrigerator or an oven. Cooking is usually done on one- or two-burner kerosene stoves or hot plates. Some volunteers have made ovens from five-gallon kerosene cans. These fit on kerosene burners and can be used to bake the potatoes found in many parts of the Philippines.

If he can justify his need for it, a volunteer is issued a bicycle, typewriter, battery-operated tape recorder, or *Encyclopaedia Britannica.*

Swimming is excellent in many parts of the islands, and is especially popular with most volunteers. There is plenty of surf on the Pacific east shores. The western shores on the China Sea have some beautiful white sand beaches and coral reefs that are exciting to explore with a face mask.

There is also freshwater swimming in a few places. Los Banos has many hot-spring swimming pools, and the pool at the University of the Philippines in Dilliman, Quezon City, is open to volunteers. Swimming in lakes and rivers is discouraged, for they are often contaminated with the parasites that cause schistosomiasis.

Though some volunteers like to brag that they put in a hundred hours a week on their jobs, most have plenty of leisure time.

This can be a problem in the *barrio,* where there are often only limited ways of passing time—especially for girls and especially after dark. Reading, even if by kerosene lantern, is the major leisure activity of most volunteers. Many read their way through the Peace Corps book locker and then through vast quantities of the wares of Alemar's or Erewhon bookstores in Manila.

Social activities also occupy a great deal of time. In

the *barrio,* these are often limited to fiestas, school functions, family parties, and visits. Dating between volunteers or between volunteers and Filipinos is common in the cities but rare in the rural areas. Rural Filipinos don't understand casual dating.

Many volunteers take part in sports, but here, too, girls in rural areas are handicapped, for in the Philippines, women are not expected to be active. Because of this and the starchy diet, most Peace Corps girls gain weight.

Bicycling, hiking, and tennis, though ranking far behind swimming, are also popular with volunteers. Many also play basketball, organized or unorganized.

Bowling alleys abound—though they are of the type known in the States as tenpins, with small balls and pins. Pool halls are also common. Many theatres show American movies, but there is also a good supply of "Filipino Westerns."

For entertainment, Manila is a big attraction. Nightclubs feature American and Spanish music. There are many concerts. In one recent week the Manila Symphony Orchestra presented a program of Shostakovich, Saint-Saëns, and Wagner; the Yale Glee Club appeared, and a *rondalla* (Filipino orchestra) performed the works of a contemporary Filipino composer—all in the same auditorium.

—CHARLES KRATZ

Lois and Stephen Hirst, married volunteer teachers from Miamisburg, Ohio, in front of their home in Liberia.

A continuing debate in the Peace Corps concerns the pros and cons of life in the city versus life in the "bush," as volunteers call the nonurban areas. The debate is well summed up in this discusison of life in Dakar versus life in the boondocks of Senegal. Gary Engelberg, author of the discussion, is from Brooklyn, and as a PCV helped train secondary school teachers in Dakar.

Dakar has so often been called the Paris of Africa that some people now jokingly reply that Paris is the Dakar of Europe. Every joke has its grain of truth. Dakar, though typically African in many ways, is nevertheless one of the "Twentieth-Century Modern" African capitals based on Western models and concepts. As in many other developing countries in Africa, the second largest city does not compare to the capital in wealth or extent of development, and the degree of development of the rest of the country does not seem to justify the existence of a glittering white capital. Dakar is the jewel in the crown—but the crown is yet to be forged. There are, in effect, two "countries" here, Dakar and Senegal.

Thus, there are two kinds of volunteers—the Senegal volunteer and the Dakar volunteer. They share the general problems of the volunteers around the world. But their specific problems are products of their vastly different environments.

In June, there were seven volunteers in Dakar—three teachers, three social workers, and a volunteer secretary. Most of them were cliff dwellers, living in apartment houses scattered throughout the city, or in new government-sponsored housing projects on the outskirts of town. Though they enjoyed the generally comfortable living conditions in the city, they also paid the capital city prices. Jim Toliver, an English teacher, has felt the pinch of prices in one of the world's most expensive cities:

"Financially speaking, I find myself in the hole. No adjustment is made between the salaries of "bush" and city volunteers. My sympathy goes to the "bush" volunteer who often suffers from lack of sufficient recreation. But I wonder whether the city volunteer, who is tempted daily by taxis, movies, and various other types of amusement, does not suffer more. If he avails himself of these amusements, he will plunge himself hopelessly into debt."

To the volunteers living in the bush with no running

The "great debate" among Peace Corps volunteers is life in the city versus life in "the bush." (*Opposite page*) Jan Anderson, a PCV teacher in Maracaibo, Venezuela, changes cabs. She took four taxicab rides in her daily round trip to and from work. (*Right*) John Calkins and a visitor, Betsy Norton, two volunteers who taught in Nigeria, sit outside Calkins' bush home in Taboye.

water, the problems a Dakar volunteer has with his plumbing or his water heater must sound ludicrous. The complaints of the Dakar volunteer often do, in fact, take on a tone similar to the complaints of apartment dwellers in New York or Chicago.

Toliver says: "I live in what might be called a modern apartment house, situated ten minutes outside of the city. The other people who live in the building all have very noisy children. The kid upstairs is another Caruso. I'm on the ground floor, next to the parking lot which serves as an alarm clock and major distraction when I'm preparing lessons or trying to correct papers. I have an electric refrigerator, a water heater, lights, and approximately four huge cockroaches daily."

Physical problems of city living are easier to adapt to than the social and psychological problems. In a bush village, the sense of community is strong and always evident. In Dakar, the community is a vague, perhaps nonexistent entity, almost impossible to define. Fran Pilzys is a social worker. She spent her first year in the bush, and now works in a hospital in Dakar. Comparing the two lives, she says, "In the 'bush' village you know everyone. You're always entertaining your neighbors, or they're entertaining you. Sometimes I had to lock my door and pretend I wasn't there so I could get some work done. Here in Dakar, I live in an apartment. I know my neighbors, but they're French."

The Dakar volunteer does not have the ready-made community into which he can fit himself. Any contacts with the Senegalese beyond work are immediately handicapped by the nature of city living in general, and the living conditions of the volunteer in particular. Technical assistants are usually housed by the Senegalese government. Volunteers, therefore, often find themselves in apartment houses, surrounded by French or other non-Senegalese technical assistants. The Dakar volunteer then either becomes involved in the French community or falls back into the sometimes frightening anonymity that big-city living engenders.

"In the city, I'm a little person. I go to work, and I come home," says Miss Pilzys. She is expressing very simply the alienation that one has come to expect in a highly developed society, but that one is surprised to see here.

The Dakar volunteer also encounters these big-city problems in his work. He is often dealing with the sophisticated problems of a highly developed society, while at the same time, in the same country, the bush volunteer is teaching equally important basic skills. The Dakar volunteer is already working in the offices of the "skyscraper," while the bush volunteer is building the foundation upon which this "skyscraper" must eventually stand or fall.

Often it's a case of letting the people in the "skyscraper" know what's happening down below.

In the hospital where she works with a Senegalese counterpart, Miss Pilzys tends to cases needing quick aid—usually financial. The poor who come in from the bush with no money or clothing, and who need help such as an artificial limb, are the people she deals with. "My job is not only letting the people know what is available to them but also letting the government know what cases need help," she says.

Donald Patriss teaches English and Spanish in a non-sectarian private school organized by Canadian brothers. He says, "It is more important for me to be in the

But no matter where he lives, the day in the life of a volunteer develops a pattern—certain things are the same the world over. (*Above*) Volunteer Ken McLean starts the day off in Ndjobe, Gabon, with a shower. (*Right*) Nomenee Robinson gets his morning milk delivery in Chandigarh, India.

(*Above*) A volunteer in Bahia, Brazil, makes his bed.

(*Below*) Dane and Judy Smith from Albuquerque, New Mexico, two volunteers who taught in Ethiopia, have breakfast before leaving for school.

Then it's off to work—by whatever means of transportation available. (*Above, left*) PCV Nancy Wallace used a motorcycle in Ibadan, Nigeria. Motor bikes in most countries are now restricted unless they are necessary to do the job. The preferred means of transportation is the bicycle, which the Peace Corps will provide. (*Above, right*) Ann Schmidt, a Community development worker and teacher in Malaysia, works her way through a muddy spot in the road on her way to work. (*Left*) Nancy Holland grabs a ride on the principal means of transportation in the village of Kundis, Afghanistan, where Nancy taught English.

city than in the bush. Here, I'm training an elite that is going to use the English I have taught, whereas in the bush, many students can barely speak French.

"The idea of teaching an elite sounds, at first, contrary to democratic Peace Corps goals. But, despite the undemocratic connotations the word 'elite' may carry, it must be understood that in a country where there are not yet enough facilities to enforce the desired compulsory education, those who are educated form an elite. Only the fact that this elite will, in turn, aid in the development of the country and, in so doing, contribute to its own downfall as an elite, justifies our part in its formation.

"I work in a school roughly equivalent to an American teachers' college, preparing English teachers for secondary schools," Donald says. "Like the other Dakar teachers, I concentrate on the oral method of language instruction. I sometimes think I'd rather live in the bush, but I couldn't do this job there. If I'm successful here, and if my students learn to use the oral-aural teaching methods, they will in turn affect many students each year.

"In a world crying for communication, the academic knowledge of a modern living language is not sufficient. Here my job is facilitated by a modern school, equipped with projectors, tape recorders, and a twenty-four-seat language laboratory. I don't think any teaching I could do in the bush would have such long-range effects as my work here."

Brian Young, who spent his first year coaching in the southern region of Senegal, worked in a Dakar center for the rehabilitation of young delinquents—boys who

In the hills of Latin America, the horse is preferred. (*Above*) Earl Williams, who worked on a rabbit project in Colombia, rides out to pay a morning call on one of the *campesio* families with which he worked.

In Africa the "mammy wagon" is the most common means of public transportation. (*Above*) Carol Waymire, of Santa Rosa, California, gets aboard. Some volunteers, when their jobs call for it, have the luxury of a jeep. But like cars everywhere, sometimes the Peace Corps jeeps won't start in the morning. (*Left*) Florence McCarty, of Solvang, California, checks the motor of her jeep in Comilla, East Pakistan.

When nothing else is available, hitch-hiking is recommended—by Robert George of Stony Creek, Connecticut, who catches a ride in a pickup truck near Mirpur, East Pakistan. And when all else fails (*right*), volunteer Bill Myers, of Moorpark, California, walks off to work in the jungle near Nargana, Panama, where he was a community development worker.

For lunch you might be lucky enough to be the guest of the *Illalos*, the Somali bush police. (*Above*) Peace Corps Representative Bob Blackburn (*left*); volunteer Steve Frantz; Administrative Assistant Ali Essa; Peace Corps Representative Charles Overholt, and Volunteer Ted Rideout (*right*) eat *bariss iyo helib*, which is camel's meat and rice washed down with *anogel*, fresh charcoal-flavored camel's milk. (*Below*) After lunch there might be time to work in the school garden, as volunteer teachers Duke Talbot (*left*) and John Roberts did at their school in northern Somalia . . .

had either been in some kind of trouble, or whose parents found under the pressures of urban living they could no longer supervise or control their children. Much of the students' time at the center was spent learning mechanical or woodworking skills, and preparing for tests that would allow them to enter or reenter the normal public education facilities. In addition to his coaching, Young taught English.

Most social workers, in fact, enter some form of teaching in their work, whether it be literacy, puericulture, nutrition, or sewing. Rosalee Black was also working in a social center in Dakar. She, like many female volunteers in community centers throughout the country, worked with women in health, nutrition, and sewing. But unlike the bush volunteers, she worked through a highly organized social center.

This connection with some sort of institution seems to be typical of the work of the Dakar volunteer. For social workers, it's the hospital or the community center. For the teachers, it is simply the school, the Order of the Sacred Heart, to which the Canadian brothers are attached, or UNESCO. The work situation of the Dakar volunteer is clearly more highly structured, and

is more likely to have regular hours and set duties. Where the creative energies of the bush volunteer are concentrated on trying to set up a self-perpetuating institution that will satisfy a community need, the Dakar volunteer finds the institution already created, and devotes his energies to working within the institution and improving it.

—GARY ENGELBERG

Judith Nordblom taught two years in Asmara, Ethiopia. In her opinion, "the real job of helping can best be achieved in the city."

It is my contention that the job of the city volunteer offers more of a challenge and can bring as much fulfillment as life in the way of developing one's sensibilities.

Drummed into volunteers' heads at training, in publications, and by staff members is the notion that the real Peace Corps volunteer is not the city volunteer but the young man or woman in the rural post. The poor city fellow is attacked by those volunteers who come in

. . . or time to join in a game of volleyball, as community developer Everett Snowden did at the Chijnaya school in **Peru.**

The day's work over, Herbert Hoffritz, an agricultural worker in Ludhiana, India, heads home to his hostel four miles away.

Margaret Gallen, a nurse in Tunis, stops to do some shopping on her way to the house she shares with volunteer nurse Sandy Ketner.

from the villages once a month to get supplies *and* be luxurious, and who see little of the city but the main street, and by latter-day Thoreau fans who are still tied to the glories of the Golden West.

Obviously these well-meaning romantics know little about the average New York apartment or American history. And so it is hard for the city volunteer himself to believe that where he is *is* worthwhile.

But the city is worthwhile. The trouble is that in order to come to that conclusion, the volunteer has to reexamine completely what self-denials he should have to make, if any, and he also has to take another look at the city.

As far as the material comforts of a city proving to be debilitating, this has been an oft-considered part of Peace Corps policy. I suppose it is typical of Americans always to be aware of material things. The disease of complacency has its roots in the individual rather than in his possessions, and I doubt if anyone could accuse the majority of volunteers of having this defect.

Criticism has encouraged the Peace Corps staff to move volunteers out of cities. One argument is that the native teacher or health worker does not want to be in the provinces, while the Peace Corps volunteer has a special desire to do so, and because of his wish for this kind of challenge, he can do an especially effective job. I do not think Americans should necessarily go where no one else wants to go.

There is a little disciplinary value in forcing people to do their own dirty work (I assume that going to the provinces for the native of any country is such). And to create real progress at the village level takes understanding of the villager, which, no matter how great his enthusiasm, the American just cannot have. He can build wells, give superior education while he is there, and help a few bright, barefooted boys to get to America or Europe. But because he cannot really communicate with the people, language speaker or not—why he is there to change them and why change is important— the effect he has will usually be only skin deep. The less educated African who may be forced to go into the village will still be enough above the villager to create the desire for improvement, and they will understand why he has improved. Not only do I think that the American of today is too far from the village situation economically and emotionally to comprehend it (and living the way the locals do does not make you one of them), but I do not believe in sustained provincial equality or development until the centers of wealth create enough capital to be able to give some away.

(*Below*) Vince Martin, of Inverness, Florida, pauses in the marketplace in Pesqueira, Brazil, where he listens to a public reader tell of the news of the day in poetic rhyme. Martin gives a brief description of *faz mal* on page 238.

At home after work, Robert Cuddy (*above*) in Gabon stops to read the mail and Arnold Zandstra in Niger (*below*) feeds his pet, "Bitty."

The real job of helping—and I assume that *the* most important task of a volunteer is to provide a skill—can best be achieved in the city, though again I believe that the native peoples, when there are enough of them trained, will do more even here.

First of all, the students in the cities are closer to the foreigner, and especially the American, in attitude and comprehension of the modern world. If the city is a typical postcolonial one, the students are in between cultures. The village priest of the Moslem family has taught them one thing and the European has taught them another.

But how can we help when both of us seem to be questioning? As older people, and here I refer to the student-volunteer-teacher relationship, we have gone through some of their problems already, though not too long ago—the advantage of youth in the Peace Corps—and can suggest solutions or considerations. There is a common language of distress. And we can communicate through knowledge of city life and the newspaper. Students living in the city are not naïve about politics and people, and do read more books and know current events.

There is concern that because so many volunteers are concentrated in cities, they take the easiest way out and associate only with one another. Few attempts are made to search out friends and acquaintances among host country people. This, say Peace Corps officials, not only prevents volunteers from coming to understand the country, but makes the people consider the Peace Corps as they do any foreigners: isolationist and condescending. I admit that this tendency to clan is usually not overcome among city volunteers, and that in many cases this person knows less about the customs of his students than the fellow stationed in a village. But more clarification of this criticism is still needed.

The individual volunteer and his ways of performing are at the bottom of most considerations. While there are cases of volunteers in the cities who have only

(*Opposite page*) Kathryn Fitch, on the island of Panape in Micronesia, takes a swim, using a palm leaf to cover her head from a tropical shower.

American friends, many village volunteers fit the same pattern. Now while these actions may limit the anthropological knowledge of the person or prevent his fame from growing, I do not necessarily think that this preference lessens his effectiveness in his job.

For the city volunteer, the number of total host country acquaintances is usually smaller, and the knowledge of the "feel" for the traditional society will certainly be less, but the number of people one could call "friends" will probably be greater if only because a city has a greater number of educated people. These friendships will probably be deeper because of the increased experiences of the city dweller and the fact that the most qualified people in developing nations migrate to the cities. And, in an African city with its social life, offices, and bars, volunteers have a hard time *not* getting to know people.

The city provides a source of personal contacts impossible to get elsewhere. Other than trying to suggest change at the bottom by working with the village people, the city volunteer can meet the people who are involved with or control policy change. As adult teachers and as members of the clubs for civil servants, the volunteers can come to understand the working at the top, the most influential people, and because of the greater basis for communication, achieve some results.

One comment should be made about the relationships volunteers develop with one another. The en-

. . . (*Opposite page*) Dale Myers, a small business adviser from Colorado, explores a World War II Japanese Zero sunk in 25 feet of water off Ibeye in the Marshall Islands. (*Above*) Fred Carlson, also in Micronesia, does a little reading. The book locker in the foreground is given to all Peace Corps Volunteers. (*Below*) Beth Halkola, a health worker in Sabah, just unwinds . . .

236

forced closeness of a group in a city is often a rewarding experience for the volunteer. A person without
props—such as constant busyness or the feeling of being part of a mass society, to protect him from himself
and others—becomes dependent upon everyone else,
and hence more exposed. If this situation is recognized,
the volunteer can develop relationships that he had
never been able to have before. I suppose the experience is like the camaraderie of men on the battlefield.
To volunteers, these friendships are an important part
of their experience, and a reason why some prefer to be
stationed in the city.

The urban volunteer is sometimes accused of not
being a "full-time" volunteer. The volunteer in the
village is probably forced to participate in extra activities in the community. But the city volunteer can lead
the separate lives of school and home, and usually finds
himself doing this.

Some volunteers will be "full-time" volunteers in the
village or in the city. Some in the city work so hard for
their students or their ideals that they have little social
life. One could work for the Peace Corps twenty-four
hours a day no matter where he was. But according to
a Peace Corps myth, as popularly interpreted, "full-
time" is interpreted not in terms of hours but emotional commitment, and the size of a city prevents a
volunteer there from having it. I have often felt sepa-
rated from the life and growth of the city because of
little things like not being able to know the home life
of my students.

The myth assumes that it is possible to lose onself in
a village small in physical size or number. There are
basic lines of communication between people, it says,
and because these can be explored closely and completely (all phases of life) in a village, one can learn
another way of life and help modernize it.

I disregard the notion that the problem of communication is governed by geographical or numerical size.
The controlling factor seems to be the size of the emotional gap separating people. Living among a people
may reveal their daily schedule and help one understand why they think the way they do. But I really
question whether they, because of their lack of sophistication, can ever determine why we act the way we do.
A fruitful discussion must entail understanding on
both sides.

The volunteer should be encouraged to regard the
experience of two years as a deeply human encounter

. . . And Earle and Rhoda Brooks, in Manta, Ecuador, relax
in their courtyard before dinner. After leaving Ecuador,
where they adopted two little Ecuadorians, the Brookses
returned to Minneapolis and wrote a book about their
Peace Corps experience—*The Barrios of Manta.*

Dinner may be at home, where Howard Gard (*above*) of Sacramento, California, dines with a Thai co-worker in Mahasarakham, Thailand, or at a neighbor's house (*below*) where Volunteer Dolores Tadlock, a poultry worker in Habra, India, helps fix a meal.

where he is constantly comparing cultures and reactions, and remaining open to whatever is needed to help him and his "adopted" country communicate with each other. This alone is a twenty-four-hour job. If it demands that the person separate his lives or have privacy and free time, then this is right. And this makes living in the city an advantage—one can get away from the situation to see it in new ways.

So, then, having tried to break apart the "golden calf" of the Peace Corps, what special tasks remain for the volunteer? First, he is a person interested in providing a skill needed by the host country. His job is most important, and he should be judged by how thoroughly he does this task, not by the number of hours he spends at it or where he does it. The successful volunteer is the person who did or will do his work as well at home as he now does it in the Peace Corps, whether or not his Peace Corps work has been his former occupation. He is basically serious about getting on with the business of life and its improvement.

Next, he is committed to an honest study of himself and others as part of a quest for knowledge of human nature. To what extent he realizes this, how much actual emotional maturity he brings to the job, and the resulting amount of sympathy he has for the people will determine his success.

—JUDITH NORDBLOM

No matter where they live, sooner or later most volunteers are confronted with faz mal. *Below, volunteer Vince Martin, a member of a four-man public health team in Pesqueira, Brazil, discusses the care and treatment of the* figado *in Brazil.*

No sketch of Brazil, or more particularly of the northeast of Brazil, would be complete without mention of what we might call the *figado*-complex—health beliefs the *Nordestinos* have adopted to prevent illness to them and their *figados,* the Portuguese word for livers. Actually, some people might call *faz mal,* under which heading we group the *figado*-complex, just another system of folk taboos. Unfortunately, it may not be as simple as this; *faz mal,* translated loosely into English, means generally "it's bad for you!" A better translation might be "what is bad for your liver."

As volunteers working in a health project, we have at numerous times been accosted, cautioned, and especially warned by local friends about various *faz mals,* and how to prevent them and their spread. There seem to be two kinds of *faz mals* to beware of: the pure *faz mal* is a treacherous thing, because it directly aims for the *figado,* an organ which people esteem very highly. The other *faz mal* can impair the bodily system in general, depending on what *faz mal* is violated, and can even render one *doido* (translated loosely as "a little off the rocker").

My first brush with *faz mal* occurred in a *pensão* (boardinghouse) in a small town in the central region of Pernambuco where I am stationed with another volunteer. After finishing supper one evening, my volunteer co-worker asked for the key to unlock the door to the shower (the only one available); he was quickly told that the key couldn't be found, and perhaps it would be better if the *senhór* waited until the next day to take his shower. The *senhór,* in his broken Portuguese, explained that he didn't want to wait and proceeded to get the key himself despite a general protest. The shower over, the volunteer dressed and walked out to face a group of anxious Brazilians, including the proprietor and his wife, who nervously inquired about his health.

The next day the proprietor confided to me in a horrified tone, "We didn't think he'd live!" Not understanding Portuguese well, I still didn't catch on to exactly what was worrying them. It was not until one volunteer went three consecutive nights without being able to get into the shower, and a visiting volunteer nurse had to go to bed one night with shampoo in her hair, that we finally discovered the danger that we were in! "Never take a shower after you eat," we were advised, "especially a cold one." "Why?" we asked blankly. *"Porque faz mal ao figado"* (because it's bad for the liver), they fired back.

"How does it offend the *figado?*" we ventured to in-

For many volunteers, the day ends about the way it did in college. (*Above*) Peace Corps Representative Larry O'Brien (*left*) and volunteers Ed See and Craig Kinzelman (*with back to camera*) finish the day with an old-fashioned bull session. The volunteers worked on a school construction program in Gabon.

quire. Unfortunately, the answer was a little beyond our vocabulary at the time; the only statement comprehensible was something about "hot and cold."

During the months that followed, even after our transfer to another site farther in the interior, we were barraged constantly by a variety of *faz mals* of all shades and classifications—many of them that changed and differed in form from town to town and area to area, but just like the proverbial itch, they constantly emerged in differing contexts. All of them, however, had one main preoccupation—to keep the *figado* safe from attack. A typical conversation would usually go like this:

"How are you today, Carlos?"

"More or less. To tell you the truth, I've been feeling a little sick."

"What's the problem, Carlos? A little cold?"

"No, but I'll tell what I think it is! It's this damn *figado* acting up again."

"*Figado,* eh! Well, what did you do this time?"

"I don't know! Everyone thinks it was that mango I ate before I went to bed last night! But, personally, I think it was that cold water I drank after taking hot coffee this morning!"

Common *faz mals* include the following:

- Cutting one's hair or nails after eating.
- Eating fruit of any kind after physical exertion and sweating.

- Drinking an alcoholic beverage after eating a watermelon.
- Eating a mango or pineapple or nearly any fruit after drinking coffee or before going to bed.
- Going to sleep after eating goat tripe (particularly fatal).
- Opening a refrigerator or letting a cold breeze hit you after drinking coffee.
- Eating certain varieties of hot fruit (especially bad). In some quarters it is strongly believed that eating hot *pinha* (a common northeastern fruit) will definitely cause asthma.
- Anything in general that involves a mixture of eating something hot and then something cold. Eating ice cream after drinking coffee is practically unheard of in some places.

Faz mal and the *figado*-complex cut across both social classes and professional lines with little distinction. Upon seeing a man with a particularly bad case of palsy and tremors passing through the local market, one volunteer asked his Brazilian co-worker about it. "Oh, you see it all the time," he replied. He then went on to explain how the unfortunate man once came home after a hard day's work and immediately took a cold shower. "Ever since then, the poor fellow has been like this—lack of education, you know!"

Shortly afterward, a fairly well-to-do and educated member of our local community was a little hung over

Saturday morning, for most volunteers, will probably begin with a trip to the marketplace. In Morocco, volunteers Polly Rightmire (*left*) and Virginia Wolfe (*right*) set out to do their weekly shopping on market day.

the morning after a local *festa* in which he had overdone it a little on the *cachaça*. "That's what finished one of my cousins, you know!"

One final thing about *faz mal* and the *figado*-complex that needs to be mentioned is the duration of time involved to cure the *figado* once it has been invaded. Normally the cure is very brief, depending on how strong the *figado* is to start with. The worst case that we have heard about was revealed to a volunteer who was having his hair cut in a local barbershop. During the course of a conversation, the barber casually mentioned that his *figado* was in a bad state.

"What happened?" the volunteer asked cautiously, "did you eat a mango before going to bed?"

"No," the barber quickly countered. "In February of 1941 in Alagoas I drank a cold *guarana* after eating and haven't been the same since." The volunteer then asked him pointedly if it couldn't have been his *rins* (kidneys) instead of his *figado* that offended.

"The *rins?*" he repeated in a puzzled tone. "Yes, the *rins*. They aren't far from the *figado*, you know!" After thinking this over for a little while, he finally said with a little uncertainty, "Well, it could have been the *rins*, but even if it was, I know the *figado* had something to do with it."

—WILLIAM L. MARTIN

Earle and Rhoda Brooks at the marketplace in Manta, Ecuador . . .

Nancy Tucker is from Montclair, New Jersey, and was graduated from Mount Holyoke College with an A.B. in Religion and English. She spent two years in the village of Matru, in Sierra Leone, as a volunteer teacher. Below, she describes a Saturday morning visit to the marketplace.

In contrast to the bustling liveliness of Freetown, life in Matru, a small town on the Jong River, is slow-paced and even sleepy, but for a Peace Corps volunteer it is hardly dull. A Saturday shopping trip into the center of town, for example, provides changing and panoramic views of small-town West African life.

The first time I sallied forth to shop in Matru, I was armed with only two Mende (one of the major tribal languages in Sierra Leone) words of greeting: *"Boa!"* and its response, *"Mmm, bise."* As I stepped off the athletic field that marks one side of the school compound, I met some men on their way to the ferry across the Jong River. *"Boa!"* I said, somewhat timidly and feebly, half hoping that the men would not reply. *"Mmm, bise,"* the men cheerfully returned, and then broke into a stream of Mende. *"Mmm . . . mm,"* I said weakly, glad that this response acceptably covers a multitude of Mende questions and comments. *"Boa!"* I said with increasing confidence as I turned onto a residential street lively with Saturday morning household activities. Startled that this strange new white person should know their language, the adults were a little slow to respond. But the children looked up from their play and waved frantically or ran off their porches to surround me and touch my hand.

As I approached the plank bridge that crosses the stream which serves as the local water hole and laundry spot, I stopped to survey the houses of Matru. There are still a few of the round native houses made of wattle and mud, and thatched with tall elephant grass or palm branches, but most of the town's dwellings are rectangular with thatched or corrugated zinc roofs. All of the houses on the hill opposite me stood at different angles, accommodating themselves to the curves of the terrain they had been set on.

Though it was still before 7:00 A.M., it looked as if washday had already been going for some time. Women and their daughters, schoolboys, and small children of all shapes and sizes had come to the stream to pound their clothes on the rocks or to beat them mercilessly with sturdy wooden paddles. Many of these industrious launderers were also bathing themselves; their black bodies gleamed, and little beads of water caught in their hair winked at me in the brightening sunlight. School had been in session for four days, and I wondered whether I might see some of my students at the river. However, since I had 215 different stu-

. . . Harry Tobias, from Jericho, New York, in Nahuata, Guatemala . . .

dents, I figured that I would hardly recognize one in a sea of unknown faces. *"Boa!"* I said to the assembled company in general. Over the chorused response, *"Mmm, bise,"* came one clear and recognizable call, *"Bonjour, Mademoiselle Tucker."* One of my students, at least, had already learned something from me.

I climbed the rutted and rocky slope beyond the stream in the company of little girls sent to the river to fetch water; their brimming basins wavered uncertainly to and fro with each of their steps which occasionally sloshed some of the clear water onto their straight little bodies, while the dipper on the surface of the water bobbed gaily around. On the porch of one of the more substantial houses sat an elderly Muslim man in his flowing gown of electric-blue poplin. He was surrounded by tiny boys and girls who were dutifully chanting parts of the Koran in high-pitched and monotonous voices, not one of them keeping time with the others, each one hardly looking at the wooden plaque with its faint Arabic letters that was to guide his chanting and instruct his mind in the truth.

A little farther on, I passed a Protestant pastor's house. At least two radios were blaring from inside the parsonage, one with gospel hymns and another with highlife music.

As the sounds of the parsonage faded behind me, the noise from the market grew. I went straight to the screened-in corner of the raised platform at one end of the market, and joined the noisy crowd jostling there for a place at the butcher's window. Above the bobbing heads I could see that a full side of beef, half of two legs, a head, a tail, and a basketful of pieces of cowhide were still for sale from the beast that had been slaughtered earlier that morning. The butcher, a tall, strong man of the Fullah, a cattle-keeping tribe of northern Sierra Leone, presided forcefully over his sales, hacking out fair, though hardly generous, portions of meat. Not being able to argue in Mende with my fellow shoppers, I contented myself with inching my toe forward and gaining a foothold nearer the window. After twenty minutes of persistence, I got the butcher's attention and placed my order for six pounds of steak (at 38 cents a pound). Then, with the meat stowed in my green handbag, I turned to the counters that held displays of vegetables. Sometimes during each transaction, I paused a few moments to exchange greetings with the woman who was selling to me. Inevitably, she would carry the conversation past what I could understand, and we would laugh together, a deep, full laugh of friendship and simple delight. I was beginning to see how village life in Sierra Leone is both simple and rich.

For things that I could not buy at the market, I went to Jalloh's and Brainard's, general stores run by prospering African businessmen who stock everything from worm powders and refrigerated 7-Up to drip-dry shirts and pineapple jam. In contrast to these stores, I discovered that the Matur post office was not so completely stocked.

"You get some airforms?" I asked the postmaster, knowing that when a fellow volunteer had asked earlier in the week he had been told that airforms would be stocked shortly.

"No, next week."

"Oh. You get some 10-cent or some 7-cent stamps?"

"No, next week."

"You get some 5-cent stamps?"

"No."

"Some 3-cent, some 2-cent, some 1-cent?"

"No, madam, I no get *anything*."

"Oh—oh, I see. Well, we go see, next week," I said resignedly as I walked out. Well, I had been warned that Matur is somewhat remote.

Though I had not bought any stamps, my shopping trip had been reasonably successful; but my book bag was certainly not bulging.

At the moment I was content to return to the school compound and to its Saturday activities. Perhaps "Penny Kerosene," a blind man who comes around to beg each week, would already be at the house; I felt in my pocket to make sure that I still had some small change left to give him. Perhaps some students would be waiting to ask for tutoring help, to beg a book for extra reading, or simply, as is their charming custom, to "greet" a teacher.

I knew that I was not returning just to a quiet round of household activities; I was also going back to the turmoil of the local zoo. The Matur Zoo is maintained by three volunteers; we are famous (and sometimes notorious) throughout the school and the town for our collection of animals. Actually we have only one chimpanzee, three monkeys, a baby mongoose, and a household pussycat. Before they died, we also had a baby duiker (small antelope) and another cat. But with a chimp to take on walks or canoe rides, or a mongoose constantly underfoot, or two monkeys lying on the ground and cleaning each other or stirring up a playful fight, domestic life in this Peace Corps household is always at least as varied and interesting as life in the town.

—NANCY TUCKER

. . . Shopper's indecision is just as common in Accra, Ghana, as anywhere else. (*Above*) Volunteer Dorothy Vellenga, of New Concord, Ohio, who taught in Accra.

Boredom may hit some volunteers, but for most of them there are new experiences, new sights and sounds, strange and fascinating things to see and do, and a new way of life, different from the one they left behind, to discover. (*Bottom*) In the village of Nkhota Kota, Malawi, Severin Hochberg, who grew up in Cuba, sits beneath an ancient fig tree—the same tree under which Dr. David Livingston sat when he negotiated an antislave trading pact with the African chief Jumbe in 1863. (*Left*) Volunteer teachers Tom and Ruth Nighswander talk with Mpheto Banda, the witch doctor at Nkata Bay, Malawi. Behind them is Lake Nyasa. (*Below*) Ardis Gaither, of Sweetwater, Texas, watches two women grind corn in Tukuyu, Tanzania, where he taught.

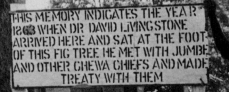

THIS MEMORY INDICATES THE YEAR 1863 WHEN DR DAVID LIVINGSTONE ARRIVED HERE AND SAT AT THE FOOT OF THIS FIG TREE HE MET WITH JUMBE AND OTHER CHEWA CHIEFS AND MADE TREATY WITH THEM

Charles Whalen keeps up with traffic on a road near Bannangstar, Thailand. Chuck is from Mahanoy City, Pennsylvania, and before joining the Peace Corps as community developer in Thailand, he was a mechanical engineer at Pratt and Whitney Aircraft Corporation in Hartford, Connecticut.

246

"Transculturation" in Four Not-So-Easy Stages

The impact of the Peace Corps experience on the volunteer is still a much-studied thing, and one sociologist who attempted to evaluate it is Dr. Maurice L. Sill, a graduate of Pennsylvania State University and an acting Peace Corps director in Pakistan, who later became Peace Corps training officer. Dr. Sill found that a volunteer passes through four stages of "transculturation," as he calls the process of adjustment: discovery, self-alignment, participation, and devolution. Below, Dr. Sill discusses his four stages:

Discovery (0–4 months)

The volunteer faces a major adjustment during his first few months in the host country. At first, he is a foreigner, looking but not seeing. True, he excitedly sees, hears, and smells all the things that are different—the camels, noisy night watchmen, and cow dung; but he misses human relationships. He misses so many cues that the realities behind structure and behavior are not apparent. As one volunteer put it, "It was a full three months before I began to *see* the country."

A volunteer writes:

"Until I get to know my village better I guess I really won't know how to predict how much is happenable.' I was sincerely invited to breakfast by a village young man on school vacation, but the invite did not come off. I waited until 11:30—got good and hungry. I finally started on my village rounds and came upon him by accident. I discovered 'face' that day. He was too socially chagrined to tell me that as an untouchable he could not entertain me while I was a guest of a Brahmin."

Discovery is an exciting process, and the anticipation of its delights is part of the attraction of the Peace Corps for many applicants. It is not without hazards, however. One who opens himself to the volunteer experience is also expected to abandon the protective shield of beliefs, values, and customs that he has relied on to make sense of the world. When a volunteer lands in the host country, his commitments to transcend cultural barriers expose him to an assault on his personal way of seeing the world to which other visitors rarely lay themselves open. As another volunteer said:

"I'll never forget my first trip to the teeming bazaar, with all the wild, strange people, its mutilated beggars straining and pushing one another to get a look at us.

A pictorial chart reprinted from the Peace Corps publication, *Volunteer*, shows Dr. Sill's four stages of "transculturation."

MONTHS

I acted unimpressed and nonchalant, of course, in front of my fellow volunteers, but that night I had a nightmare. I dreamt I was strapped naked to a stretcher, and two attendants were carrying me to an insane asylum. As we entered the place, the inmates, all dark-skinned, covered with filth and running sores, and wearing coarsely woven gray cowls, crowded around me to leer and touch my clean, white body. I squirmed to get away but the straps held me tight, and as the attendants carried me farther and farther inside, the multitudes became bolder until they were poking their oozing, mutilated limbs into my face. I woke up in a cold sweat, and instantly realized the obvious connection between my dream and my trip to the bazaar. I also realized what people meant when they talked about (I hate to use this term) culture shock."

The excitement and discovery cascade into frustration. A volunteer resident in a new culture is living and working still on American terms. By opening himself to experiencing the conditions of life and the view of the world of the host country, he has brought his own beliefs and values into question. He faces the necessity to realign his convictions to fit the experience into which he has plunged. A volunteer may go through a deep depression at this time, a "dark night of the soul," and refuse to see the hope or significance of giving himself to the situation. The feeling at this stage was summarized by a volunteer nurse at the end of four months in Pakistan:

"The lady health visitor (co-worker) has her own way of doing things, and has been doing them that way for a long time. Like performing D and C after an abortion with unsterile gloves and prescribing glycerine for a post-injection abscess. I don't consider her very receptive to teaching or even casual suggestions. Every time I try to do something, I run into a brick wall."

Self-Alignment (4–8 months)

The second stage begins when a volunteer decides to cross the threshold between an American value orientation and a host country value orientation. A volunteer reassesses himself, his skills, his expectations, his values; and he chooses more delimited, attainable goals. He aligns himself with a host country view of the situation. He finds a crack in the "brick wall," and discovers some way to participate in his new culture. Some comments at this stage:

"I am learning not to be so hard on myself by continually criticizing my own endeavors and undermining my mental capacity to cope with myself, my husband, and village life."

"I'm not sure of just what has worn off . . . the newness of the romantic notion that somehow creeps its way into training, despite all the best effort of the instructors. Or perhaps it's a more realistic attitude that

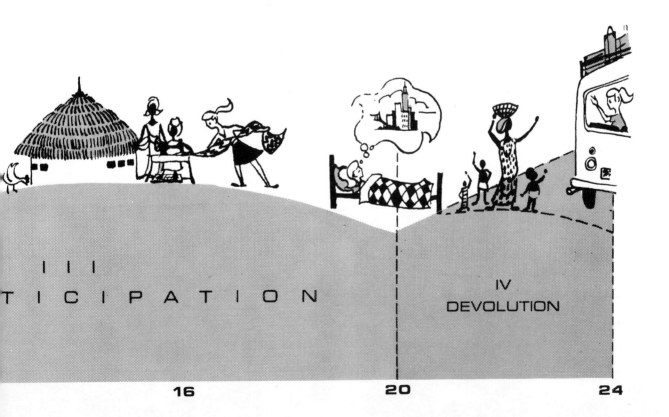

III
TICIPATION

IV
DEVOLUTION

16   20   24

Social life can be a trip to the Zamboanga Zoo in the Philippines as enjoyed by Jerry Poznak (*above*), from Newark, New Jersey, and Jennifer Grant, from Armonk, New York; or joining in an Indian fiesta as Emory Tomor (*below*) did in Chile . . .

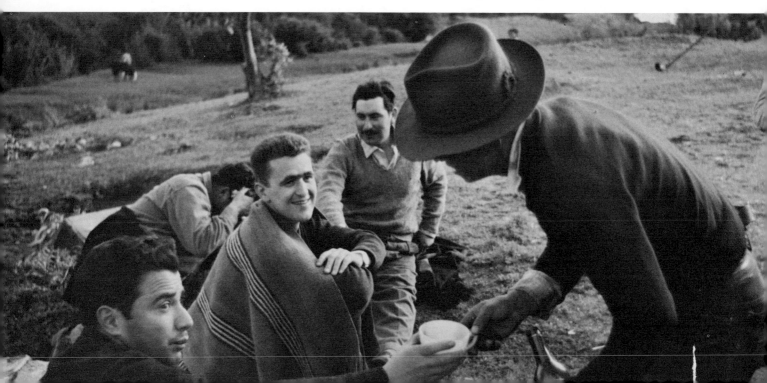

. . . It can also mean dates with host country girls, such as these lovely Thai ladies, although as Harvey Price of San Francisco points out (*below*), dating in Thailand is not quite the same as it is back home.

"I met her, an attractive Thai who speaks no English, in downtown Bangkok. I started talking to her, and she was quite friendly. She was waiting to meet her older brother. She suggested that I write down her name and phone number. I didn't ask her for it—she offered it. She asked me to call her.

"There is no dating of the Western sort in Thailand. Normally young men and women go out together only in large groups. I decided to experiment, however.

"A few days later I called and asked her out. She asked me if I was going to bring anyone with me. When I replied no, she seemed pleased.

"She said she would come alone also. She told me not to tell anyone I was meeting her. Our rendezvous was to be the lobby of a theatre. The date was for 6:00 p.m.

"I arrived at the theatre a little early. At 6:00 p.m. she arrived. She immediately asked me if I had told

anyone about our meeting. I assured her I had not.

"Having established the complete secrecy of our date, we then proceeded out of the lobby, into the street. I followed her, having no idea where she was taking me.

"We walked about a block, and then she said we should take a bus. I agreed, and we climbed aboard. We rode for about fifteen minutes, then got off the bus and continued walking. I still had no idea where she was taking me.

"It was then we approached a yellow bus.

" 'This will take you home,' she said. 'It's starting to get dark. I have to get home before my older brother . . . Goodbye . . . Thank you.'

"In a state of confusion, I got on the yellow bus. I glanced at my watch. It was 6:20 p.m."

—Harvey Price

Dating, of course, often leads to marriage, and dating in the Peace Corps is no exception. There have been dozens of marriages in the Peace Corps. (*Above*) Robert Shaw, a volunteer teacher in Kabul, married the daughter of the Peace Corps staff doctor in Afghanistan. The Peace Corps has no objection to married volunteers; in fact, one field officer, when asked to describe the "ideal volunteer," replied: "All else being equal, a happily married couple"—such as Chris and Evie Lotze (*below*), who taught in Sousse, Tunisia. The Lotzes examine some sheep heads, which are considered a delicacy in Arab countries.

(*Above*) When this picture of the Lotzes visiting ruins of a Roman coliseum was taken, Evie was four months pregnant. While the Peace Corps prefers that the volunteers wait until they return home to have children, they do not forbid it—although Peace Corps Director Jack Vaughn (*below*) appears to be considering a policy revision as he is greeted by volunteers Susan and Bob Slattery and their new son in an Ethiopian airport. At least one Peace Corps baby has been born in nearly every one of the fifty-three countries where the Peace Corps serves.

The biggest part of the volunteer's life abroad is spent getting to know the people of the host country. (*Above*) PCV John Metcalfe (*second from left*) talks with a group of Indian students. On his left is Tonia Koloski, a young American student studying at Ahmednagar on a Grinell College scholarship. On the right is Milton C. Rewinkel, then U.S. Consul General in Bombay. (*Below*) Lois Fenzl, from Schenectady, New York, talks with a neighbor in the Peruvian village of Chimbote where she was a community developer.

William Brandon (*left*), Hickory, North Carolina, and John Seligman, Los Angeles, community developers in Shiraz, Iran, chat with one of their neighbors.

Andrew Conaway, of Sykesville, Maryland, stops to talk with a child in St. Lucia.

Lawrence Dobson, of Seattle, attired in the customary dress in the Kempur region of India, where he worked on a poultry project, visits with a neighborhood child.

For meeting people, music is always a good ice-breaker, as Prudence Ingerman (*above*), a teacher and folk singer, and Gayle Standring, a volunteer nurse in Coroico, Bolivia, found out . . . or games (*below*): Michael Bailkin, from Philadelphia, tries a fast game of table tennis at the neighborhood settlement house in Bombay, India.

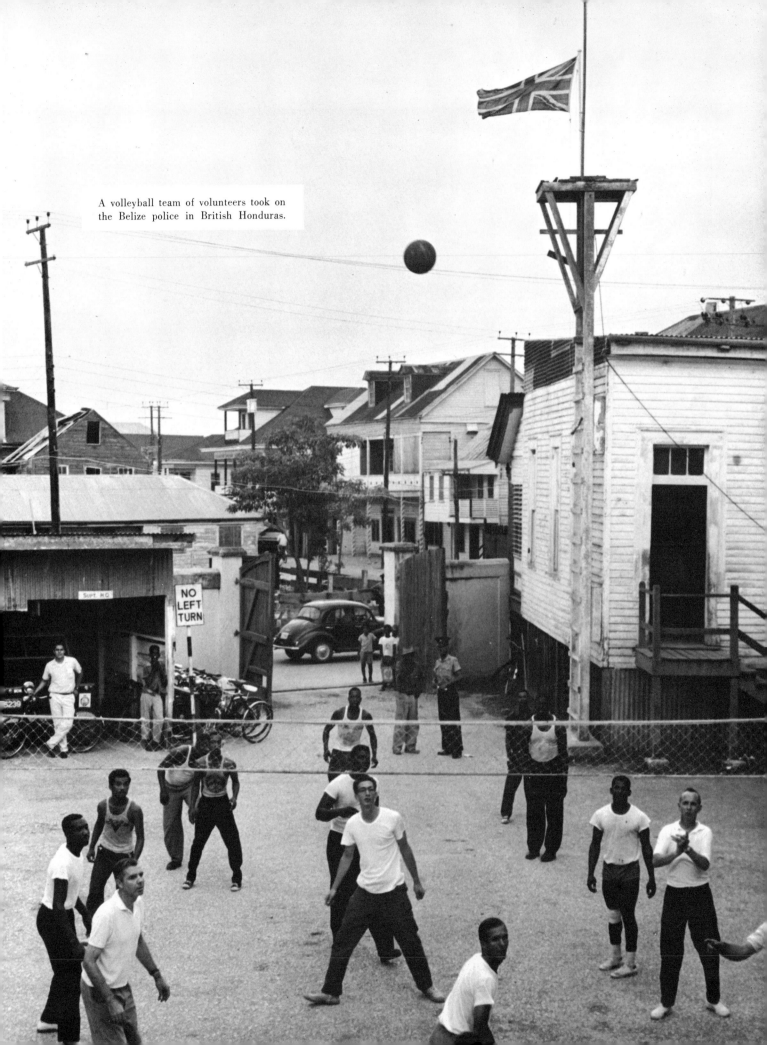

A volleyball team of volunteers took on the Belize police in British Honduras.

And when all else fails, there's always baseball. (*Above*) John Soldate, from Santa Barbara, California, teaches the kids around Bopolu, Liberia, the basics of the game. Organizing a Carnival also brings you into a community—fast. (*Below*) James Fisher acts as barker at a Carnival in Katmandu, Nepal, that raised $130 for a boys' school.

A Dominican musician, on the way to see his girl, is stopped in the road by volunteer John Greenough, of Fort Smith, Arkansas, who asked him to play a tune.

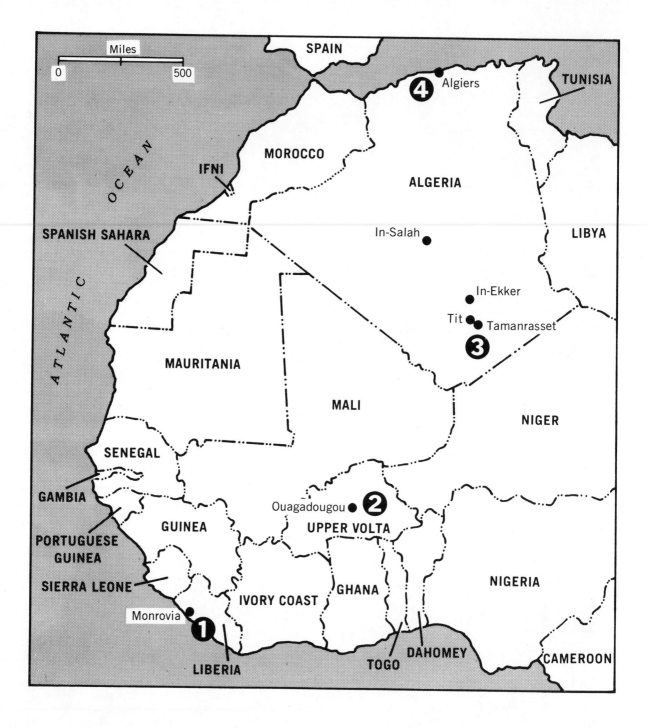

Miles
0   500

SPAIN

TUNISIA

④ Algiers

MOROCCO

IFNI

ALGERIA

LIBYA

SPANISH SAHARA

In-Salah

In-Ekker

Tit ● Tamanrasset
③

MAURITANIA

MALI

NIGER

SENEGAL

GAMBIA

Ouagadougou ● ②

GUINEA

UPPER VOLTA

PORTUGUESE GUINEA

SIERRA LEONE

NIGERIA

GHANA

IVORY COAST

Monrovia
①

DAHOMEY

CAMEROON

LIBERIA

TOGO

OCEAN

ATLANTIC

Some volunteers have been able to do a little sightseeing on their vacations, and one such trip by five Peace Corps teachers in Liberia made history of a sort and the pages of *Time*, *Life*, and the *New York Times*. The five girls, pictured above in their black jebbas with the local innkeeper on the oasis of Agadez in the Sahara Desert, hitchhiked 2,000 miles across the Sahara in early 1964. From Monrovia (1) (see map, opposite page) to Ougadougou (2) to Tamanrasset (3), they traveled by auto, train, and bus; from Tamanrasset, they hitched rides across the Sahara, mostly on the thirty-ton trucks that ply the desert. They found out who was going where by checking at each oasis with the local police who clear all desert traffic. The girls took the trip simply because they wanted to see more of Africa than they had been seeing in and around Monrovia, the capital of Liberia, where they taught. The result of the trip, which was for the most part without incident, was that they learned "how nice people could be." When they got back to Monrovia, they were in a little hot water because they were late for the new school semester, but eventually all was forgiven—especially after they donated the $5,000 they received for their story from *Life* to a scholarship fund for training Liberian teachers in Liberian colleges. *Left to right*, the girls are: Barbara Kral, San Lorenza, California; Barbara Prikkel, New York City; Barbara Doutrich, Seattle; Evelyn Vough, Scottsdale, Pennsylvania; and Geraldine Markos, McKeesport, Pennsylvania.

For creative volunteers and the performers there is plenty of time to exercise their talent. The woodcut (*left*) is from a series called "The Aymara Wedding," by Volunteer Irwin Zagar who taught arts and crafts in the Peruvian village of Chucuito. Zagar's Peruvian woodcuts received favorable comment when they were put on display in a Washington, D.C., art gallery. (*Below*) A Peace Corps barbershop quartet was included in a variety show honoring President Tubman of Liberia during his inauguration. *Left to right* are volunteers Frank Cunning, Lee Giles, Dr. Donn Leaf, Peace Corps staff physician, and volunteer Bill Staab. (*Opposite page*) Dennis Hershbach, who taught at the Technical Training Center in Ombe, Cameroon, poses behind one of his creations.

No matter where they are serving—in the city or the bush—there is always the possibility of a distinguished visitor. (*Left*) Colombia Country Director Larry Horan and Volunteer Tom La-Belle visit with artist Norman Rockwell. Rockwell was in Colombia to sketch volunteers for *Look* magazine, and the experience made a Peace Corps enthusiast out of him. "Shakespeare said something about a candle in a wicked world," Rockwell commented. "I think volunteers are like that." (*Below*) Emperor Haile Selassie, of Ethiopia, pays a visit to classes taught by Peace Corps volunteers in Diredawa. (*Opposite page*) New York Senator Robert Kennedy and his wife Ethel stop to visit with volunteers in the Mbeya region of Tanzania on a 1966 trip to Africa. When he returned, Kennedy said: "The Peace Corps is the most effective operation the United States has in Africa."

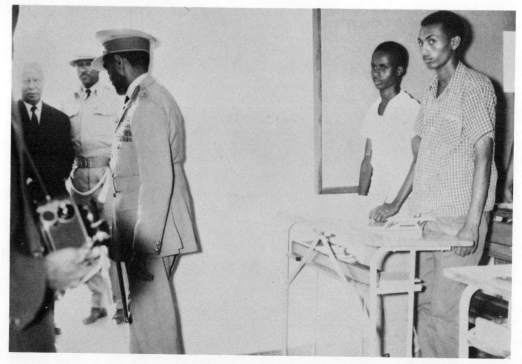

When young men are out in the bush for long stretches of time, many react by growing their own. Some of the more distinguished Peace Corps beards were those of (*above left*) Gene Kirschner, in Somalia; (*above right*) Alton Scarborough, in the Cameroons; and (*left*) Stuart Siegel (*left*) and Donald Walker, in Gabon. The Peace Corps prohibits beards in some areas, especially where they violate local customs, but tolerates them in others.

is exerting itself and forcing some of the naïveté of idealism out. I honestly like my former idea of the world better, but to the extent that it wasn't real, I am changing it."

"We've been in Pakistan four months now, and it seems to me as if the haze or fog is lifting and we're starting to see our way more clearly—or we're getting a

better idea of how to go about accomplishing things. Or I at least hope that that is the case."

"This month will mostly be spent just building up rapport and making friends. I think this is the hardest job of community development, coupled with communication problems . . . I'm finding it difficult to get [my fellow volunteer] motivated to do anything. She's

Despite the difficult circumstances in which the volunteers often live, morale in the Peace Corps is remarkably high. However, with a certain amount of alienation, frustration is inevitable, as the cartoon drawn in 1963 by Philip Durand, a volunteer in Africa, suggests. The cartoon is reprinted from the Peace Corps magazine, *Volunteer*. Morale is most likely to be a problem when communications break down between Washington and the field. One such crisis occurred in 1966 in Nigeria where a breakdown of the morale of nearly 700 volunteers necessitated a special trip by Jack Vaughn to Nigeria (*see following page*).

got good ideas, but seems to have a defeatist attitude about our success here. Time will tell, I guess. I'm not ready to give up yet, but I am anxious to get more under way."

Participation (8–20 months)

During this stage the volunteer settles into his job, and finds new ways to feel that he is fulfilling the aspiration that motivated him initially. He is beginning to consolidate his broadened view of the world and to regain confidence in his ability to make sense of it. This growth frees him for more complete participation in the host country culture.

The volunteer's agony of definition and search revealed much to his Pakistani colleagues and friends that was helpful to them and provided a role model for their own part in nation-building. These co-workers sensed the volunteer's concern to understand, to find a real job, and to include as many people as possible in planning and growth processes. A volunteer's comment: "After my initial eight months of setbacks and frustrations, I now feel that I am starting to realize some of the idealistic goals that were uppermost in my mind when I left home. As to how worthwhile my Peace Corps experience has been, I cannot dispute the fact that during my first year of service I was virtually on the receiving end at least 90 percent of the time, but for my second year I believe that I can actually make a contribution."

Another volunteer writes of communication beyond the job: "Along with the knowledge and understanding comes the most trite-sounding and yet the most significant experience of all—the mere fact of living in another country and trying to understand what makes it tick. We are all human beings, true, but there are differences, and these differences are important to understand in the world of today. Things beyond our comprehension in our snug bungalows on Main Street, U.S.A., are coming to have a profound effect on that snug, tranquil life. Now maybe we will have a more sympathetic attitude toward such things. While we have been here, perhaps for the first time in our lives we have tried to serve others and have learned the joys and sorrows that go along with it. We have had successes and we have had failures, but I think we will remember the successes longer. What's more, I have made friends, not only with those who work with me, but also with some who work against me; nonetheless, both are equally valuable."

Devolution (20–24 months)

Toward the end the Peace Corps term, the volunteer begins to think about that nice life back home. But he is not ready to leave the people with whom his lot has been so intimately cast and the projects which he has helped develop without wondering whether the pro-

. . . On his arrival in Nigeria, Vaughn said: "I came because a dialog was missing." In three weeks of travel and discussions, Vaughn met with 600 of the 699 Volunteers in Nigeria. He found that most of the difficulties centered around living allowances, which had been cut; hostels, which Vaughn had ordered closed; and motorcycles, which the Peace Corps had prohibited except when they were essential to the job assignment. After extensive review, the problems concerning the Nigerian program were worked out and relative peace was restored. (*Above*) Vaughn meets with Nigerian Volunteers in Onitsha.

grams will remain a people's program and live after him. After all the effort which has gone into assessing the situation, the volunteers begin to ask whether the situation is sufficiently theirs so that they and their leaders will continue to give it time, resources, and guidance. Having incorporated some of the values of his hosts, the volunteer wonders whether they, in turn, have in fact incorporated some of his.

An illustration of this stage is found in the planning, near the end of the tour, of a volunteer who had built a community development project, out of an adapted leather tooling hobby. He writes:

"The leather project seems to be moving along nicely. I have just about cleared the debts, and the orders are holding up well. Several of the boys are developing a real skill and pride in their work, which is most satisfying. Our supply of raw material is improving in both quality and dependability, and although we have not been able to obtain any good-quality belt leather, we have hopes. Bob is making progress on the machines for producing tools and lacing, and I am confident that we will soon be able to obtain all our supplies here in Pakistan.

"The cooperative society is all set up on this end, and I hope to be in Lahore at the beginning of March to try to get the papers through the registration procedures (red tape is a better word) required. I am convinced that, to ensure a successful functioning of the industry in Pakistan, this society is necessary."

Conclusion

Volunteers have "joined the human race," but not as they thought they would, for those first expectations were hometown ones. If they decided to join on the host country's own terms, they grew more personally and became more effective. The job they did was not the job they would do, but the end results were deep involvement in the life of their two-year land of adoption, and a new synthesis of values uniquely theirs— neither passively accepted from their own culture nor docilely drawn from the host culture.

Deep understanding, wide communication, and some friendships have resulted, and this is what the volunteers wanted. After a few months back in the United States, most volunteers agree that they gave and got about what they really had hoped for. A sample taste of the socioeconomic revolution which rages around the earth whetted the appetite of many volunteers for more effective tackling of basic issues now on their consciences. Many of their jobs had demonstration value. Their new shoulder-to-shoulder relationship with and orientation to the problems of "the people" drew co-workers, supervisors, and even higher officials into more active, democratic, nation-building activities.

The transculturation implied in the second and third goals of the Peace Corps Act is not unrelated, then, to the first goal. The better one understands, the better he serves.

—MAURICE L. SILL

Despite the difficulties of "transculturation," when their tour of duty is over, most volunteers, as Maurice Sill says, "agree that they gave and got about what they really had hoped for." (*Right*) Among Maureen Orth's projects during her twenty months in the province of Medellin, Colombia, was a schoolhouse which she helped build by organizing fund-raising activities and work parties. The school, located in the little village of Aguas Frias, was christened by the villagers *Escuela Marina Orth*. On her last day in Aguas Frias, Maureen says good-bye to the children who attend the school she helped to build.

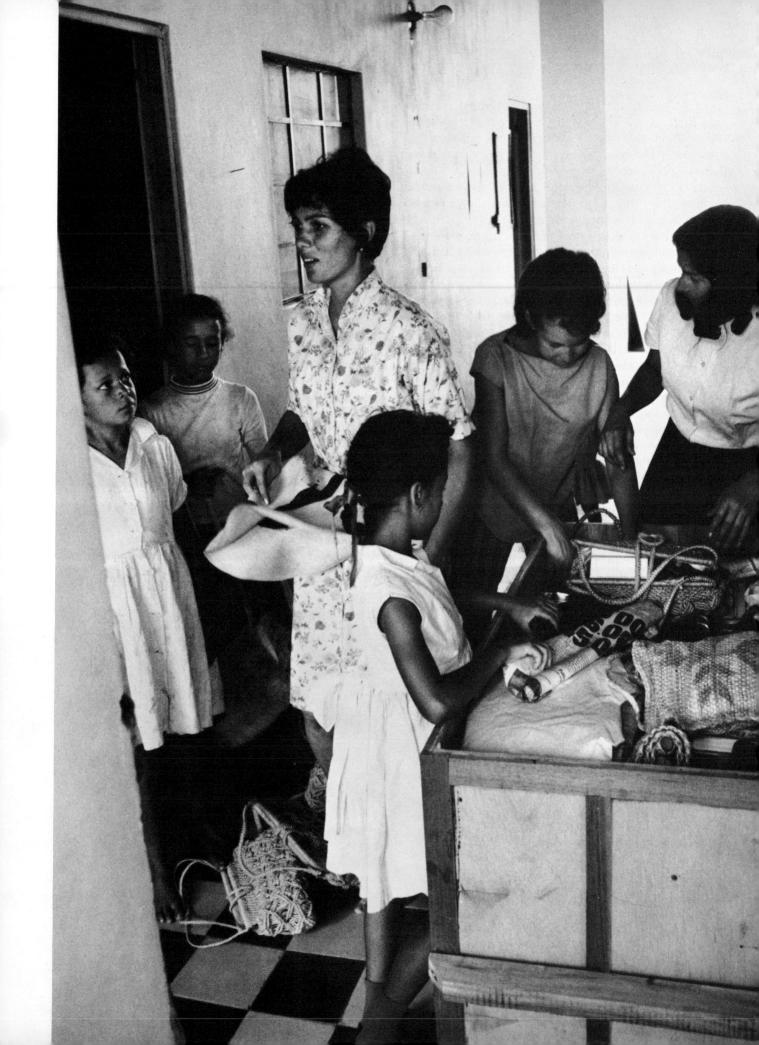

(*Opposite page*) Maureen, who is from Piedmont, California, packs for her return to the States. The sorrow of parting is evident on her face.

(*Below*) Maureen bids her many Colombian friends goodbye at the Medellin airport. The villagers presented her with a farewell gift in appreciation of her work in Aguas Frias: a little gold medal which was inscribed simply *Acción Comunal.*

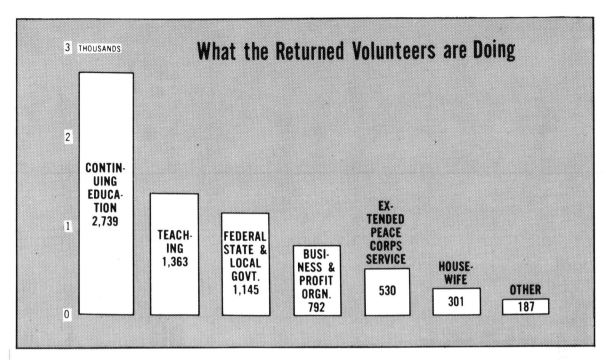

What the Returned Volunteers are Doing

3 THOUSANDS

CONTIN-
UING
EDUCA-
TION
2,739

TEACH-
ING
1,363

FEDERAL
STATE &
LOCAL
GOVT.
1,145

BUSI-
NESS &
PROFIT
ORGN.
792

EX-
TENDED
PEACE
CORPS
SERVICE
530

HOUSE-
WIFE
301

OTHER
187

Much has been made of the Peace Corps "reentry crisis." "The first month was hell." "I was depressed for six weeks." "I don't feel at home anymore," were some of the remarks quoted by a national magazine when the Peace Corps volunteers began coming home in 1963. "We have everything. But so much of it seems like cheap veneer."

Today there are more than 10,000 returned volunteers; by 1970 there will be more than 50,000. Although some volunteers have had difficulty, usually temporary, adjusting again to American life, it has not developed as a serious problem, and the early reports of a "reentry" crisis were overplayed in the press. There is no such thing as a typical returned volunteer. However, a certain pattern has emerged—"almost invariably," as one Peace Corps official says, "the returned volunteer seeks a job, education, or a personal mode of life that will enable him to make a contribution. The chances are he is the sort of person who would have done so anyway, but there is no doubt that two years of Peace Corps service propels him ever more strongly into a way of life where service never really ends."

The above chart shows the result of a study of the first 7,057 returned volunteers. The majority of volunteers end up back in the classroom—either continuing their own education or teaching.

(*Opposite page*) Gene Schreiber, shown walking down one of the long State Department corridors, taught math, English, and road building in Tanzania. When he made his "reentry" in the summer of 1963, he spent a year working with the Peace Corps headquarters in Washington. Then he took the Foreign Service exam and passed. Today, Schreiber is one of more than twenty volunteers working in the State Department, most of them as Foreign Service Officers. He says of his Peace Corps experience: "When I went into the Peace Corps, I was a civil engineer. I hardly knew what the Foreign Service was. I pictured it as made up of striped-pants diplomats. But the Peace Corps literally and completely switched my career plans. It got me overseas. It put me into teaching. It exposed me to a developing country. It broadened me. No longer was I solely an engineer. After two years in the Peace Corps, I had new foundations from which to branch out. I consider my Peace Corps experience a perfect transition. . . .

"There are things I learned in the Peace Corps which serve me well now. We were taught by the Peace Corps to be flexible, to work within a system, and to maintain enthusiasm. It's the same thing here—you find freedom in your job by combining tact with enthusiasm.

"I don't want to sell tractors or something the rest of my life. I don't want to be confined to a narrow field. I need to try new and different things. I had met Foreign Service people overseas in the Peace Corps and was impressed by them and by their enthusiasm. That's how I first got interested. . . .

"People ask me if I didn't lose two years by being in the Peace Corps. I don't think so. I have different insights and motivations than someone who didn't share the experience. I have a feeling about people, about growth and development, that others may lack.

"To me, the United States Government will never be successful if it is to be an institution. Only as a very human institution will it work. You have to work with people—not with ministries and embassies, but with people.

"I might have thought this way anyway, without serving in the Peace Corps. I probably would have. Who knows?

"I only know that by helping others, you indirectly help America. It has nothing to do with nationalism; it's a matter of what I call national pride. I felt that when I joined the Peace Corps and I feel the same thing now."

In March, 1965, one national magazine tried to make volunteer Janet Hanneman (shown on the opposite page talking with a patient in the government Mental Hospital in Lahore, Pakistan, where she served as a volunteer nurse) a prototype of the volunteer suffering a "reentry crisis." Says Janet: "There is no reentry crisis peculiar to Peace Corps; it's simply a matter of change. How can you reenter something you never did leave?

"Each individual who becomes a volunteer brings with him the complete experience of his life. He does not discard it during two years of service . . . ."

When Janet returned home, she married a widowed Montgomery Ward executive, the father of four children. She lives in a North Shore suburb of Chicago, is a member of three PTA's, a "hospitality mother" at the junior high school, and the regional alumni director for the University of Kansas nursing school. She still does volunteer work on a variety of projects. Looking back, she says, "The Peace Corps is a vehicle by which one can express a philosophy. It gives purpose to the search for self-fulfillment and the desire to express humanitarianism." (*Below*) Janet at home with her stepchildren.

With more than 50 percent of the Peace Corps volunteers engaged in teaching, the ex-volunteers represent a valuable pool of potential teachers. Many states have recognized this and are making every effort to help ex-volunteers get their teaching certificates, and some are giving them credit for teaching time overseas. Many of the special teaching programs, such as the Cardoza High School project in Washington, D.C., the Cleveland Elementary Training program, the Teachers Corps, and VISTA, have attracted returning volunteers. (*Below*) Ex-volunteer Bill Plitt with his class at Washington's Cardoza High School. Most textbooks prove useless at Cardoza, so Plitt designed his own curriculum materials. "There's no limit," said one administrator, "to the time they are willing to spend with pupils after **hours**."

"The burden of finding a place in society rests primarily on the volunteer himself. Volunteers tell me of difficulty in communicating the essence of their experience when they return home. They seem often to find problems in making the transition, in reestablishing relationships with Americans and with America. Thus, they sometimes seek companionship among other Peace Corps returnees. But if friendships are limited in this way, the danger arises that the only other Americans who will benefit from the Peace Corps experience are members of the volunteer's family who may listen in at home gatherings. The entire community will gain only if the volunteer is willing to apply this experience *wherever* he is—the backyard, the settlement house, on Madison Avenue. The young Peace Corps returnee unestablished in a career may upon return feel a bit reluctant to enter fields not directly related to social service. Shouldn't he be reminded that there is no place, no job, no position where the Peace Corps spirit is not needed?"

—Esther Peterson, Assistant Secretary of Labor, in a statement to the conference of returned volunteers. (Mrs. Peterson's son, Eric, served as a volunteer in the Philippines.)

Ann Kessler, who served as a nurse in Brazil, looks on the reentry crisis simply as "immaturity." She now attends the St. Joseph's Hospital School of Nursing in Phoenix, Arizona.

Someday she hopes to go back overseas as a nurse, or work in slums or with Indians in the Southwest. "Except for my parents," Ann says, "I have never been asked a really intelligent question about the Peace Corps."

Chapter 10

The Peaceful Revolution

"In search of meaning, some believers have desperately turned to psychiatry, Zen or drugs. Thousands of others have quietly abandoned all but token allegiance to the churches, surrendering themselves to a life of 'anonymous Christianity' dedicated to civil rights or the Peace Corps."
—From *Time* article, "Is God Dead?"

Why does a volunteer join the Peace Corps? David Schickele, one of the first young Americans to volunteer for the Peace Corps (see page 54), says he really couldn't answer that question until after he had served abroad. Schickele was born in Ames, Iowa, grew up in Fargo, North Dakota, and attended Swarthmore College where he earned his B.A. in English in 1958. He joined the peace Corps in 1961 and spent twenty months teaching in Nigeria. When he returned, he wrote about his experience in an article which first appeared in the Swarthmore Bulletin and has since been reprinted many times by the Peace Corps. According to Harris Wofford, former Deputy Director of the Peace Corps, Schickele's article "has probably led more good

Fred Carlson from Brooklyn with his students on the island of Panape in Micronesia. Fred is a TESL—Teaches English as a Second Language.

(*Opposite page*) Another TESL teacher, Kathryn Fitch of Bakersfield, California, talks with her students on Panape.

volunteers into the Peace Corps than any other single publication." The article, reprinted below, was entitled, "When the Right Hand Washes the Left."

The favorite parlor sport during the Peace Corps training program was making up cocky answers to a question that was put to us seventeen times a day by the professional and idly curious alike: Why did you join the Peace Corps?

To the Peace Corps training official, who held the power of deciding our futures, we answered that we wanted to help make the world a better place in which to live; but to others we were perhaps more truthful in talking about poker debts or a feeling that the Bronx Zoo wasn't enough. We resented the question because we sensed it could be answered well only in retrospect. We had no idea exactly what we were getting into, and it was less painful to be facetious than to repeat the idealistic clichés to which the question was always a veiled invitation.

I am now what is known as an ex-volunteer (there seems to be some diffidence about the word "veteran"), having spent twenty months teaching at the University of Nigeria at Nsukka in West Africa. And now I am ready to answer the question.

My life at Nsukka bore little resemblance to the publicized image of Peace Corps stoicism—the straw mat and kerosene lamp syndrome. The university, though fifty miles from anything that could be called a metropolis, was a large international community unto itself, full of Englishmen, Indians, Pakistanis, Germans, Americans, and, of course, Nigerians. I lived in a single room in a student dormitory, a modern if treacherous building with running water at least four days a week and electricity when the weather was good. I ate primarily Western food in a cafeteria. I owned a little motorcycle and did my share of traveling and roughing it, but the bulk of my life was little different from university life in the States, with a few important exceptions.

In the first place, the university was only a year old when I arrived, and a spirit of improvisation was required at all times and in all areas, particularly the teaching of literature without books. The library was still pretty much of a shell, and ordered books took a minimum of six weeks to arrive if one was lucky, and I never talked to anyone who was. The happier side of this frantic coin was that in the absence of organization many of us had practically unlimited freedom in what and how we were to teach, and we made up our courses as we went along according to what materials were available and our sense of what the students needed. This was tricky freedom which I still blame, in my weaker moments, for my worst mistakes; but it allowed an organic approach to the pursuit of an idea

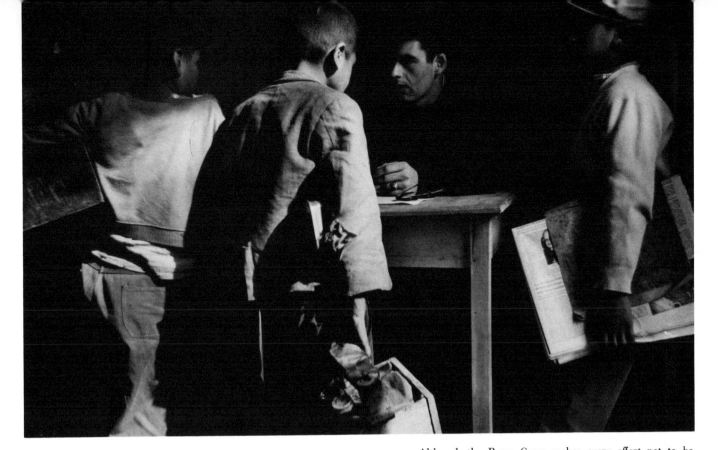

Although the Peace Corps makes every effort not to become involved in political change, officials are quick to point out that the volunteers are involved in social and economic change—and they are not unaware of the narrow line between social change and political upheaval. "Our relevance to the world," former Deputy Peace Corps Director Warren Wiggins told a national magazine reporter, "is not that we are a nice bunch of people offering low-paying overseas fellowships." The Peace Corps, said Wiggins, is a "critical element in the evolution of a society" and the results will bring changes so great, he said, that "we might as well talk about revolution."

(*Above*) PCV Sam McPheters, of Juneau, Alaska, did community development work in Quito, Ecuador, where he helped the *betuneros* (shoeshine boys) get uniforms and recognition from the government.

(*Opposite page*)

Mrs. Dudley (Mary Jo) Weeks dances with her students at the school in Mile Ten, a remote village in Northern Borneo. Her husband, who also taught in Borneo, wrote in an article intended for a national magazine: "The minds of most of the people with whom Peace Corps volunteers are working are minds that are open to growth. There has been a void of challenge and now the PCV represents the freshness and meaningfulness of the opportunity to grow. So it is with grave responsibility that each volunteer must accept this challenge. The way he lives daily in relation to the people he is serving will determine the growth or stagnation of these people. His moment-by-moment decisions will determine the success or failure of the Peace Corps and/or the ideals in which our country is rooted. But just as important are the American people at home. Their daily lives must speak of brotherhood, concern and awareness. For if the American at home betrays the ideals of his country, the Peace Corps volunteer must then overcome suspicion and a lack of trust before he is allowed to help meet the realistic needs of his new community."

Wiggins is not the only ex-Peace Corps official who talked of revolution. Frank Mankiewicz, who was the Peace Corps Representative in Peru and Latin American Director in the Washington office before leaving to join the staff of Senator Robert Kennedy, wrote a paper on community development —"A Revolutionary Force"—which has become required reading in the Peace Corps. However, Mankiewicz goes a little further and talks of political revolution. The ultimate aim of community development," said Mankiewicz, "is nothing less than complete change, reversal—or a revolution if you wish—in the social and economic patterns of the countries to which we are accredited. . . . This is the mission of community development—a mission which consists of nothing more than a political turnabout. . . . We are talking about situations in which 3 percent of the people function effectively and 97 percent do not. If that situation is to change to one in which the great bulk of the outsiders become insiders, the nonparticipants become participants, and the oppressed and forgotten become a functioning part of the country, then that is nothing less than a revolution; and it is one that will be accomplished by political means." (*Below*) Community Development volunteers James Welcome (*right*) and Ronald Atwater (*second from right*) discuss details of a construction project in a Colombian village.

(*Opposite page*) James Allen, of Bunker Hill, Illinois, worked on a school construction project in Bolivia, where he is having lunch. Jack Vaughn, Peace Corps Director, tells this story about a trip he took to Bolivia in 1958. "I reached the point where I was reluctant to go up on the high plains near Lake Titicaca to hunt and fish because of the menacing attitude of the Indians," says Vaughn. "They were all armed, they seemed resentful, didn't speak Spanish and didn't change. That was seven or eight years ago. I visited five villages in that very same area in 1965. In all five, I was carried into town on the backs of the Indians who wanted to show me that they were in the human race. They had all built a new school, the first school in a thousand years. They all had a clinic for child deliveries, the first clinic in a thousand years. They all had potable water piped in, and they had done it themselves. . . . But more important was their attitude, the openness, the willingness to look you in the eye and tell you about who they were and what they had done, and the pride and self-respect of citizenship. This was done by the Peace Corps. What the Spaniards and the Incas and the Western miners and the diplomats and the AID people couldn't do in a thousand years the Peace Corps had helped to do in about three years. This is real revolution."

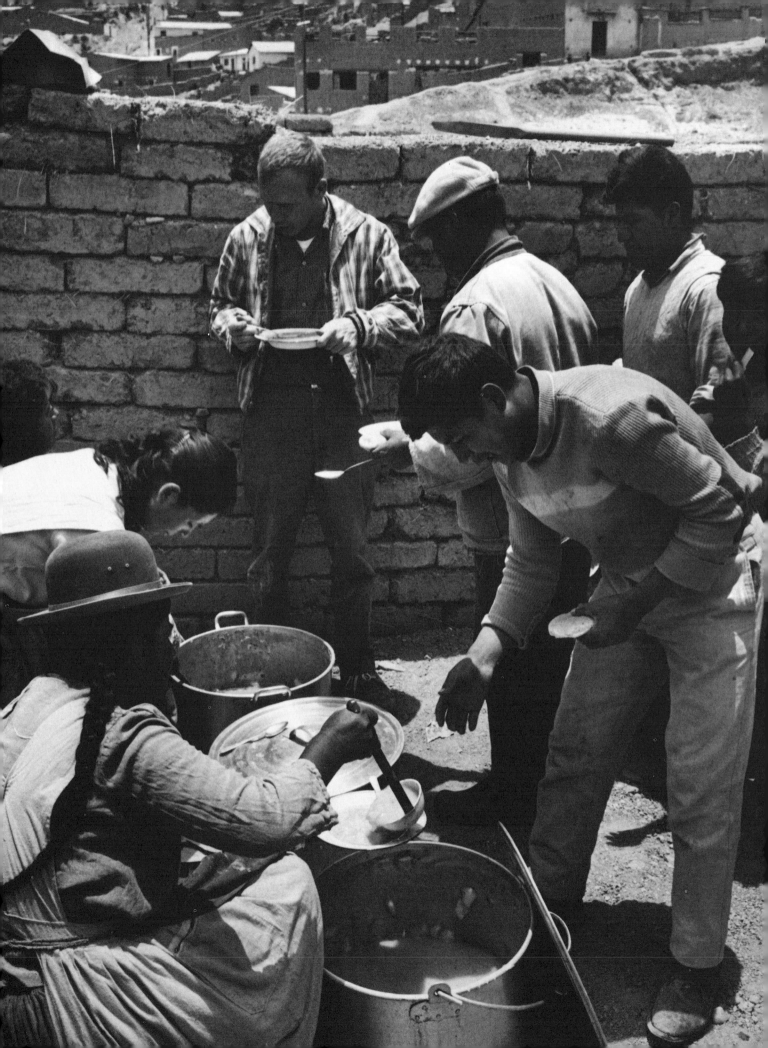

282

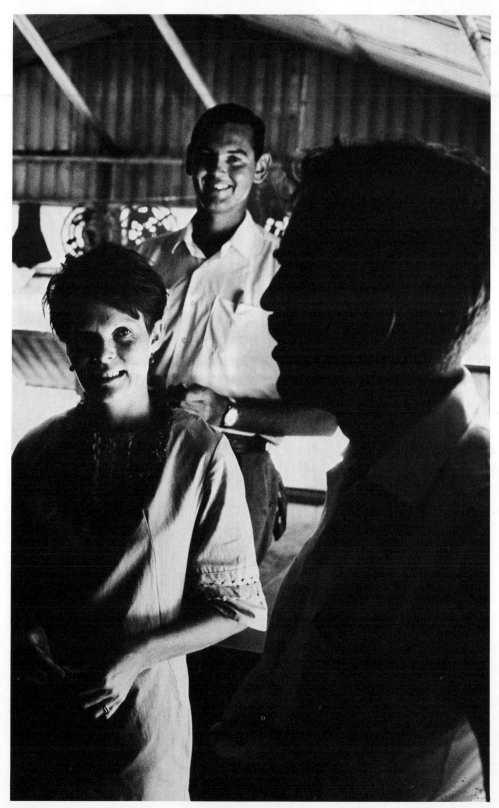

Vaughn concedes: "I may end up running a revolution: successful Peace Corps volunteers cannot help but teach that change is possible, and what is more, that change is not a fearsome unknown, but a responsibility to be shared and encouraged by the governments of lands in which they serve. They also spread the word that peace invites adventure, mobility and self-expression." (*Right*) Vaughn talks with volunteers in Micronesia.

with all its nooks and crannies, an approach long over-due for students trained in the unquestioning acceptance of rigid syllabi.

The longer I was there, the more I became involved with a nucleus of students, and the weaker became the impulse to disappear over the weekend on my motorcycle in search of external adventure. My social and professional lives slowly fused into one and the same thing. I shared an office with another volunteer, and we were there almost every evening from supper until late at night, preparing classes and talking to students, who learned that we were always available for help in their work, or just bulling around. We sponsored poetry and short story contests and founded a literary club which was the liveliest and most enjoyable organization I've ever belonged to, joyfully subject to the imperative of which all remote areas have the advantage: If you want to see a Chekhov play, you have to put it on yourself.

In some ways I was more alive intellectually at Nsukka than I was at Swarthmore, due in part to the fact that I worked much harder at Nsukka, I'm afraid, than I did at Swarthmore; and to the fact that one learns more from teaching than from studying. But principally it has to do with the kind of perspective necessary in the teaching of Western literature to a people of a different tradition, and the empathy and curiosity necessary in teaching African literature to Africans. It is always an intellectual experience to cross cultural boundaries.

At the most elementary level, it is a challenge to separate thought from mechanics in the work of students who are not writing in their native language. Take, for example, the following paragraph, written, I would emphasize, not by a university student but by a cleaning man at the university in a special course:

"It sings a melody in my poor mind, when a friend came to me and said that: I enjoy certain tasks in my work, but others are not so enjoyable. I laughed and called him by his name, then I asked him what is the task in your work. He answered me and then added, for a period of five years. I have been seriously considering what to do to assist his self as an orphan, in this field of provision. That he should never play with the task

Of course, when Peace Corps officials talk of revolution—social, economic, or even political—they mean *peaceful* revolution. (*Above*) Volunteer George Seay, from Buffalo, engages in a little peaceful combat with a member of his "Exercise Club" in Conceição de Castelo, a Brazilian village near Vitória.

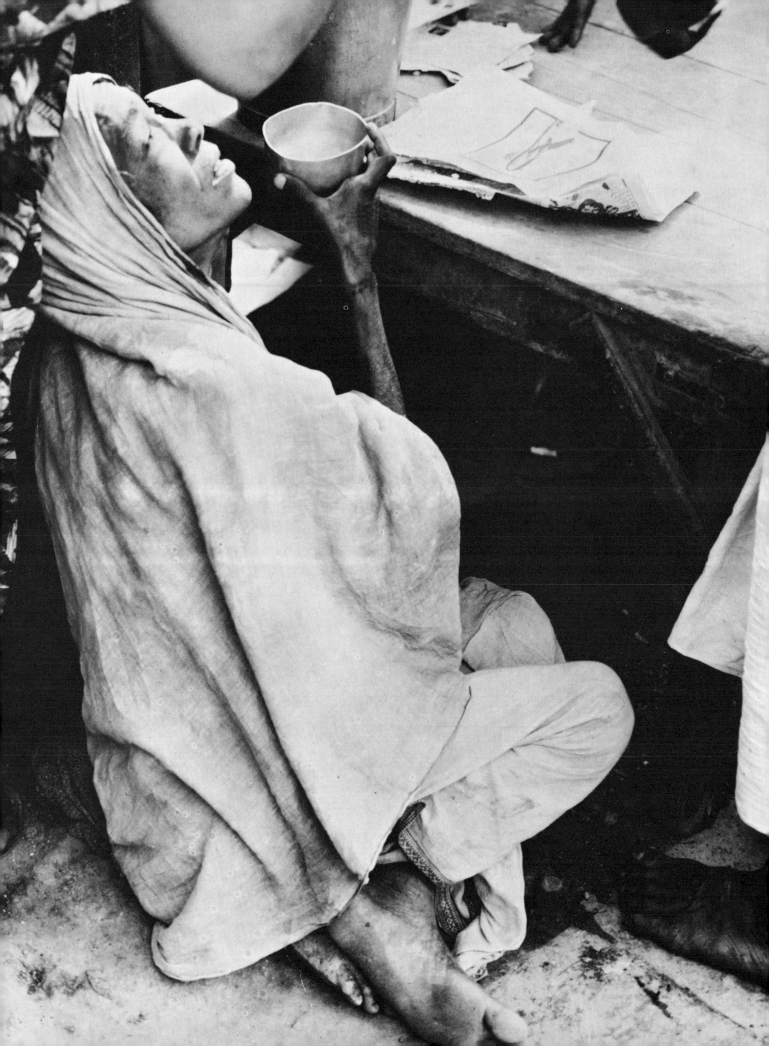

of his work. But others who are not so enjoyable could not understand the bitterness to his orphanship. He said to those who are not so enjoyable that they have no bounding which hangs their thoughts in a dark room."

I regard this passage with joy, not to say a little awe, but beneath its exotic and largely unconscious poetic appeal there is a man trying to say something important, blown about in the wilderness of an unfamiliar language by the influences of the King James Version and the vernacular proverb. Where writing like this is concerned, it is impossible to be a Guardian of Good Grammar; one must try to confront the roots of lan-

guage—the relationship between thought and word, with all the problems of extraneous influences and in many cases translation from a native tongue.

At another level, the intellectual excitement came from a kind of freshness of thought and expression in minds that have not become trapped by scholastic conventions, or the fear of them. I remember times at Swarthmore when I kept a question or thought to myself because I feared it might be in some way intellectually out of line. But most of my Nsukka students had no idea what was in or out of line, what was a cliché and what was not, what critical attitudes were forbid-

But even revolution, peaceful or otherwise, will have no meaning unless poverty, hunger, and disease are eliminated from the earth. As President Johnson has said: ". . . What does freedom mean—when famine chokes the land, when new millions crowd upon already strained resources, when privilege is entrenched behind law and custom—when all conspire to teach men that they cannot change the conditions of their lives?"

Under such conditions peace is an illusion. It has not served man—only nations. "Seven million Indians have lived in the mountains and jungles of Peru," says Vaughn,

"hardly moving out of the eighteenth century—almost entirely in times of peace. Millions of human beings of so-called lower caste have starved to death or died of a dread disease in India and Pakistan—in times of peace. Nine hundred million adult men and women alive today will pass through life without ever having read or written a word in their own or any other tongue—almost all in times of peace. And how many countless millions will not so much as lift a finger to change their lot, because they have no comprehension of even the gentlest revolution, in times of peace?"

den or encouraged (though I did my share, I confess, of forbidding and encouraging). They were not at all calculating, in a social sense, in their thought. They spoke what was in their heads, with the result that discussion had a lively, unadulterated, and personal quality which I found a relief from the more sophisticated but less spontaneously sincere manner of many young American intellectuals. It was also a little infuriating at times. I am, after all, a product of my own culture. But one has only to look at a 1908 *Phoenix* (the Swarthmore student newspaper) to realize how much sophistication is a thing of style and fashion, and how little any one fashion exhausts the possible ways in which the world can be confronted and apprehended.

In Nigeria, literature became the line of commerce between me and my students as people, a common interest and prime mover in the coming together of white American and black African. Ours was a dialogue between equals, articulate representatives of two articulate and in many ways opposing heritages. Because literature deals more directly with life than other art forms, through it I began to know Nigeria as a country and my students as friends.

An idealized case history might read something like

In the face of such overwhelming worldwide poverty, hunger, disease, and ignorance, many people justifiably ask: How successful has the Peace Corps been; is it really making a difference? These are not easy questions to answer because it will be years before all the returns on the Peace Corps effort are in. However, a few serious attempts to study the effectiveness of the Peace Corps programs have been made, and for the most part they are favorable. For instance, a group of social scientists under the general direction of Robert Textor and the Massachusetts Institute of Technology, studied thirteen developing countries in which the Peace Corps was operating. In the case of Somalia, for example, Frank Mahoney wrote that "about one year after the Peace Corps was organized, someone asked Sargent Shriver which of all the countries in the world was proving the most troublesome for the Peace Corps to work in. Without a moment's hesitation, Shriver named the Somalia Republic. Though he could not possibly have known it when he spoke—worse was yet to come." According to Mahoney, "everything went wrong in Somalia One. Yet, despite all the problems the Peace Corps had in Somalia, Mahoney concluded that without any doubt the Peace Corps effort in Somalia was successful. "For the first time in the history of United States relations with the Somali Republic, Somalis began to regard Americans as genuinely friendly, likeable people," Mahoney reported. (*Below*) Volunteers Ann Jorganson (*left*) from Silver Spring, Maryland, and Susan Barr of Summit, New Jersey, use the *Somali News* as the textbook in their adult literacy class in Hargeisa, Northern Somalia.

this: A student brings me a story he has written, perhaps autobiographical, about life in his village. I harrumph my way through a number of formal criticisms and start asking questions about customs in his village that have a bearing on the story. Soon we are exchanging childhood reminiscences or talking about girls over a bottle of beer. Eventually we travel together to his home, where I meet his family and live in his house. And then what began, perhaps, as a rather bookish interest in comparative culture becomes a real involvement in that culture, so that each new insight does not merely add to one's store of knowledge, but carries the power of giving pain or pleasure. If there is any lesson in this, it is simply that no real intellectual understanding can exist without a sense of identification at some deeper level. I think this is what the Peace Corps, when it is lucky, accomplishes.

This sense of identification is not a mysterious thing. Once in Nsukka, after struggling to explain the social and intellectual background of some classic Western literature, I began teaching a modern Nigerian novel. Achebe's *No Longer at Ease.* I was struck by the concreteness of the first comments from the class: "That

In two of the three basic measures of Peace Corps success —projecting a better image of America, and promoting an understanding by the volunteers of another culture—the MIT study concluded that the Peace Corps has been overwhelmingly successful. As to the third measurement—a significant contribution to the host country's development program—although the study acknowledges the difficulty in evaluating this contribution, it concludes that the contribution "has in most respects been smaller than originally envisaged by many early senior staff members of Peace Corps/Washington. . . . Many volunteers, too, have started out with unrealistic aspirations. Before long, however, they usually learn how unreasonable their initial ambitions were. More important, they learn a good deal about what *can* be done." (*Above*) PCV Fred Schmidt from Closter, New Jersey, surveys a goat cooperative he helped establish in Sungei Tiang in northern Malaysia, one of the areas studied by the MIT sociologists.

Peru: Measurable Progress and a Model Volunteer

One of the most publicized, and certainly the most comprehensive, study of Peace Corps volunteers was one made by Cornell University anthropologists of the volunteers serving in Peru. Fifteen communities with volunteers working in them were studied; three were in large cities, the rest were small, rural villages. In addition, five communities that had no volunteers were studied. The Cornell Report did not try to gloss over Peace Corps mistakes—in fact, the report was so hard-hitting that one newspaper, unfriendly to the Peace Corps, used it as evidence that the Peace Corps was proving unsuccessful, which was incorrect. However, the Cornell team did find that volunteers were sloppy and wasteful with equipment, and that some girls withdrew from the pressure of their work to spend hours primping in front of a mirror. But the Report's general conclusion was encouraging: Although little or no progress was recorded in the three cities where volunteers worked, in the countryside the Cornell anthropologists found that villages which had volunteers progressed more than three times as fast as those that did not have volunteers. They also found that this progress was not carried out by the volunteers alone, but by volunteers having material and technical support from Peruvian and United States agencies.

A Peruvian farmer near the village of Pisac in the Andes.

(*Above*) A *compesio* works his farm in the Urubamba Valley high in the Peruvian Andes. (*Below*) PCV Julia Zagar, from New York, works with the women of the Peruvian village of Chucuito. "We started small," says Julia, "by designing products incorporating traditional knitting skills of the Andes." The Cornell University study of Peace Corps Volunteers in Peru concluded: "The evidence before us certainly supports the hypothesis that . . . if Andean communities receive material United States aid through the direct personal intervention of United States citizens—in this case, Peace Corps volunteers—then they will move toward economic self-sufficiency, capital formation, political autonomy, and initiative."

Although the Cornell anthropologists found that no measurable increase in development was noted in the three urban areas studied, they did report that existing institutions were strengthened by the addition of Peace Corps volunteers. (*Above*) Nancy Fletcher, of Oakland, California, who worked as a community development worker in a Lima *barriada*, holds a weekly singing class for teen-agers.

Vicos: The Village That Voted to Throw the Peace Corps Out

By 1962, when Peace Corps Volunteers first arrived in Vicos, one of the Peruvian villages studied by Cornell anthropologists, the village had already made considerable progress. Thanks to work already done by Cornell and the efforts of the Peruvian government, Vicos had a school with 250 regular students and eight teachers, a health clinic, an agricultural extension service, and an electric generator. The Vicosinos had also obtained their own land and had elected their own officials. It was probably the only village in the Peruvian Andes where democracy had begun to function. How well it was functioning was demonstrated by the fact that seventeen months after the Peace Corps volunteers arrived, the Vicosinos met and voted that the volunteers be asked to leave. The reasons were a combination of insensitivity on the part of the volunteers and misinformation on the part of the villagers. Four weeks later, the villagers met again and voted that the volunteers be invited back. "But that was not nearly as great a triumph," says Frank Mankiewicz, then Peace Corps Director in Peru, "as the fact that they felt confident enough to take that vote and throw us out in the first place." Mankiewicz calls the Vicos revolt against the volunteers a "great victory for community development."

Volunteers Tom Mon Pere, from Fresno, California (*facing camera in white straw hat*), and John F. O'Brien, of New York City (*standing*), help put up a small church in a Peruvian village.

Model Volunteer

The Cornell Report anthropologists also uncovered a "model volunteer"—Perry, as he was called in the Report; actually his name is Ralph Bolton. Here is an account of Perry's achievements, as extracted from the Cornell Report by the Peace Corps magazine, Volunteer:

Perry's first community project as a Peace Corps volunteer in the Peruvian Andes was to set up a barber in business. When he left Peru two and one-half years later, Perry had organized one village and transformed another.

In his two assigned areas, Huancollusco and Chijnaya, Perry tried more than a dozen projects including anthropology classes, consumer cooperatives, and windmill irrigation. He had a fair share of failures. But his successes were formidable enough for Cornell researchers to call the way he worked "truly a model of the Peace Corps ideal image."

Perry's first home was a rented one-room house in the Jatun Ayllu section of Huancollusco in southeastern Peru. Huancollusco is an Indian settlement in the district of Taraco, situated near the town of Taraco. Jatun Ayllu has an estimated 1,200 inhabitants.

For nine months, Perry divided his time between Jatun Ayllu and the city of Puno, where on weekends he taught anthropology at the National School of Social Work. He devoted his earnings there to financing community improvements in Jatun Ayllu.

One of his first projects was a financial investment which paid off. Perry loaned $18.65 to a local resident who had acquired the skills of a professional barber while a temporary migrant outside Huancollusco. Jatun Ayllu soon enjoyed for the first time the services of a professional barber, resident in the community of Huancollusco. Also, the barber charged other members of this Indian community less for haircuts than did the Mestizo barbers in nearby Taraco. In one year, the barber was able to repay the loan to Perry, and he became a completely independent operator.

Perry took an active interest in the education and the recreation of the people of Huancollusco. Within three months, he was teaching literacy classes in three neighborhoods of Jatun Ayllu. The enrollment was 96, 50, and 29 in the respective neighborhoods, with attendance running about 50 percent of enrollment. Perry found that about half his students could read and merely required practice in order to improve their reading skills.

He began lending members of his classes and other peasants reading materials after each class session. Old textbooks, copies of *Life* magazine in Spanish, and newspapers were eagerly borrowed. Perry made 279 loans of reading materials during the first five weeks of the library.

Perry also found that the Indian settlements lacked recreation aside from festivals, dances, and market days. Sports were played in only some settlements. Concluding that the lack of activities to break the monotony of rural life led to a high rate of alcohol consumption by the peasants, Perry set out to organize sports clubs. He felt that team play might also foster habits of working together.

Perry succeeded in organizing clubs at a school in Huancollusco, and in two neighborhoods of Jatun Ayllu. These groups met weekly to play soccer, basketball, and volleyball with equipment supplied by the Peace Corps.

The people of Jatun Ayllu were enthusiastic about Perry's idea for a community center where various activities might be carried on under the same roof, and they contributed materials and labor to construct the four-room building.

The tool for community action used most by Perry was the cooperative. He started several consumers' co-ops in Jatun Ayllu. Each cooperative made its own purchases, and consolidated purchasing was eventually tried, but the cooperatives did not prove to be enduring organizations. Perry transferred to a different program before his work had had sufficient time to jell.

Perry also became interested in forming a producers' cooperative among the women, to weave and knit alpaca wool scarves. This effort took more time, but it appears to have more chances for lasting success than the consumer ventures, the report says.

In December, 1963, Perry left Huancollusco, having effected the most rapid rate of change of any highland Indian community where Peace Corps volunteers worked during 1962–1964. The only exception, cites the Cornell Report, was Chijnaya which, because of its newness, was "an artificially swiftly improving settlement." Perry moved to Chijnaya. Through July, 1965 (he extended his Peace Corps service), he worked among the 315 people of that transplanted community.

(Opposite page) Volunteer Everett Snowden tries out a water-powered spinning wheel near Chijnaya, a village founded by another volunteer in 1963. The volunteer who preceded Snowden in Chijnaya and who founded the village was the legendary "Perry" who, according to the Cornell Report, "achieved one of the most remarkable records of individual volunteer achievement in Peru to date."

Chijnaya's birth was itself an exercise in community action.

Early in 1963, Lake Titicaca overflowed and destroyed large sections of the Taraco district. Indian peasants had to move, leaving their homes and lands under water. Perry, along with the subdirector and other representatives from the Puno Development Corporation, devised a plan to move some of the families to safer ground. Preparations were made for a resettlement project in Chijnaya, then an estate owned by the church and situated near the town of Pucará, 62 miles from Taraco.

At first, most of the people were suspicious of the offers to help. Rumors circulated that this was a Communist plot, or that the Indians would be slaughtered by the *gringos* to make grease for their machines, or carried off to work in the jungles. But some were not disturbed by the rumors, and 74 families committed themselves to the experiment.

The first task for the settlers was to build temporary sod houses, since there was no housing. Perry helped them form a cooperative organization through which loans were handled for new houses, a school, and a community center. Perry also helped start a consumers' cooperative, a small retail store to cater to their immediate needs.

Chijnaya mushroomed.

Community plantings were increased. The scrawny cattle belonging to the members of the new settlement were pooled, forming another cooperative designed to upgrade livestock and improve grazing procedures. One immediate result of cooperative cattle management was that children were no longer required to shepherd animals, allowing them to attend school.

The community actively supported the educational programs under Perry's guidance, and school attendance surpassed that in larger neighboring towns. After a campaign of petitioning the Ministry of Public Education, the community obtained recognition for its school, and the Ministry sent three teachers.

Chijnaya is most famous for its alpaca wool and its tapestries. Perry conceived the idea of creating a cooperative for marketing handspun alpaca wool for local weavers in the coastal cities and abroad. The women of Chijnaya, idled by the cooperative management of cattle and lacking homemaking chores to occupy them, readily joined in the project, even though spinning was traditionally a male specialty.

Another Peace Corps Volunteer, not working at Chijnaya but interested in handcraft activities, suggested that the children try their hands at embroidery. Perry encouraged some children to sew multicolored tapestries depicting local scenes on plain homespun cloth. At first these tapestries were a novelty. Then Perry discovered that he could sell them, and he encouraged the children to expand their efforts. They did so eagerly, and now more than 200 children embroider tapestries for "fun and profit."

Perry arranged marketing in Lima and in the United States. By August, 1965, this enterprise had earned almost $10,000 and is expanding. The arts and crafts industry of Chijnaya is also paying back to the Peruvian government the funds used to found the community (an investment totaling some $200,000).

Of Chijnaya, the Cornell Report says, "Without Perry, the project would not even have started, much less enjoyed the success that it has to date."

Perry was successful as a volunteer because of the way he worked, say the researchers. "Perry consistently lived among the people with whom he was working, and largely at their own economic level," the report adds. "Both in Jatan Allyu and Chijnaya his housing could not in any way be distinguished from that of his neighbors."

Especially important, according to the report, was Perry's command of Spanish, which allowed him to communicate his ideas effectively and when necessary, to utilize an interpreter (from Spanish to Quechua) to full advantage. Perry also learned enough Quechua to "know what was going on most of the time."

Perry conducted preliminary studies prior to undertaking any large-scale program. He talked widely with the people of Jatun Ayllu before initiating any project with the people in the area of his first assignment. "He showed great patience and persistence in dealing with the sluggish local bureaucrats and the people themselves," the researchers say.

"The trust and confidence placed in him by the people of Chijnaya and the Puno Development Corporation," they conclude, "were equaled in degree in the case of few, if any, other volunteers studied by the Cornell Peru Project."

Tapestry (*above*), embroidered by a child in Chijnaya, is one of many embroidered by the villagers to help pay back a $200,000 loan. The tapestries are now being sold in New York for $50, and the Smithsonian selected 35 of them for an exhibit which toured the United States and Canada.

place where the Lagos taxi driver runs over the dog because he thinks it's good luck . . . it's really like that. . . ." It seems that the joy of simple recognition in art is more than an accidental attribute—not the recognition of universals, but of dogs and taxicabs.

Before going to Africa I read another book by Achebe, *Things Fall Apart*. I enjoyed it and was glad to learn something about Ibo culture, but I thought it a mediocre work of art. I read the book again at the end of my stay in Nigeria, and suddenly found it an exceptional work of art. It was no longer a cultural document, but a book about trees I had climbed and houses I had visited in. It is not that I now ignored artistic defects through sentimentality, but that my empathy revealed artistic virtues that had previously been hidden from me.

We in America know too much about the rest of the world. Subjected to a constant barrage of information from books, TV, photographers, we know how Eskimos catch bears and how people come of age in Samoa. We gather our images of the whole world around us and

The Cornell Report's "model volunteer" showed what one imaginative, energetic volunteer can do when he happens to be in the right place at the right time. But most volunteers get their satisfaction from simply providing a service, such as nursing the sick, as volunteer nurse Christine Krutenat, from Nantucket, Massachusetts, did in a hospital in Tunis . . .

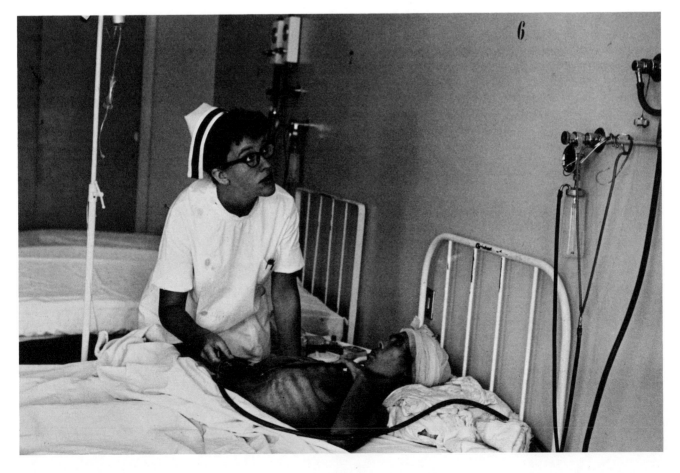

succumb to the illusion of being cosmopolitan. We study comparative literature and read books like *Zen and The Art of Archery* and think of ourselves as citizens of the world when actually vast reading is simply the hallmark of our parochialism. No matter how many Yoga kicks we go on, we still interpret everything through the pattern of our own American existence and intellectual traditions, gleaning only disembodied ideas from other cultures.

If, as the critics have it, ideas are inseparable from their style of expression, it is equally true in the cultural sense that ideas are inseparable from the manner and place in which they are lived. This to me is the meaning of the Peace Corps as a new frontier. It is the call to go, not where man has never been before, but where he has lived differently; the call to experience firsthand the intricacies of a different culture; to understand from the inside rather than the outside; and to test the limits of one's own way of life against another in the same manner as the original pioneer tested the limits of his endurance against the elements. This is perhaps an impossible ideal, surely impossible in the

... or Larry Clarke (*opposite page*), from Key West, Florida, a Peace Corps teacher in Somalia who invented a piece of playground equipment from ordinary water pipes which were put together with common plumbing tools. The playground structures, which the children had never seen before, were built on all the playgrounds of all schools built by the Peace Corps and quickly became known as "Clarkesvilles," thereby giving Larry a measure of immortality in Somalia.

... or Linda Wilson (*above*), from Brewster, Washington, who taught adult literacy in a leprosarium outside of Santo Domingo in the Dominican Republic.

And those volunteers capable of identifying with larger movements get their reward from the many testimonials which have honored the Peace Corps, such as the comments by the Foreign Minister of Thailand when the Chulalong-korn University presented Sargent Shriver with an honorary degree. "Many of us who did not know about the United States," said the Foreign Minister, "thought of this great nation as a wealthy nation, a powerful nation, endowed with great material strength and many powerful weapons. But how many of us know that in the United States ideas and ideals are also powerful. This is the secret of your greatness, of your might, which is not imposing or crushing people, but is filled with hope of future good will and understanding. It is indeed striking that this important idea, the most powerful idea in recent times, should come from this mightiest nation on earth—the United States." (*Below*) Peggy Berg, of New Ulm, Minnesota, taught at the teachers' training school in Nakhom-Patom, Thailand.

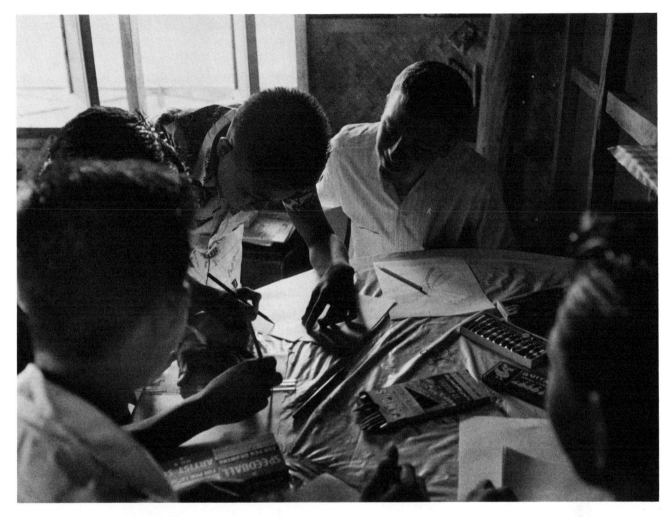

Allen Pastryk, of Chicago, taught in an elementary school on Samar in the Philippines. The volunteers were given the Ramón Magsaysay Award, the first time non-Asians received this honor. In explaining its selection, the Magsaysay Board said: "The problem of achieving peace amidst the tensions and dangers of a nuclear age occupies the mind of much of the human race, yet few within it discover a useful way to contribute. In reaffirming the essential community of interest of all ordinary people, regardless of creed or nationality, the Peace Corps volunteers belong to that small but growing fraternity who by their individual efforts do make a difference."

narrow scope of two years; but it was an adventure just the same. It was an adventure to realize, for instance, to what extent irony is an attribute, even a condition, of Western life and thought; and to live for nearly two years in a society in which irony as a force is practically nonexistent. But that is too complex a thing to get started on right now.

Life at Usukka was not always the easiest thing in the world, and the friendships I talk of so cavalierly were not the work of a day. Our group arrived at Nsukka shortly after the Peace Corps's first big publicity break, the famous Post Card Incident, which was still very much on Nigerian minds. We were always treated with a sense of natural friendliness and hospitality, but there was also quite a bit of understandable *mistrust.*

Nigeria became a nation only in 1960, and the present university generation is one bred on the struggle for independence and the appropriate slogans and attitudes. I tended to feel guilty rather than defensive, except when the accusations were patently ridiculous, such as the idea that we were all master spies—hundreds of twenty-three-year-old master spies—or when facts were purposefully ignored, as in the statement that the Peace Corps was run by the CIA. America is a large, rich, powerful, feared and envied nation; Nigeria is a new country naturally jealous of its independence and autonomy. All things considered, I am a little amazed at the openness and frankness of our reception.

There were other problems. Many Nigerians have an overdeveloped sense of status and found it hard to believe that we were paid practically nothing. Many reasoned that because we lived in the dormitories with the students instead of in big houses as the rest of the faculty, we must be second-raters, or misfits that America was fobbing off on them. But insofar as we made names for ourselves as good teachers and made ourselves accessible as people (something that few of my friends had ever known a white man to do), our eventual acceptance into the community was assured. Shortly after our arrival a petition circulated among the students asking the administration to dismiss the Peace Corps. Months later student grievances erupted into a riot that forced the school to close down for more than

"The Peace Corps," said Sierra Leone's Minister of Education, "has built a bridge between the developed world and the underdeveloped world." (*Below*) PCV Mario di Santo, from Brooklyn, helps villagers in Sierra Leone build a road. (*Opposite page*) In his *Thousand Days*, Arthur Schlesinger, Jr., wrote of meeting a volunteer from Denver, Colorado, in Caracas, Venezuela, and how impressed he was at the way the volunteer was treated in an area bristling with anti-American feeling. The volunteer was Jerry Page, a Community Development worker, who is shown talking with a young Venezuelan. Later Schlesinger asked the American Ambassador, Allan Stewart, about the Peace Corps. Stewart replied: "It has been wonderful here. It has worked miracles in changing the Venezuelan image of North Americans. Before the Peace Corps, the only Americans the poor Venezuelans ever saw were riding around in Cadillacs. They supposed them all to be rich, selfish, callous, reactionary. The Peace Corps has shown them an entirely different kind of American. It is transforming the whole theory they have of the United States."

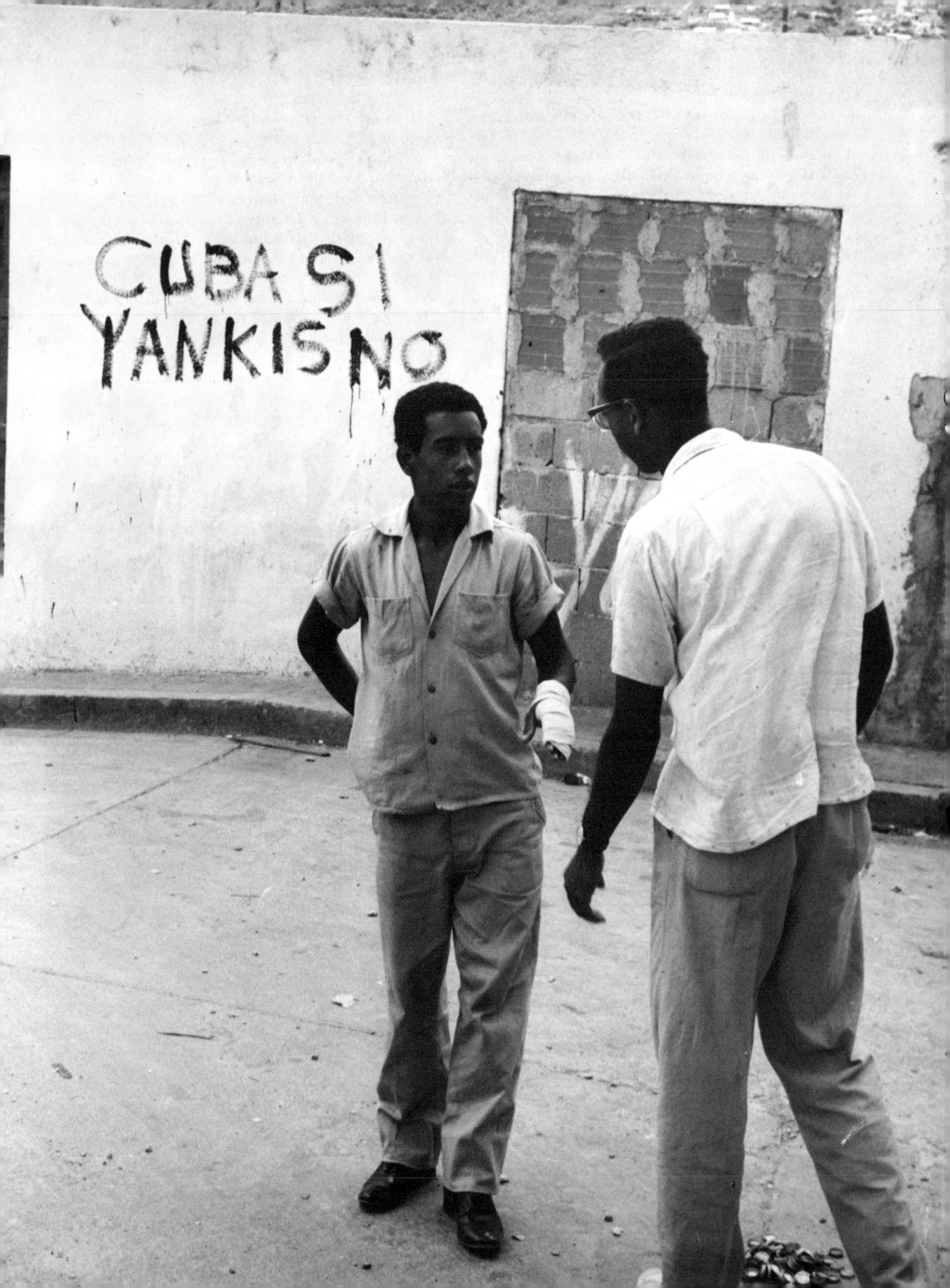
CUBA SI
YANKIS NO

two weeks, but in the long list of grievances, the Peace Corps was not then mentioned.

I do not wish to imply that we "won them over"; indeed, I think they won us over in the final analysis. It's just that the intransigence of our preconceptions of ourselves and others gradually dissolved into a kind of affectional confusion. Ideas often try to live a life of their own, independent of and separate from the people and objects with which they supposedly deal. In the intellect alone they are self-proliferating, like fungus under glass, without regard for what the weather is doing outside. But the kind of personal contact we had with Nigerians helped break up the false buttressing of formal thought, and when that happens, personal friction creates a warmth conducive to further understanding and not a heat with which to light incendiary fires. A glass of beer can make the difference between fanatics and worthy opponents.

I was at first surprised by how little I felt the presence of any racial feeling in Nigeria. What little I did notice had a kind of secondhand quality, as if it were merely a principled identification with the American Negro or a historical commitment. Though well informed about civil rights events in the United States, most Nigerians I talked to showed little understanding of the state of mind of the American Negro as differentiated from themselves. Most Nigerians have had little contact with hardcore prejudice backed by social force. They have good reason to resent, sometimes to hate, the white man in Africa, but they have never been subjected as people to the kind of daily and lifelong injustice that confronts the American Negro.

Racial feeling sometimes crops up in strange circumstances. A friend writes me, "Before Nsukka, the only whites I had ever known were reverend fathers in school who interpreted everything I did as a sure sign

Many volunteers, of course, feel that the most significant aspect of their Peace Corps experience was what happened to them. For instance, Maureen Orth, who did community development in Colombia, says: "Before I joined the Peace Corps I saw its challenges as being the changes I could make within a given set of circumstances. Now I realize that the most important result of volunteer service was what happened to me. I changed more than they did. My commitment to them—to people besides myself—will always be part of my life." (*Above*) On her last day in Las Violetas, a slum *barrio* on the outskirts of Medellin, Colombia, Maureen goes out to take a final look at the water system which had been dug at her urging.

of fast-approaching eternal damnation. . . ." In Africa as in America all whites are, to a certain extent, guilty until proved innocent, but in a very short time we were joking about our respective colors with a freedom and levity which is not always possible in America. Color has its own pure power, too; and I soon felt ashamed of my chalky, pallid skin against the splendor of the African's.

Much has been written recently about the contradictory feelings of the Negro toward the white man—hating him and yet buying facial creams to be more like him—and I think the same sort of contradictory relationship exists in Nigeria, but with a cultural rather than a racial basis. The African stands in a very delicate psychological position between Western industrial

In listing the Peace Corps's many achievements and the compliments the volunteers have received, it is too easy to leave the impression that the Peace Corps has all the answers and that the volunteers never make mistakes. As Robert Textor wrote in the conclusion to the MIT study: "The temptation should be firmly resisted to regard the volunteers as paragons of perfection. Among returnees whom I know, many a ripe anecdote circulates, indicating beyond doubt that the PCV's have been guilty of numerous cultural gaffes, and are susceptible to the usual human foibles and peccadillos." (Above) The look on volunteer Tom Eamann's face (left) suggests that even agricultural cooperative experts can be stumped occasionally. With Eamann, who is from Rochester, New York, is Al Hageman, from Auburn, New York. They are watching the cotton being weighed as it is brought in from the fields at Chiromo, Malawi.

culture and his own. He is driven to a comparative evaluation and must build a society out of his decisions. America is not so much interested in changing as exporting its society; Nigeria is interested in change and is of necessity much less parochial than ourselves in the source of its inspiration.

"Africa caught between two worlds"—it is a cliché, but it is no joke. To the race problem it is at least possible to postulate an ideal resolution: racial equality and the elimination of intolerance. But in its cultural

aspect—the struggle between African traditions and the heritage of the West—there is no indisputable resolution, not even in the mind. If I have learned anything from living in Nigeria, it is the unenviably complex and difficult position in which the young Nigerian finds himself; and if I have learned anything from the poems and stories written by my students, it is the incredible grace, honesty, and sometimes power with which many Nigerians are examining themselves, their past, and their future.

Would they do it again? A survey of 4,000 returned volunteers revealed that 94 percent would volunteer again—although only 80 percent said they would serve in the same country, 91 percent were satisfied with their experience, only 44 percent felt they had given all they could to their job, and 84 percent felt their work had made a contribution to their host country's development. One English teacher wrote from Tessenei, Ethiopia: "Meanwhile, we would have to be content with the small hints of success: three graduates (representing a 200 percent increase); a greatly improved level of English, a lot of new books, a school-wide passion for touch football, and many deep and lasting friendships. We will also remember the offhand comments, such as the one delivered by a wizened old sheikh at Village 13 on the Sudan border. 'I have never met an American before,' he said, 'but I have heard of your conduct at Tessenei, and I believe that Americans must be good people.'" (*Above*) English Teacher Ash Hartwell, from Honolulu, meets with his secondary school class in Ethiopia.

I don't know how friendship fits into all this, but somehow it does. My instincts revolt against the whole idea of having to prove in some mechanistic or quantitative way the value of the Peace Corps. If the aim is to help people, I understand that in the sense of the Ibo proverb which says that when the right hand washes the left hand, the right hand becomes clean also. E. M. Forster has said that "love is a great force in private life," but in public affairs, "it does not work. The fact is we can only love what we know personally, and we cannot know much. The only thing that cuts a little ice is affection, or the possibility of affection." I only know that when I am infuriated by some article in a Nigerian newspaper, I can summon up countless images of dusty cycle rides with Paul Okpokam, reading poetry with Glory Nwanodi, dancing and drinking palm wine with Gabriel Ogar, and it suddenly matters very much that I go beyond my annoyance to some kind of understanding. That my Nigerian friends trust me is no reason for them to trust Washington or forgive Birmingham; but something is there which was not there before and which the world is the better for having.

—DAVID SCHICKELE

(*Above*) Priscilla Bauguess, from Muscatine, Iowa, makes a house call in the Bolivian village of Coroico, where she served as a volunteer nurse. One volunteer who served in Bolivia wrote home: "Looking back over the last fourteen months I find it almost impossible to give a critical evaluation either of the impact of my work on Bolivia or Bolivia on me. It is still too soon to tell. It appears that the Peace Corps may be an enduring and complementary support to United States foreign aid. I don't believe the Peace Corps to be the final solution but it certainly can be a part."

Returned volunteer Roger Scheidewind, teaching at the Cardoza High School Project in Washington, D.C. Many people are beginning to see in the Peace Corps experience a model for all higher education. As Harris Wofford says: "The fusion of education and work, of theory and practice, of book learning and experimental learning that comes in the challenging settings of Peace Corps assignments is far from the present practice of most conventional education."